WITHDRAWN

WORLDS APART

# WORLDS APART

## MEASURING INTERNATIONAL AND GLOBAL INEQUALITY

*Branko Milanovic*

PRINCETON UNIVERSITY PRESS PRINCETON AND OXFORD

Published by Princeton University Press, 41 William Street, Princeton, New Jersey 08540
In the United Kingdom: Princeton University Press, 3 Market Place, Woodstock, Oxfordshire OX20 1SY


Library of Congress Cataloging-in-Publication Data

Milanovic, Branko.
Worlds apart : measuring international and global inequality / Branko Milanovic.
p. cm.
Includes bibliographical references and index.
ISBN 0-691-12110-9 (alk. paper)
1. Income distribution. 2. Economic development. 3. Globalization. 4. Equality.
I. Title.

HC79.I5M55 2005
330.9—dc22 2004058312

British Library Cataloging-in-Publication Data is available

This book has been composed in Palatino Typeface
Printed on acid-free paper. ∞
pup.princeton.edu
Printed in the United States of America

10 9 8 7 6 5 4 3 2 1

# *Contents*

# *Acknowledgments*

THIS BOOK has been "under construction" for several years. For me, it all started with the idea that I had in the mid-1990s of combining the many household surveys available at the World Bank for almost all of the less developed countries in the world with those, generally available, of the rich countries, thus creating the first "true" world income distribution of all individuals—in the same way as if state-level distributions were collated to obtain the all-U.S. distribution of income among individuals. The process took several years, and in 1999 the first draft of the paper was published. The results showed both a very high level of global inequality (Gini index of inequality of about 66 in 1993), and a rather significant increase of some three Gini points between 1988 and 1993. The first finding is more important, but it was not surprising: previous approximations have all come up with a Gini number in the mid-sixties range. The second finding generated much discussion. Some people saw it as proof that globalization was leading to increased inequality in the world (although I did not deal with causality), and it seemed to agree with many people's "feeling" of rising inequities. Others criticized the finding and felt compelled—using at time dubious statistical practices—to come up with numbers that showed global inequality on the decline. Some papers and magazines peddled this Panglossian vision with even less inhibition that the authors of the original papers.

During the ensuing debate I realized not only the highly contentious nature of these calculations but also the tendency to use the same terms ("international," "global," "world" inequality) to mean different things. As in any other branch of human knowledge, no progress is possible until we all agree at least on what different terms mean. So, I tried both to clear some misunderstandings, for example, to distinguish inequality in mean incomes of the countries from inequality among all individuals living on this Earth, and to proceed to additional calculations.

The need for the methodological clarity, as well as the debate on global inequality into which I was at first somewhat reluctantly drawn (although later I joined it, at times with gusto), have led me to the two areas that I originally did not plan to cover. First to the issue of differences in economic performance among the countries, the so-called "convergence debate," since, obviously, convergence (or divergence) in countries' mean incomes indicates that inequality among countries is decreasing (or increasing). And second, to the long-term relationship between, on the one hand, globalization and, on the other hand, inequality in mean countries' incomes and inequality among world individuals.

The book is very much organized along the lines that I have sketched here. After the first three chapters, which deal with definitions and measurement, in chapters 4 through 8, I discuss the empirics of incomes and growth of some 140 countries over the last fifty years, using National Accounts data (GDP per capita). In chapters 9 through 10, using household survey data, I deal with incomes of individuals in the world during the past two decades. Both parts deal with figures, facts, calculations. In the concluding comments (chapters 11 and 12), I look at the evolution of several types of inequality during the past two centuries, and briefly address the issues of association—I dare not say causality—between different inequality outcomes and the two globalization episodes. I also address some more speculative questions as to the perception of inequality during the era of globalization, why inequality may (or may not) matter, and, finally, what to (or not to) do about it.

It is truly a difficult, or more exactly an impossible, task to acknowledge the help of so many individuals whom I often consulted or sought out for data, and to make sure that no one is omitted or forgotten. Literally dozens of my colleagues in the World Bank helped with the household survey data, providing many hard-to-obtain surveys, explaining how income or consumption aggregates were constructed, and, in some cases, even doing decile calculations from the micro data themselves (when the micro data could not be released). They are acknowledged in the detailed Data Sources, a companion database (available at http://www.worldbank.org/research/inequality/data.htm) that provides disaggregated statistics (mostly deciles) from some 360 surveys I have used to calculate global inequality in 1988, 1993, and 1998. Without my colleagues' generous help and assistance, this book literally would not have been possible.

Then, Prem Sangraula, and, at an earlier stage, Costas Krouskas and Dimitri Kaltsas, provided excellent research assistance. As the reader will appreciate, the "data intensity" of the book is very high. It was not always easy for them, or for me, to keep all these files straight, to avoid mistakes as far as possible, to link many distributions together, and to do the same calculations many times over just because we had received a new survey or added a new country. I am extremely grateful to all of them.

I have also benefited from comments that I have received from many of my colleagues in the World Bank and elsewhere—at conferences and talks—where I have presented this book at its various stages: from very early to almost complete. Let me mention some: the Bellagio conference on global inequality in February 2001; lectures at the Royal Institute of International Affairs in London and at Nuffield College in Oxford in

May 2001; the World Bank ABCDE Conference in May 2001; the Globalization and (In)equality Conference at Warwick University in March 2002; Globalization and Inequality workshops at the Brookings Institution and World Bank, both in June 2002; the Institute G17 Summer School in Belgrade in July 2002; and talks at the Economic Policy Institute in Washington and at the Kennedy School of Government at Harvard, both in September 2002, at the Institute for Social Studies at the Hague in October 2002, at Yale in February 2003, at a conference on globalization and inequality at Brisbane, Australia in February 2003, at a meeting on global poverty at Columbia University in New York in March 2003, at the Siena Summer School, and at the Observatoire Français de Conjonctures Économiques in July 2003. I am grateful to participants at these conferences as well to many people with whom I have corresponded for their comments and suggestions. Again, I can mention only some of them: Sudhir Anand, Isabelle Bensidoun, Nancy Birdsall, François Bourguignon, Samuel Bowles, Ian Castles, William Cline, Guillaume Daudin, Yiri Dikhanov, Steven Durlauf, Dag Ehrenpreis, Francisco Ferreira, Glenn Firebaugh, James K. Galbraith, Carol Graham, Mansoob Murshed, Barrie Pittock, Thomas Pogge, Graham Pyatt, Gustav Ranis, Martin Ravallion, Sanjay Reddy, Robert Wade, Michael Ward, Bernard Wasow, and Shlomo Yitzhaki. I am particularly grateful to K. S. Jomo, who has consistently supported me in my work and has encouraged me to address in writing some of the issues that we have discussed informally. It is also a pleasure to thank Tim Sullivan, associate editor at Princeton University Press, who helped shape the book from its very early stages, Linda Truilo, who did an excellent editing job, and Jill Harris, who skillfully directed the book's production.

The book was written as a continuation of the Research Project 684-84 financed by the World Bank Research Grant. This is the proper place, I think, to mention that without World Bank's immense resources, in particular access to hundreds of household surveys from many countries around the world (many of which were conducted jointly by the World Bank and countries' statistical agencies), it would have been impossible to produce a data-intensive book such as this. The World Bank is indeed the only place in the world where this kind of information could be accessed, assembled, processed, and even possibly written about. Despite the sometime lack of enthusiasm in this line of research by some of my colleagues at the World Bank, I dare to believe that this may be one of the instances where the World Bank indeed played the role to which it aspires to, that of a "knowledge bank." The views expressed in the book, however, are my own and should not be attributed to the World Bank or its affiliated organizations.

# WORLDS APART

# Prologue

## The Promise of the Twentieth Century

> This is a world in which everyone . . . is sensitised to risk but indifferent to fate.
>
> —David Runciman, "The Garden, the Park and the Meadow," *London Review of Books* online

In 1963 French economist Jean Fourastié published the book *Le grand espoir du XX siècle.* I read the book in 1973 or 1974, after the first oil shock, and around the time Fourastié's "thirty glorious years" (les trente glorieuses) were coming to a close. "Thirty glorious years" was Fourastié's name for the period of sustained and high economic growth that, from the end of World War II to the mid-1970s, transformed the economies of Western Europe. Many of them were within a generation catapulted from predominantly agrarian to modern postindustrial societies. When I read the book, despite the gloom brought about by the oil crisis, the horizons still seemed bright and Fourastié's optimistic message rang true. The second half of the twentieth century seemed full of big promises: vast increases in productivity brought about by technological progress and accumulation of capital would open up new vistas to humankind. Development would spread to the four corners of the world, and penury and want would be (almost) a thing of the past.

And indeed when one surveyed the horizon then, things did not seem to contradict too much the beautiful promises painted in the book. Western Europe, North America, Oceania, and Japan were already affluent societies. Latin America and Eastern Europe, coming next in the development hierarchy, seemed to be getting there themselves. India continued with its stable, if not dazzling, "Hindu" rate of growth of some 4 percent per annum. China was in turmoil, and no one really seemed to know how much of its propaganda was believable. But the rest of Asia (with the exception of war-torn Vietnam) and most of Africa were growing, thus apparently demonstrating the benefits of newly acquired independence. The world seemed to be both moving forward and getting more equal, as poorer countries were catching up with the rich.

But with the second oil shock, the increase in interest rates, and the debt crisis, there ensued the "lost decade" in Latin America, ravages of transition in Eastern Europe and the former Soviet Union, and almost apocalyptic declines in the poorest continent of all—Africa. The promise of the twentieth century—from just beyond the century's end—has not quite held up. For sure, India's growth accelerated during the last decade of the century. And China experienced twenty years of the most remarkable growth ever recorded in history. Yet stagnation and abrupt declines in Africa, Latin America, and transition countries underlined a remarkable unevenness in outcomes: the world seemed at the same time to be rushing forward and going backward.

The average world growth rate has declined during the past twenty years. Even as large numbers of Indians and Chinese were joining the consumer society, many in the two countries were left behind. The gaps among the regions, and indeed among individuals, were growing. While a part of the rich world was discussing techniques that would prolong the human life-span to over 100 years, millions were dying from easily preventable diseases, lack of safe water, or infections. Tuberculosis, syphilis, and other diseases that seemed to be a thing of the past returned on the heels of economic crises and social anomies. Scholars were seriously debating to what extent poverty and deprivation were behind the many civil wars that erupted after the end of the Cold War, as well as behind terrorist acts.

The second half of the twentieth century that had seemed in the 1970s to offer a promise of an almost universal betterment was ending on a much more ambiguous note. New opportunities were unleashed, and they were seized by many; the artificial division of the world into the two hostile camps had ended; but for those who found themselves born in wrong countries, in wrong social groups, and of a wrong race or sex, a large part of the promise went unfulfilled.

# Introduction

## A Topic Whose Time Has Come

World inequality is a topic whose time has come. There is more talk and writing than ever on globalization. The post–Cold War world is truly a globalized world. And with globalization on the agenda, our view as to what is the proper object of study changes too. Topics of interest are now global in their scope: global public goods, difficulty of pursuing national macro policies in a world of globalized capital flows, global environment issues, and then, of course, global inequality. One may conjecture whether in some not-too-distant future we would reach the situation where we would be interested in global inequality—treating all individuals in the world the same, simply as world citizens—the way we are currently interested in national inequality. This book explores the extent of inequality among nations and among individuals in the world and relates the observed changes in inequality to the process of growth over the past half century.

But before we embark on our journey, we need to pause and ask, What is global or international inequality? There are a number of recent papers that have addressed it, all using terms such as "world" or "global" or "international" inequality. Do they all mean the same thing? As we shall see, they do not. And, moreover, conclusions that are obtained by using one set of definitions are often different from conclusions obtained with another set. That is why we often see apparently contradictory claims: that world inequality is decreasing (Boltho and Toniolo 1999; Melchior et al. 2000; Sala-i-Martin 2002), or is stable (Bourguignon and Morrisson 1999), or is increasing (Milanovic 1999). Consider figure 0.1, "the mother of all inequality disputes," to which we shall return frequently in the pages that follow. The data there are the same: GDPs per capita (or Gross Domestic Income GDI in the more recent terminology) of some 140 countries in the world for the period 1950–2000. Both lines depict levels of inequality expressed by the Gini coefficient, the most common measure of *in*equality.[1] One line shows inequality rising: in this case, each country's GDP per capita is treated as one observation. So, is world inequality definitely rising? Not necessarily. The second line—which begins its steady decline at about the same time the first line begins its steady increase—weighs each country's GDP by its population.

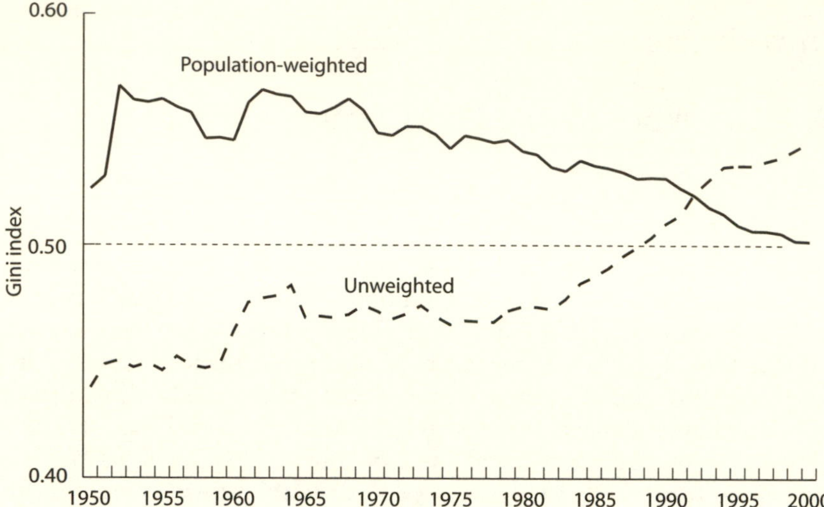


**Figure 0.1.** Two mother-of-all-inequality disputes: the Gini coefficient of countries' per capita GDPs.

So, is world inequality then decreasing? Which one is true? These are only countries' average incomes; where are incomes of the individuals? The objective of the book is to answer these questions. But before we do so, we need to take the reader through some indispensable definitions.

# Part I

## SETTING THE STAGE

# 1

# The Three Concepts of Inequality Defined

THERE are three concepts of world inequality that need to be sharply distinguished. Yet, they are often confounded; even the terminology is unclear. So, we shall now first define them and give them their proper names.

The first (Concept 1) is unweighted international inequality. This concept takes country as the unit of observation, uses its income (or GDP) per capita, disregards its population, and thus compares, as it were, representative individuals from all the countries in the world. It is a kind of UN General Assembly where each country, small or large, counts the same. Imagine a world populated with ambassadors from some 200 countries, each of whom carries a sign on which is written the GDP per capita of his/her country. These ambassadors are then ranked from the poorest to the richest, and a measure of inequality is calculated across such ranking of nations (ambassadors). Note that this is properly a measure of *international* inequality, since it is compares countries. It is "unweighted" because each country counts the same. Concept 1 is not a measure of inequality among citizens of the world.

Since it is reasonable to hold that if China becomes richer, this event should have more impact on the world than if Mauritania were to become so, we come to the second type of inequality (Concept 2): population-weighted international inequality, where we still assume that everyone in a country receives the same income but the number of representative individuals from each country reflects its population size.[2] Note that this is still *international* inequality because we compare mean incomes among nations, but it is now weighted by the population of each country. The difference when compared to Concept 1 is that the number of ambassadors from each country in our fictional assembly is proportional to the country's population. Otherwise, everything else is the same: each ambassador carries a sign with the GDP per capita of his/her country, and income ranks–a concept crucial in the calculation of every inequality measure—are the same. Concept 2 assumes that "within-country" distribution is perfectly equal: all Chinese have the same mean income of China, all Americans, the mean income of the United States, etc. This is the distribution that is often billed as "world" income distribution (e.g., Melchior et al. 2000), but, as we have just seen it is not.

Concept 2 is only a halfway house to the calculation of a true world income distribution (Concept 3), where inequality is calculated across all individuals in the world. Concept 3 treats, in principle, everybody the same. We no longer have ambassadors from the countries: we line up all individuals, regardless of the country, from the poorest to the richest. Now, Chinese individuals will no longer be crowded together: the poor Chinese will mix with poor Africans, the rich Chinese with the middle-class or rich Americans, and a few rich Africans may even mix with the U.S. "top dogs." If one thinks that this is impractical because we cannot array all 6 billion individuals, one is right. But what we can do, as we would in any household survey, is interview individuals or households selected in a worldwide random sample (such that the Chinese will have a chance to be selected proportionally to their population size), and rank all such individuals from the poorest to the richest. World distribution (Concept 3) goes back to the individual as the unit of analysis, ignoring country boundaries.

In terms of Jan Pen's (1971) parade, which is similar to the idea of our fictional assembly but where in addition the height of each individual is proportional to his income, in Concept 1, only countries' ambassadors parade, each having the height of that country's GDP per capita. The number of participants in such a parade is small: at most 180–200, as many persons as there are countries in the world. In Concept 2, each country has a number of participants proportional to its population. Thus if the entire parade consists of 1000 people, China would have some 200 participants, and Luxembourg 1/150 of a participant, but all participants from a given country have the same height—equal to that country's GDP per capita. In Concept 3, the number of participants from each country remains as in Concept 2, but the participants' height now reflects their true income: there are tall and short Chinese just as there are tall and short Americans.

The idea of the parade is illustrated in figure 1.1, where we suppose that there are three countries with different average incomes given by the height of each individual in the top row. Concept 1 inequality is calculated across them. In the second row, we let each country be represented by all of its population. The poorest county has five people (men with briefcases), the middle-income country has two (women), and the richest country three (men with hardhats). Concept 2 inequality is calculated across these ten persons, each assigned the average income of their country. In the bottom row, finally, we let each individual come into the parade with his or her true income. Concept 3 inequality is calculated across the ten people in the bottom row. Not all people from the poorest country are poor; in effect, the poorest person is from a middle-income country. Note that the total height of people from each country

**Concept 1:** three countries and three representatives with mean incomes (height)

**Concept 2:** entire population included but with mean incomes (height)

**Concept 3:** all individuals with their actual heights (incomes)

**Figure 1.1.** Three concepts of inequality illustrated.

in the bottom row must be the same as their total height in the middle row—for obviously the total income of each country is given. The example shows how Concept 2 inequality indeed stands between the other two: the height of people from a given country in the middle row is the same as their height in the top row (Concept 1), while the number of people from each country is the same as their number in the bottom row (Concept 3).

**TABLE 1.1.**
Comparison of the Three Concepts of Inequality

| | *Concept 1: Unweighted International Inequality* | *Concept 2: Weighted International Inequality* | *Concept 3: "True" World Inequality* |
|---|---|---|---|
| Main source of data | National accounts | National accounts | Household surveys |
| Unit of observation | Country | Country (weighted by its population) | Individual |
| Welfare concept | GDP or GNP per capita | GDP or GNP per capita | Mean per capita disposable income or expenditures |
| National currency conversion | Market exchange rate or PPP exchange rate | | |
| Within-country distribution (inequality) | Ignored | Ignored | Included |

Clearly, we would like to know Concept 3 inequality if we are interested in how world *individuals* are doing, even if the other two concepts have their uses too. Concept 1 answers whether nations are converging (in terms of their income levels). When we talk of convergence, we are not, necessarily or at all, interested in individuals but in countries. Concept 2 is perhaps the least interesting. It deals neither only with nations nor individuals but falls somewhere in between. Its main advantage is that it approximates well Concept 3 inequality (which, although a concept we would like to know, is the most difficult one to compute). Once Concept 3 is available, however, Concept 2 inequality will be (as the saying goes) history.

Table 1.1 summarizes our discussion of the differences among the concepts.

But how do these concepts perform empirically and how big are the differences among them? Before we turn to this issue, comparing the three concepts at the world level, let's compare them at a level where this is easy. Take the United States and break it down into fifty states. Concept 1 is simply inequality calculated after ranking all states from the poorest to the richest and giving them equal weight. Concept 2 inequality is the same except that weights are now proportional to the

**TABLE 1.2.**
The Three Concepts Applied to the U.S. Data: Gini Coefficients, 1959–89

| | *Concept 1* | *Concept 2* | *Concept 3* |
|---|---|---|---|
| | *Unweighted Interstate Inequality* | *Population-Weighted Interstate Inequality* | *Interhousehold Inequality* |
| 1959 | 11.4 | 10.7 | 36.1 |
| 1969 | 9.1 | 8.1 | 34.9 |
| 1979 | 7.6 | 5.8 | 36.5 |
| 1989 | 9.8 | 8.3 | 40.1 |

*Note:* Calculated from the 1960–1990 Censuses of the population; state per capita incomes given at www.census.gov/hhes/income/histinc/state/state3.html, interhousehold inequality from www.census.gov/hhes/income/histinc/f04.html.

states' populations. Concept 3 is our usual U.S. inequality that we obtain from the Bureau of the Census's *Current Population Survey*. Why is it, then, that neither researchers nor ordinary people ever speak of Concept 2 (or even Concept 1) inequality when they discuss income distribution in the United States? Simply because we have a reasonably good estimate of "true" income distribution (Concept 3) thanks to the Bureau of the Census surveys.[3] The reader has already seen my point: once we have such an estimate of Concept 3 inequality for the world, hardly anyone would bother about Concept 2 inequality. (We might still find it interesting to look at Concept 1 inequality to know whether mean incomes of the countries are converging.) And, of course, the three concepts can move in very different directions.

Table 1.2 shows the three concepts calculated for the United States and the fifty states over the period 1959–89 (per capita incomes by state are available at decennial intervals only). First, note the huge difference in Gini values between Concept 3 inequality and the other two. For sure, we do not expect to find such a big difference in results for the world as a whole because mean per capita incomes among countries are much more diverse than mean incomes of U.S. states, and thus both Concept 1 and Concept 2 inequality will be closer to Concept 3 inequality. We note, though, that in the United States, Concepts 1 and 2 do not even display the same trend as "true" inequality (Concept 3). While "true" inequality increased between 1969 and 1979, the other two concepts show a decline. Notice, too, that if one were to make conclusions about "true" U.S. inequality based on the first two concepts, one would be led to believe that inequality in 1989 was less than in 1959. The reverse is true: in 1989, inequality was four Gini points (or 11 percent) higher than thirty years ago.

# 2

## Other Differences between the Concepts

Do DIFFERENT STUDIES of world or international inequality differ only by the concept they use? Unfortunately not. Other differences also complicate comparisons. If readers or even researchers are not aware of these differences, comparing the results is difficult. And even when these differences are taken into account, comparisons remain difficult because the relationship among different variables (e.g., between GDP per capita and mean income or expenditures from household surveys) is not clear or obvious.

### What Currency?

First, when we compare incomes of individuals who live in different nations, we need to express them in a common currency. Some studies use the simple exchange rate of the local currency into dollars to convert national incomes. This is fine: it gives us a comparison of people across the world in terms of their *international* purchasing power. When an Indian travels abroad, he faces world prices. It is of little solace to him that hotels in India may cost only $20 per night. Once he is in London he needs to shell out more than $100 per night, maybe his entire monthly salary. This is why the middle class from poor countries have a hard time traveling abroad as tourists. Exactly the opposite is true when a Swede travels south. He can enjoy nice wine, excellent human services, and tasty food for a fraction of what he would have to pay at home. However, most people most of the time do not face international prices: they face prices of the place where they live. This is why another conversion makes more sense: national currency income is converted into "welfare" (available consumption) using the domestic price level. In other words, we need to account for the fact that the price level in India is lower than the price level in Sweden. Luckily, we have such information: since the mid-1980s the International Comparison Project (ICP) has been collecting information on relative price levels in different countries. This information is used to calculate Purchasing Power Parity (PPP) exchange rates. We thus know that price levels tend to be lower in poor than in rich countries, and when local currency incomes are converted using PPP rather than market exchange rates, poor countries' incomes get a boost, and the difference between rich and poor countries' incomes is less than when calculated using market exchange rates. The use of PPP exchange rates will give us a much better handle on the real welfare of people. Thus, not surprisingly, almost all studies of world or international inequality use PPP exchange rates. We shall do the same here.

## What PPPs?

But just when we thought that the problem has been solved, that a comparison of the welfare of people living in different countries would require the use of dollars of equal purchasing power, several technical problems appear. These problems are of two kinds: the appropriateness of PPP in cross-country comparisons, and the transitivity in time between PPPs calculated for different years. The first problem is essentially an index-number problem. PPP values are most often obtained using the Geary-Kramis method of construction of "average international prices." This method gives greater weight to price structures existing in rich countries because the weights that enter into the construction of average international prices are based on quantities consumed by different countries. Since rich countries are greater consumers of goods and services, they will influence the international average price of each item much more than will poor countries. Consequently, the "international" price structure will be closer to that which obtains in rich than in poor countries. Once this point is realized, we immediately face the Gerschenkron effect, namely that the income (or GDP) of a country will be greater (biased upward) whenever it is estimated at somebody else's prices (the prices of another country). The greater the difference in price structures, the greater the bias or the boost to incomes. The economic reason behind this is that "importing" another country's price structure fails to allow for substitution in consumption—that is, if people in a poor country were really faced by the price structure of a rich country, they would have changed their consumption and consumed more of relatively cheaper products and less of relatively expensive products. The use of Geary-Kramis PPPs will overstate real income of the poor countries, and thus understate inequality between rich and poor nations. Dowrick and Akmal (2001) discuss the importance of this bias,[4] and use Afriat's "Ideal Index" instead of the Geary-Kramis method. They show that Concept 2 inequality calculated over the period 1965–98 using the Geary-Kramis PPP displays a downward trend (something we shall see also in chapter 8) while with Afriat "ideal" index, Concept 2 inequality shows a mild upward trend (see Dowrick and Akmal 2001, 26). However, PPP numbers generated by the International Comparison Project are (still) based on the Geary-Kramis index.

This problem is even more serious if one engages in poverty comparisons, an area in which Reddy and Pogge (2002) have argued that the general consumption-based PPP index is inappropriate not only because of the reasons given by Dowrick and Akmal but also because such indexes cover too great an array of goods, many of which are of no importance to the consumption of the poor. In other words, the poor may be shown to be less poor than they really are simply because services consumed by the rich in the rich countries are very expensive (and hence even their minute consumption by the poor in poor countries will unrealistically raise their incomes).

Finally, there is a problem of PPP time-intransitivity. While à la rigueur, we can establish comparisons among countries in a moment of time, comparisons across time are much more problematic. This is because the reference prices in period $t$ are some weighted average of prices obtaining in all countries of the world in period $t$; when we deal with the prices in period $t + 1$, we no longer know how to relate them to the prices from period $t$ because the shares of different countries might have changed. Although the United States is normally used as a reference country (in the sense that the GDP of the United States evaluated at U.S. prices and at "international prices" must be the same), this does not automatically mean that the inflation implicit in the PPP is the same as the inflation registered in the United States. The U.S. inflation rate is obtained using the consumption bundle and individual (relative) prices that obtain in the United States. But in the case of PPP, both the consumption basket and the relative prices change. The period $t + 1$ basket is not the same as the period $t$ basket: one reflects actual world consumption in one period, the other, actual world consumption in another period.

To use an illustration borrowed from Pogge and Reddy (2003, 3), consider two countries A and B and two base years 1980 and 2000. The within-country comparison of purchasing power is relatively easily done using the initial- (or final-) year composition of the basket and converting nominal values by thus-calculated CPIs. (The important, and reasonable, assumption is that the initial- and final-year basket are not very different, so that the Laspeyres- and Paasche-based CPIs do not differ significantly.) Thus we can move horizontally in figure 2.1 with some ease. Vertical comparisons are more difficult. They are based, as just explained, on a creation of an average "world" basket that exists in a statistical sense but is irrelevant for consumption choices

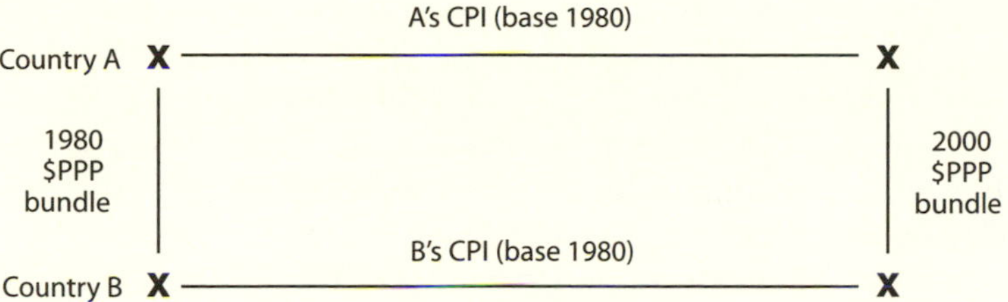


**Figure 2.1.** Price comparisons in space and time. *Source:* Pogge and Reddy (2003).

made in either country A or B. This is how the 1980 or 2000 PPPs are derived.

But the magnitude of these problems fades in comparison with problems we have to face when comparing incomes intercountry and intertemporally. Let us compare country B's income in 1980 with country A's income in 2000. The 2000 average world bundle of goods as well as relative prices are different from the bundle and the prices used to calculate the 1980 PPP. Thus, while we are used to making almost daily "horizontal comparisons," vertical ones are much more suspect, and diagonal comparisons are not, in principle, solvable. Pogge likens the problem to the issue of projecting earth's surface onto a plane.[5] We can make different assumptions and end up with different projections, but none of them preserves all the characteristics of the original.

## Survey-Based Mean Income or GDP per Capita?

We have used words "income" or "welfare" or "GDP per capita" very loosely, almost interchangeably. But they are different. First, note that Concepts 1 and 2 are always calculated using GDP per capita (see table 1.1). This is our proxy for the average welfare level in each country. We cannot use GDP per capita to calculate Concept 3 because we need *distribution* of income across individuals, which we get from household surveys. (We could "cheat" on that by taking distribution from household surveys and then multiplying it by GDP per capita, but the question then becomes, if we believe surveys to generate distributions, why not also take mean income from these surveys? We shall return to this issue later.) Thus, as soon as we move to calculating Concept 3 inequality we do not only change concepts, we also change our source of data and the *mean* value that we use: instead of GDP per capita, we use survey-calculated mean income or expenditure.

And once there, we face other problems. There is some evidence

(Milanovic 1999) that the ratio between mean income from surveys and GDP per capita will be greater in poor countries than in rich. There are several reasons for this. First, surveys focus on disposable household income, which by definition excludes direct taxes. Direct taxes in turn pay for free education and health (and police protection and other services), all of which contribute to GDP. The discrepancy between GDP and survey-mean will be larger in rich countries where direct taxes are a greater proportion of GDP. Second, companies' retained profits, inventories build-up, and capital income, which all tend to be greater in rich countries, are included in GDP but not at all or only imperfectly (e.g., capital income) in surveys.[6] Third, household surveys seem to be doing a better job of accounting for home consumption than national account (GDP) statistics. Since home consumption is relatively greater in poor countries, their incomes will be increased by more. This also raises survey mean / GDP ratio in poor relative to rich countries. The bottom line is this: the income-to-income comparison between the poor and rich countries will tend to show smaller difference than comparing GDP per capita to GDP per capita between the same countries. This, in turn, has an important implication. As we move from calculating Concept 1 or 2 to calculating Concept 3, we do not only change the way inequality is calculated (the issue we discussed in the previous section), but we also introduce a systematic difference between the mean income values that the concepts use.

**Income or Expenditures?**

The next problem is what we would like to compare: "welfare" or expenditures as an indicator of the actual living standard, or "income" as an indicator of the potential living standard.[7] The problem is that countries often "fall" into two groups depending on what information they collect in their households surveys. Western European and Eastern European countries, the United States, and most of Latin America collect household *income* information; African and Asian countries more often collect information on expenditures than incomes. If we want to have the whole world represented, we have no real option other than to combine the two indicators of welfare: income and expenditures. This creates a problem in turn because expenditures tend to be more equally distributed than income, at least over a month or a year, the two periods that the statistical offices conducting surveys generally use to record income and expenditures. The mixing of income and expenditure data will therefore introduce a bias in our results.

The problem is compounded by the differences in the definitions of income and expenditures. So long as we do not have a single world household survey, there will be differences in the definitions of income or expenditures among the countries. Generally speaking, we try to use disposable income, although the distinction between disposable and gross income is in many countries of little importance (since direct taxes are practically nil). But even the definition of gross or disposable income varies across countries. One example is treatment and valuation of home consumption, an item that can be very important in many poor countries. Another example is inclusion and valuation of imputable services, the most important being housing: if everything is the same except that in one country all housing is rented while in another all of it is owner-occupied, expenditure-based measure will yield higher "welfare" in the first country—unless we properly impute housing services. Often, however, imputation is not easy either because we lack housing information or cannot use appropriate prices (e.g., data on location or amenities are insufficient).[8] A third example is inclusion of self-employment income, coverage of agricultural and nonagricultural self-employed population, and the use of their net or gross income. A myriad of similar problems (e.g., the time-period of data collection and recall: the longer the time-period typically the less the inequality) have been extensively studied, or at least acknowledged, in the case of single-country comparisons through time (see, e.g., a number of excellent country studies—France, Germany, Israel, United States, Japan, Canada, Greece—in Gottschalk, Gustafsson, and Palmer 1997), or intercountry inequality comparisons (Atkinson and Brandolini 1999 commenting on Deininger, Squire, and Zhang 1995; Deininger and Squire 1996).

When it comes to expenditures, similar issues arise with respect to the treatment of purchases of consumer durables. Is a car that is purchased during the reference or recall period included with the entire amount expended, or is this amount pro-rated assuming some "normal" duration of the car so that it gives a proxy of utility received from the possession of the car over a period? If so, should all car owners, and not only those who have purchased the car during the survey period, be imputed a similar amount? The point is not to enumerate all these various comparability problems—but simply to state that in a panel analysis, these problems are much more serious than either in a time-series single country analysis or in a cross-section.

### Per Capita or Equivalent Adult?

All of international or world income distribution is calculated on a per capita basis. Yet one could argue that for a world where household size

**TABLE 2.1.**
Methodological Choices and Likely Outcomes

| *Choice between:* | *Used* | *Outcome* | *Why* |
|---|---|---|---|
| Exchange rate and PPP | PPP | Lowers inequality | Poor countries have lower price levels |
| PPP (Geary-Khamis) and PPP (Afriat) | Geary-Khamis | Lowers inequality | Boosts poor countries' incomes |
| GDP per capita and household survey mean income | Household survey mean | Lowers inequality | Public expenditures that are larger in rich countries are excluded |
| Per capita and equivalent adult | Per capita | Increases inequality | Greater economies of scale in poor countries are neglected |

and age of household members vary widely, comparing welfare on an equivalent adult basis would be more appropriate. Clearly, larger households and households with many children (whose prevalence is greater in poor countries) do not require as much, on a per capita basis, to be equally well-off as small households. However, moving from per capita to equivalent adult analysis meets with two formidable obstacles that make such an approach extremely unlikely—at least until a world-wide household survey is conducted. The first obstacle is technical. We often have only grouped-data information on income distribution, and such groups are formed on per capita basis. Even in cases where we do have individuals ranked by equivalent incomes, we do not usually know the scale used to convert household incomes into equivalent unit incomes. Moreover, such scales vary among the countries. Thus, if we used "equivalized" data, we may be easily combining data calculated with very different scales. In principle, however, this problem could be solved if we had access to individual-level data (with all the requisite information, including say, age of children) so that we could do all the calculations ourselves, or again if there were a single worldwide household survey.

The second obstacle is more difficult to overcome. The problem is immediately apparent if we observe that economies of scale and the cost of children relative to adults vary in function of relative prices within a country. This means that even if we had a single worldwide household survey, the "correct" equivalence scales to be used would not necessarily be the same for all countries. For example, in a country where the relative cost of children goods is high, we would need to assign a relatively high weight to children (say, 0.8), while in a country where the cost of children goods is low, the weight would be low (say, 0.5). The "correct" equivalence scales therefore vary by country. This, in turn, implies that we would need to conduct a relative price survey or to use the already collected International Comparison Project data to derive the country-specific equivalence scales. They would be, in a way, equivalent to PPPs. It is likely that they too would vary in function of country's income and that the relative cost of children goods would be lower and economies of size greater in poor than in rich countries. However, none of these results exists, and before there is (i) a worldwide household survey and (ii) an estimate, obtained within a consistent framework, of country-specific equivalence scales, we will have no choice but to stick with per capita comparisons, even if we know that they tend exaggerate world or international inequality.[9]

Table 2.1 summarizes the dilemmas and choices we make, and their likely outcomes.

# 3

## International and World Inequality Compared

To see what exactly the differences among the three concepts are we shall write out the Gini formula (since we would be using mostly the Gini coefficient to estimate inequality).[10] The Gini coefficient ranges from 0 (all recipients have the same income: full equality) to 100 (all income is received by one recipient only: maximum inequality).[11] One of the reasons for Gini's popularity is that it can be easily represented in graphical terms. It is equal to twice the area lying between the line of perfect equality (the 45° line) and the Lorenz curve (see figure 3.1). The Lorenz curve charts the percentage of total income received by the cumulative percentage of recipients when recipients are ranked by their per capita income. Thus, for example, point A in figure 3.1 tells us that 5 percent of the poorest people get 2 percent of total income (note that since they are poorest, their share must be less than 5 percent); point B tells us that the bottom 90 percent of recipients receive 80 percent of total income, or in other words, that the top 10 percent get 20 percent of total income. As can be easily verified, when the entire income is appropriated by one person, the income share of all but him will be zero, and the Lorenz curve will coincide with the $x$ axis, and then rise vertically at the point $x = 1$. Then the area between the line of perfect equality and the Lorenz curve would be twice the area of the triangle, that is, equal to 1 (or to 100 if we use percentages). On the other extreme, if everybody's income is the same, the Lorenz curve will follow the line of perfect equality, and since the two coincide, the area will be 0.

When the Gini coefficient of inequality between individuals in the world is written algebraically, and decomposed, it is shown to consist of three parts. Part A (the first term on the right-hand side of equation 1) is a weighted sum of within-country inequalities. Each country's ($i$-th) inequality is represented by its own Gini coefficient ($G_i$), and the weight is given by the product of the country's population share (in total world population) $p_i$ and the country's share in world income ($\pi_i$). Since both $p_i$ and $\pi_i$ are less than 1, their products will tend to be small. The weights assigned to $G_i$ will thus be small, and even the sum of $G_i p_i \pi_i$ will be quite small. This is the reason why the component A will tend to be small in the overall Gini decomposition.

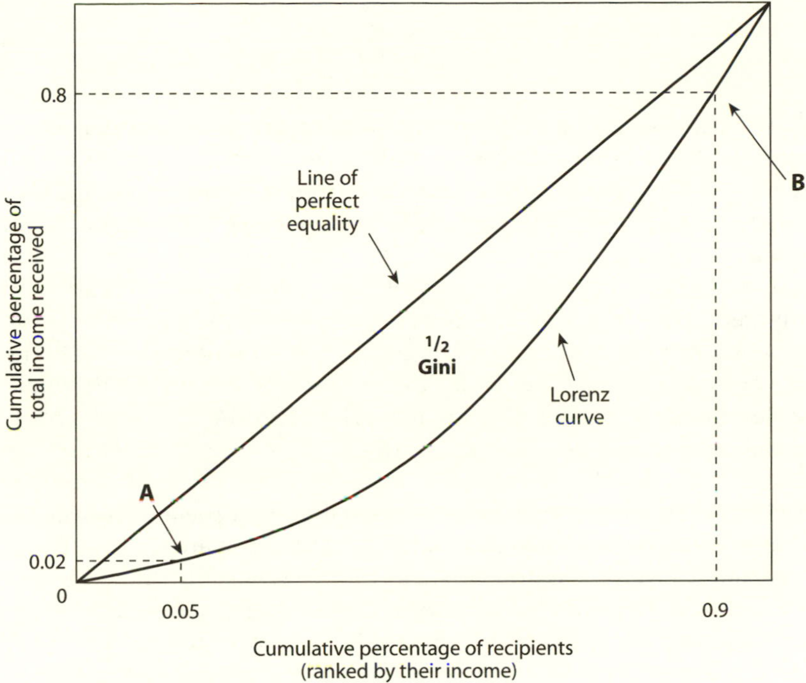


**Figure 3.1.** The Gini coefficient and the Lorenz curve.

Part B, the second term on the right-hand side of equation 1, gives the between-country inequality. All countries are ranked by their mean income (from the poorest to the richest) so that $y_j > y_i$, and the relative distance between two countries' mean incomes $(y_j - y_i)/y_i$ is weighted by the product of the poorer country ($i$-th) share in world income and richer country's ($j$-th) share in world population. We can thus immediately see that this intercountry term (ICT) will tend to be large for the pairs of poor populous countries (i.e., those with a relatively large $\pi_i$, like China) and very rich populous countries (i.e., those with a relatively high $p_i$, like the United States). After some manipulation, term B gets simplified (see equation 2; where $\mu$ represents mean world income) so that the weights are population shares.

$$GINI = \underbrace{\sum_{i=1}^{n} G_i p_i \pi_i}_{A} + \underbrace{\sum_{i}^{n}\sum_{j>i}^{n}\left(\frac{y_i - y_i}{y_i}\right)\pi_i p_j}_{B} + \underbrace{L}_{C} \qquad (1)$$

$$Gini = \sum_{i-1}^{n} G_i p_i \pi_i + \frac{1}{\mu} \sum_{i}^{n} \sum_{j>i}^{n} (y_j - y_i) p_i p_j + L \qquad (2)$$

Part C, the so-called overlapping component, is a residual. It accounts for the fact that somebody who lives in a richer country may still have an income lower than somebody from a poorer country. One interpretation of the "overlapping" component is "homogeneity" of population (Yitzhaki and Lerman 1991; Yitzhaki 1994; Lambert and Aronson 1993). The more important the "overlapping" component compared to the other two, the more homogeneous the population—or, differently put, the less one's income depends on where she lives. The more crowded (closer) the mean incomes of the countries, the more people from different countries will overlap, and the greater the overlap component will be. To see this, think of the European Union. Its member countries have very similar mean incomes: so part B cannot be very high (at the extreme, we can assume that their mean incomes differ infinitesimally, in which case part B will tend toward 0). Part A will be small because of the double weighting of $G_i$'s.[12] But there are still poor and rich people in the European Union: many people from (say) Italy will have a higher income than lots of people in (say) Germany even if Germany's mean income is higher. All of such "overlap" inequality will "feed" into part C. Contrast this with the situation between Germany and the Congo. Almost all Congolese would be poorer than all Germans, and there would be no overlap. Hence part C will be very small.

This can be illustrated by figure 3.2. Consider three countries with different mean incomes A < B and B < C. Around each country's mean income there is some distribution as given in figure 3.2a. There is some overlap in incomes between the rich people from the poor country (A) and the poor people from the other two countries (B and C). Now, let us assume that mean incomes of the three countries converge. Assume that while it is still true that A < B and B < C, the three mean incomes become much closer while the distributions do not change. Clearly, the area of the overlap will increase (see figure 3.2b). This shows that a "denser" world distribution—in the sense of mean incomes of the countries getting closer to each other—will be associated with an increase in the overlap component of the Gini.

So, in conclusion, when we decompose the Gini, it consists of three parts:

- **A.** Within-country inequality
- **B.** Between-country inequality
- **C.** Overlap

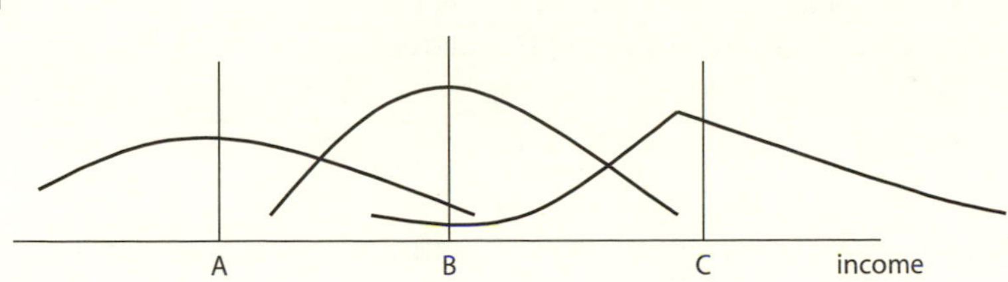


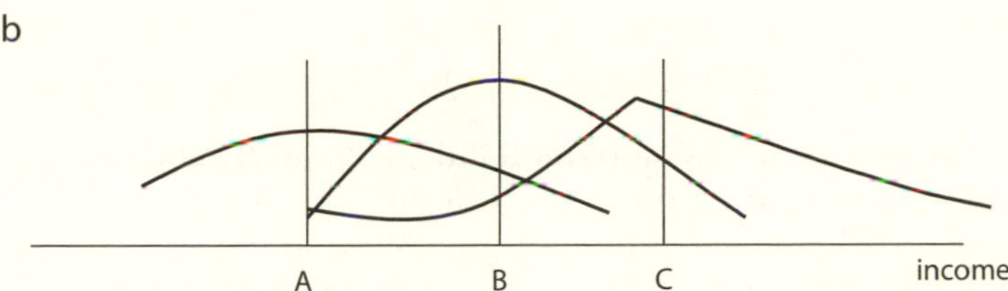


**Figure 3.2.** Small and large overlap component in Gini decomposition. Vertical lines represent countries' mean incomes. *Source:* Milanovic (2002).

So far we have discussed a general decomposition of the Gini that is valid for all cases. Let us now try to see how Concepts 1 and 2 fit into Gini equation 1. The situation is very simple. Part A is equal to 0 because, in one case (Concept 1), we take into account only the mean income of each country and in the other case (Concept 2), we assume all individuals to have the same mean income of the country. So, in Concept 1, within-country distribution does not even exist; in Concept 2, within-country distribution is assumed to be perfectly equal.

Similarly, for both Concept 1 and Concept 2 inequality, the overlap component must be 0. If there are no within-country distributions, there cannot be overlap: if all Chinese are assumed to have the mean income of China, and all Americans the mean income of the United States, then no single Chinese can have a higher income than any American. Case closed: the overlap is 0.

The difference between concepts 1 and 2 is only in the weighting of part B. In Concept 1, the weight of each country is $1/n$ ($n$ being the number of countries); in Concept 2, the weights are population shares. Thus, the Gini coefficient, in Concept 1, becomes simply

$$\frac{1}{\mu_1}\frac{1}{n^2}\sum_{i}^{n}\sum_{j>i}^{n}(y_j - y_i), \tag{3}$$

where $\mu_1$ = mean unweighted world income.

The Gini we calculate in Concept 2 is equal to

$$\frac{1}{\mu}\sum_{i}^{n}\sum_{j>i}^{n}(y_j - y_i)p_i p_j, \tag{4}$$

where $p_i$ are as before population weights and $\mu$ is population-weighted average world income. In Concept 3, of course, the Gini we calculate is equal to the entire formula (1), that is, all three parts are included. We can also easily see the relationship of Concept 2 to Concept 3:

$$\textit{Concept 3 Gini} = \sum_{i=1}^{n} G_i p_i \pi_i + \underbrace{\frac{1}{\mu}\sum_{i}^{n}\sum_{j>i}^{n}(y_j - y_i)p_i p_j}_{\text{Concept 2 Gini}} + L \tag{5}$$

Since part B (= weighted international inequality) tends to be the largest component of the Concept 3 Gini when it is calculated for the world (because differences among countries' mean incomes are large), some people have argued that Concept 2 gives a good approximation of "true" world inequality. Now, while this is true in a static sense—e.g., weighted international inequality accounts for 70 percent or more of world inequality—it does not follow that the *change* in Concept 2 inequality will necessarily give a good proxy for the *change* in Concept 3 inequality.

There are two reasons why the changes in Concepts 2 and 3 may move differently.

The first (Reason 1) is easy to see. Since weighted international inequality does not include the within-country inequality (part A), if that part changes, "true" world inequality might increase or decrease while weighted international inequality does not budge. Thus, for example, an increase in within-country inequalities in the 1980s and 1990s in countries as diverse as the United States, India, China, and Russia will increase (everything else being the same) part A but will not at all affect weighted international inequality, which, of course, reflects only what happens to mean incomes (and population and income weights), not what happens to distributions within each country. Moreover, when mean incomes do not change but distributions become more unequal, not only will part A increase, so will the overlap component. In that case, both components A and C will drive Gini up, while component B will not be affected at all.

The second reason (Reason 2) is slightly more complicated, although we have already alluded to it. Recall what we said before about how

**TABLE 3.1.**
World Gini and Its Components as China's and India's Per Capita Incomes Increase (simulations)

| | *Percent Income Increase* | | | | | | |
|---|---|---|---|---|---|---|---|
| *Inequality Components* | *0* | *10* | *20* | *50* | *70* | *85* | *100* |
| A. Within countries | 1.3 | 1.4 | 1.4 | 1.5 | 1.5 | 1.6 | 1.6 |
| B. Between countries (Concept 2) | 57.8 | 56.9 | 56.0 | 53.6 | 52.2 | 51.2 | 50.3 |
| C. Overlapping | 6.9 | 7.0 | 7.0 | 7.4 | 7.5 | 7.8 | 7.9 |
| *Total Gini (Concept 3)* | *66.0* | *65.2* | *64.4* | *62.5* | *61.2* | *60.6* | *59.8* |

*Source:* Milanovic (1999).

the overlap component changes when mean incomes become more "bunched," that is, when countries' incomes grow closer to each other. While "bunching" means that the weighted international inequality (Concept 2) goes down, there will be an increase in the overlap component. As a result, the two parts of the Concept 3 Gini will pull in opposite directions: while part B will go down, part C will go up (see equation 1). Thus, if we use the change in weighted international inequality to approximate the change in "true" world inequality, the approximation will be biased downward. In other words, "true" world inequality will not have decreased as much (or might have even increased) as implied by the change in the weighted international inequality.

We can illustrate this with the following example. Let mean incomes of India and China increase relative to the rest of the world, and keep everything else unchanged. Table 3.1 shows what then happens: while part B (weighted international inequality) decreases by as much as 7.5 Gini points as India's and China's mean per capita incomes double, part C (the overlap component) increases by 1 Gini point. And even part A increases as income weights of India and China go up. So if we use Concept 2 to assess what is happening to world inequality, we would conclude that it went down by 7.5 Gini points whereas the real change was only 6.2 points.

Of course, the reverse is true too. Were weighted international inequality to increase, the overlap component would tend to go down. Then the use of weighted international inequality would give us an overestimate of the change in "true" world inequality.

Finally, since we would be using the Theil entropy index as well, it is worthwhile giving its formulas too. Concept 2 inequality would be

$$\sum_{i=1}^{n} p_i \frac{y_i}{\mu} \ln \frac{y_i}{\mu}, \quad (6)$$

where all the terms are as defined earlier.[13] Unlike the Gini coefficient, the Theil index is exactly decomposable, and its Concept 3 formulation is as given in expression 7.

$$T = \frac{1}{N}\sum_{s=1}^{N} \frac{y_s}{\mu} \ln \frac{y_s}{\mu} = \sum_{i=1}^{n} \frac{n_i}{N} T_i + \sum_{i=1}^{n} \left(\frac{n_i}{N}\frac{y_i}{\mu}\right) \ln \frac{y_i}{\mu} \quad (7)$$

$$= \sum_{i=1}^{n} p_i T_i + \underbrace{\sum_{i=1}^{n} \left(p_i \frac{y_i}{\mu}\right) \ln \frac{y_i}{\mu}}_{\text{Concept 2 Theil}},$$

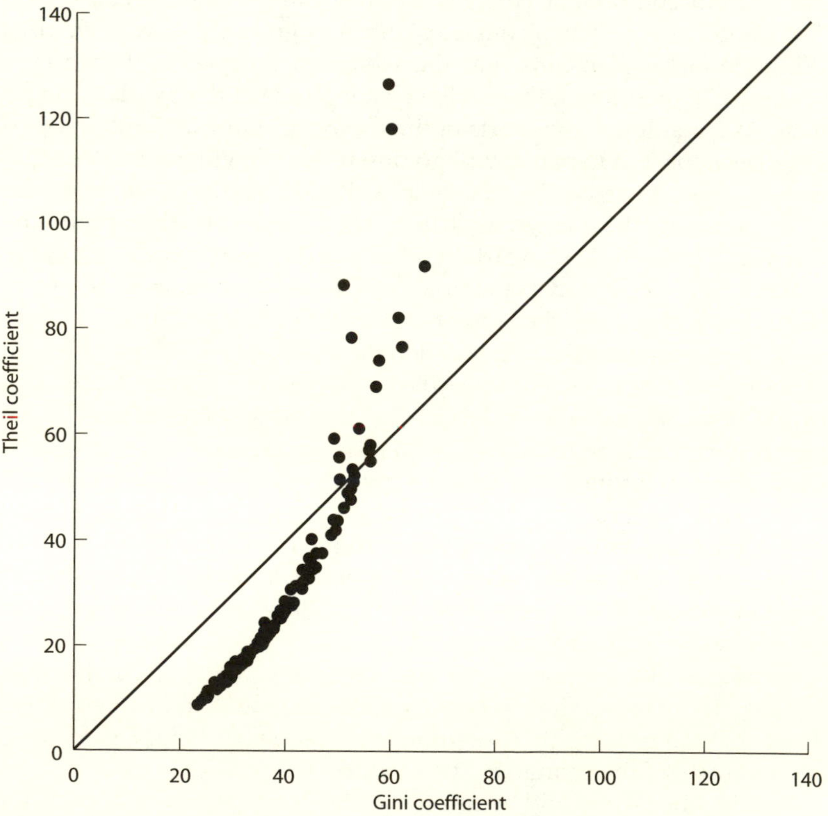


**Figure 3.3.** The empirical relationship between Gini and Theil coefficients (countries of the world; year 1998).

where $N$ = all individuals in the world, $y_s$ = $s$-th individual's income, $\mu$ = mean income of the world, $n_i$ = population of country $i$, $y_i$ = mean income of country $i$, and $T_i$ = Theil index of country $i$. The first right-hand side term gives the within-country component, which is a population-weighted sum of individual countries' Theils, and the second term gives the between-country component (our Concept 2), which treats all individuals in a country as if they had the same income. Consequently, Concept 3 Theil is equal to Concept 2 Theil plus the population-weighted average of country Theil indexes.

The empirical relationship between Gini and Theil is as shown in figure 3.3. At low inequality levels, Theil is lower than the Gini. But as inequality rises (and, of course, as both coefficients increase), Theil overtakes the Gini. The reason can be seen if we notice that in equation (7) very high incomes will produce a very high ln value, which, moreover, will be weighted also by the high value. Accordingly, for Theil, unlike the Gini coefficient, the upper bound is not 1 (or 100): if the entire income is received by one recipient, Theil index will amount to ln $N$, which is greater than 1.[14]

Now, "armed" with some intuitive and formulaic understanding of different inequality concepts, we can move to their calculation for the world in the period 1950–2000.

# Part II

## INEQUALITY AMONG COUNTRIES

# 4

## Rising Differences in Per Capita Incomes

We are trying to find out what things *are*, whether or not we like them.
—Ortega y Gasset, *An Interpretation of Universal History*, p. 162

### Definitions and Coverage

We shall consider first the easiest concept—unweighted international inequality. In the analysis in this chapter, we shall never refer to the population. We shall ignore it altogether as if the growth rate of a tiny country had the same importance for the world as the growth rate of China. This is an approach that makes sense, first, for the reasons of economic policy-making, because we can regard each country's experience as an observation on what works and why (and for that approach, the size of the country clearly does not matter), and second, because our view of the world is also influenced by how inequality among countries changes.

A few words are in order, however, to explain what countries are included in our calculations. The calculations are based on nations' per capita GDPs expressed in 1995 dollars of equal purchasing parity. The World Bank *World Development Indicators 1997* give 1995 GDP per capita values in 1995 PPP dollars for about 120 countries. This is our benchmark value. Starting from it, and using countries' GDP per capita growth rates at constant domestic prices, we fill in the values for all the years going back to 1950, and do this for as many countries as possible. Most of these values (approximately four out of five) come from the World Bank SIMA (Statistical Information Management and Analysis) database which gives GDP per capita in constant 1995 dollars.[15] These data, however, are not complete (that is, are not available for all countries), and the period begins in 1960. Thus, for the missing country/years, and in particular for the period 1950–1960, we have used a variety of sources: countries' statistical yearbooks, International Monetary Fund's *International Financial Statistics*, Summers and Heston's Penn World Tables (PWT), and Maddison (1995, 2001) data.[16]

Appendix 1 gives the years and countries that are included in our calculations. The per capita GDPs[17] are thus made comparable across time and across countries.[18] We believe that this is the most complete and consistent panel series of GDPs per capita: out of the total 7038 possible cells (138 countries times 51 years), we have the data for 6149 country-years.

Then, for each year, we calculate the Gini coefficient (and eight other measures of inequality; see appendix 6) of such national per capita GDPs.[19] Clearly, the Gini will depend greatly on the number of countries in the sample. Even if we had 100 percent coverage of the world, but the world fragmented from X countries to X + Y countries while leaving income of each individual person *unchanged*, it is very likely (although not necessary since this would depend on the way the world would fragment) that the Gini with more countries would be greater than the Gini calculated with fewer countries. One of the important things for which we therefore need to control is the number of countries. I have decided to (as it were) project the world backward: in other words, to begin with the countries that existed in 1995, and to try to find their per capita GDPs for all the years going back to 1950. This has led to three problems.

First, some of today's countries, like Ukraine, Slovakia, Bangladesh, or Eritrea, were not independent nations for at least a part of the period with which we are concerned. In such cases, I have tried to obtain their republican/state/provincial GDP per capita. Therefore, they are treated as full-fledged countries throughout the 1950–2000 period. For most of these countries, the problem has not proved insoluble. For example, the republican statistics can be culled up from the Soviet yearbooks all the way back to 1958 (with a hiatus, though, between 1961 and 1963); for the former Yugoslav republics we can go back to 1952, for the Czech republic and Slovakia, to 1984; for Bangladesh (East Pakistan), we have the data since 1960.

Second, some of today's countries were colonies, and it is difficult or impossible to obtain data on their GDP per capita. Fortunately, that problem is severe for the period 1950–60 only. After 1960, as decolonization picks up, the data for almost all the former colonies become available.

The third problem is simple lack of data, independent of countries coming into existence or disappearing. For example, Haiti or Cuba were independent countries throughout, but information on their GDP per capita is not continuously available. Thus the sample size varies simply in function of certain internal (wars, revolutions) or external developments (e.g., Cuban withdrawal from the World Bank and the IMF). However, this variation is limited to a handful of countries.

Figure 4.1 shows the number of countries and the share of world

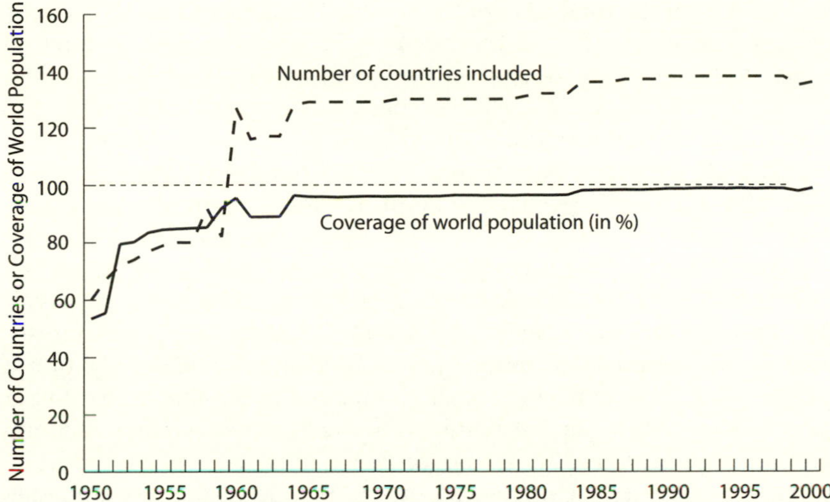


**Figure 4.1.** Number of countries and the percentage of world population included in calculations.

population included in each year. In the 1950s, the number of countries steadily rises from about sixty to a little over eighty. Then, in a step-like fashion, with the decolonization in Africa and Asia, there is an increase in the coverage in 1960 (127 countries are included). Since 1960, the number of countries slowly increases oscillating between 129 and 138. The only exception is the period 1961–63, for which we lack data for the then-Soviet republics: there is thus a decline in the sample size in these years. China is included since 1952, India, Pakistan, the Philippines and Brazil from the very beginning in 1950, Indonesia since 1954, Nigeria since 1951, most of the OECD countries since 1950. The calculations from 1960 to the end of the century are practically done across the same sample, which, of course, makes them almost fully comparable.

The same, if slightly more dramatic, evolution is exhibited by the share of world population included. It starts with about 55 percent; then jumps in 1952, when China is included, to 80 percent; and since 1960, when most of the African countries are added, it remains at almost 100 percent.

## World Growth

Before we move to a study of inequality, let us briefly consider world's growth record over the entire post–World War II period. There we distinguish between two different ways to measure growth. The first is the growth rate of the total GDP of the world. Total world GDP is the sum of all countries' GDPs (all the calculations are expressed in international dollars). This is the standard calculation. However, such a calculation is "plutocratic" in the sense that it gives greater weight to rich countries. For example, since the U.S. GDP represents 22 percent of world GDP, a 5 percentage decline in the U.S. GDP will reduce world GDP by more than 1 percentage point. It can make an obvious difference to whether the world moves into recession or not. Put differently, a country of about the same population size as the United States but poorer will matter much less in such a calculation. Indonesia, for example, accounts for only 2 percent of world GDP. Hence, a 5 percent recession in this country will reduce world GDP, almost negligibly, by 0.1 percent. But, if we look at people, in both cases about the same number of people (assuming no distributional changes) have seen their incomes go down by 5 percent.[20] To adjust for this, that is, to calculate world income growth rate as experienced by the people of the world (again, assuming no distributional changes), we calculate the population-weighted growth rate. The "plutocratic" growth rate is shown in figure 4.2, the "people" growth rate is shown in figure 4.3. The growth rates are shown starting with 1953 because the average GDP of the world drops significantly in 1952 as China enters our sample. This of course does not represent a real change, but only a change in the sample composition.

Figure 4.2 shows the five postwar global recessions: in 1954, 1960, 1975, 1982, and 1991. All five recessions coincided with the recessions in the developed world, or, more exactly, in the United States, which, as we have seen, due to the nature of the calculation of the "plutocratic" growth rate strongly influences what happens to world growth.[21] Two of the five recessions (1975 and 1982) coincided with the oil crises. The 1960 recession was the deepest: world average income dropped by 2.5 percent; the 1975 recession was the shallowest (average income decreased by 0.3 percent). The figure also illustrates some extremely high world growth rates—in excess of respectively 4 and 5 percent per capita—in 1955 and 1964 (driven by Japan, West Germany, and in the latter year by China as well).

Table 4.1 illustrates the slowdown in (standard or "plutocratic") world growth in the past twenty years compared to the period 1960–78. The average growth rate of world economy was cut almost in half: from 2.7 percent per person annually to 1.5 percent.

We use here and in the rest of the book the year 1978 as the cut-off year. This is for several reasons. First, the year 1978 was the last year of relatively fast world growth (2.6 percent per capita), and it would take another ten years until that rate would be reached again. Second, and

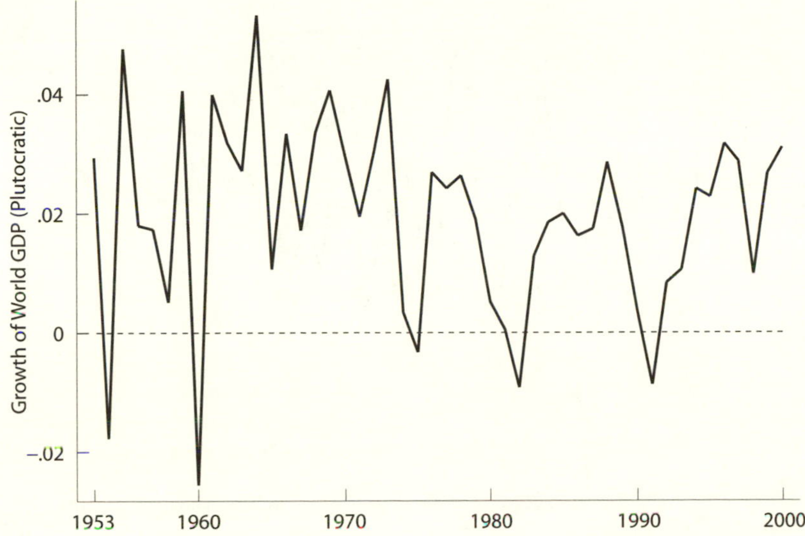


**Figure 4.2.** Growth rate of world economy ("standard" calculation), 1953–2000. Growth rate expressed in fractions: e.g., 0.04 is 4 percent per capita per annum.

more importantly, the years 1978–80 were, in the words of Paul Bairoch (1997, 3: 999), "les années charnières," the beginning of a new phase of development that "for many Third World market economies is characterized by a total failure of economic growth"—a fact which will be amply documented in the pages that follow. The year 1978 was also the last year before the second oil-crisis and the tripling of oil prices.[22] Third, it was the year when the Chinese agricultural reforms, an event of enormous significance for poverty reduction and inequality in the world, began. Finally, 1978 was only a couple of years before the quadrupling of real interest rates, which in the early 1980s precipitated the first debt crisis.[23]

The population-weighted world growth rate in figure 4.3 shows only one year of negative growth (1961), which was caused by a dramatic decline in China, whose per capita output, particularly in agriculture, dropped precipitously due to the bottlenecks, disorganization, and adverse incentives brought about by the failed Great Leap Forward and the creation of communes. China's GDP per capita plunged 26 percent, and the worst man-made famine in recent history, and possibly in history ever, ensued.[24] For all other years, population-weighted world growth was positive. Unlike the "plutocratic" growth rate, where we see a clear discontinuity at the end of the 1970s, here there is no trend. Population-weighted growth was in almost all years higher than the "plutocratic" growth rate indicating that populous countries have

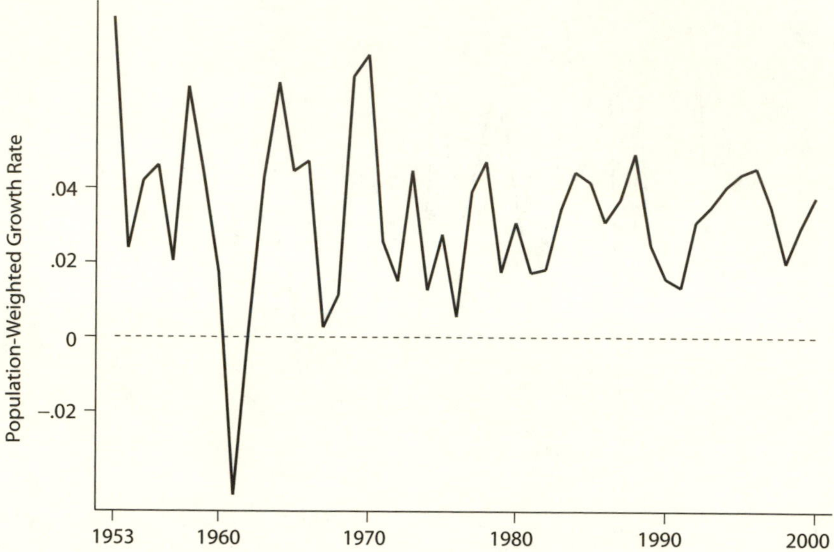


**Figure 4.3.** Population-weighted world growth rate, 1953–2000. Growth rate expressed in fractions: e.g., 0.04 is 4 percent per capita per annum.

tended to grow faster (on per capita basis) than countries with large economies. Over the entire period, population-weighted per capita growth rate was 3.3 percent per annum vs. the "plutocratic" rate of 1.9 percent per annum (table 4.1).

To focus on poor countries, we also include a population- and utility-weighted growth rate where marginal utility is approximated by the inverse of GDP per capita (figure 4.4). The assumption is the standard one of (total) utility increasing in the logarithm of income.[25] Thus calculated growth rate gives an extra bonus to the growth in populous and poor countries. Overall, this growth rate was the highest in the first period, it decelerated in the second, and then increased again during the last two decades (table 4.1).[26] It was negative in five years, although for entirely different reasons than the "plutocratic" rate. While the "plutocratic" rate is influenced by what is happening in the United States, the population- and utility-weighted rate is determined by changes in China. Thus, in each year when it was negative (1961, 1962, 1967, 1968, and 1976), Chinese growth rate was negative too. Of course, several other poor and populous countries also contributed, as for example in 1967 when Nigeria (–18 percent), Bangladesh (–4.4 percent), Indonesia (–1.2 percent), and Egypt (–1.8 percent) had negative growths. China's influence was preponderant though: the correlation between its growth rate and population- and utility-weighted world growth rate is 0.94.

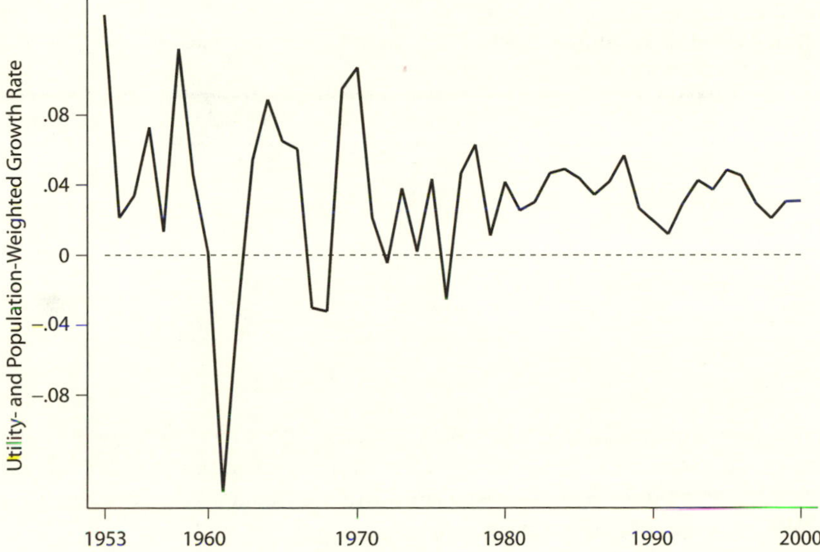


**Figure 4.4.** Utility and population-weighted world growth rate, 1953–2000. Growth rate expressed in fractions: e.g., 0.04 is 4 percent per capita per annum.

Finally, note that the last period (1979–2000) displays, regardless of the growth rate we select, much less temporal volatility, as measured by the standard deviation, than either of the two previous periods.

The analysis so far has referred to average world annual growth rates (however measured). But if we combine all countries and all their annual growth rates and break them down into the same three periods, we notice—not surprisingly—in the most recent period a significant drop in average and median growth rates amounting to between 1.5 and 2 per-

**TABLE 4.1.**
Three Growth Rates Compared, 1953–2000 (in percent, per capita; per annum)

| | *1953–60* | *1961–78* | *1979–2000* | *Total* |
|---|---|---|---|---|
| "Plutocratic" growth | 1.4<br>(2.4) | 2.7<br>(1.3) | 1.5<br>(1.2) | 1.9<br>(1.6) |
| Population-weighted growth | 4.4<br>(2.2) | 3.0<br>(2.9) | 3.2<br>(1.1) | 3.3<br>(2.1) |
| Population- and utility-weighted growth | 5.5<br>(4.7) | 2.4<br>(5.8) | 3.5<br>(1.2) | 3.4<br>(4.1) |

*Note:* Growth rates calculated as simple averages over the period. Standard deviations of growth rates given between brackets.

**TABLE 4.2.**
Annual (Real) Per Capita Growth Rates in Three Periods (each country/year is one observation)

| | *1950–60* | *1961–78* | *1979–2000* |
|---|---|---|---|
| Mean growth rate | 3.4 | 3.0 | 0.9 |
| Median growth rate | 3.1 | 3.2 | 1.7 |
| Percentage of negative growth rates | 25.4 | 22.4 | 33.1 |
| Total number of growth rates included | 670 | 2348 | 2980 |

centage points per capita (table 4.2). We also find a significantly increasing share of negative growth rates: their percentage shoots up from about 22 percent in 1960–78, to almost a third during the last two decades. This means that, on average, every year one country out of three had seen its GDP per capita decline. The negative changes in the 1979–2000 period affected the shape of the distribution of growth rates. The distribution, which in the first two periods looked practically the same, shifted to the

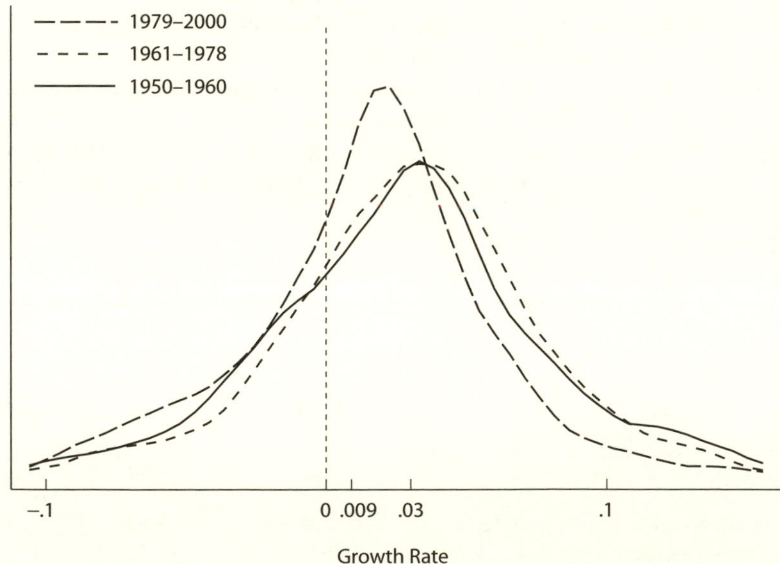


**Figure 4.5.** Distribution of annual growth rates in three periods (1950–60, 1961–78 and 1979–2000). Each growth rate is one observation, expressed as ratio (0.03 denotes a 3 percent annual per capita growth). Nonparametric kernel density function with Epanechnikov bandwidth.

left with a much longer tail and greater thickness, and, of course, with fewer positive rates at the right end of the distribution (see figure 4.5).

## Intercountry Inequality

Figure 4.6 (the top line) shows the evolution of unweighted international inequality from 1950 to 2000.[27] The detailed results for nine measures of inequality are shown in appendix 6. In the text we shall discuss the Gini coefficient, and at times Theil only. A part of the increase in inequality can be attributed to the increase in the sample size, as when the Gini coefficient in 1960 jumps from 44.9 to 46.3 (the 1960 Gini for the countries included in the 1959 sample would have been 45.0, which is practically unchanged from its 1959 value). But that cause disappears from about 1960 because the countries in the sample, and the share of world population covered, are practically constant. Between 1965 and 1982, the Gini is almost unchanged: in 1965, it is 46.9, in 1982, it is 47.3. However, after 1982 there is an inexorable tendency for inequality to increase. For twelve years, between 1982 and 1994, there is a steady and sharp increase in intercountry inequality. In other words, there is a growing divergence in countries' economic performance, with poor countries doing, on average, worse than the rich ones. After 1994, the increase is still present but is

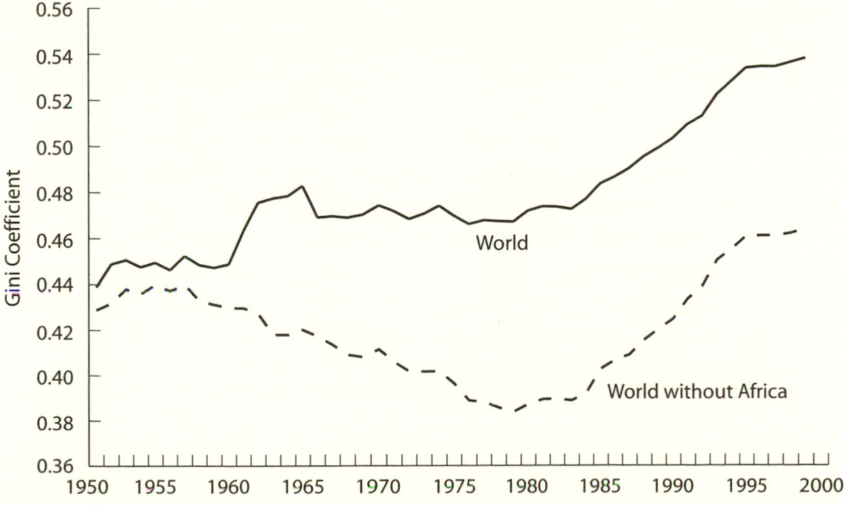


**Figure 4.6.** Unweighted international inequality I, 1950–2000.

more moderate for a few years before picking up again. By the end of the twentieth century, the intercountry Gini is 54.5. This represents a gain of almost eight Gini points, or 20 percent, compared to its mid-1970s value.[28]

### Why Is Intercountry Inequality Increasing?

At its most abstract, if unweighted international inequality increases, this indicates that poor countries are doing worse than rich countries. We explore this question next by looking at the five-year average growth rates of all countries and regressing them against their initial GDP per capita. We would expect that the period of relative Gini stability that lasted from the early 1960s to the early 1980s would produce coefficients that are not statistically different from zero, while the latter period of divergence would yield positive correlation between countries' quinquennial growth rates and their initial GDP per capita. This is exactly what is shown by the regression coefficients in figure 4.7. While the coefficients in the mid-1960s are positive, they are not statistically significant. It is only during a relatively brief period, 1986–90, that the coefficients turn positive and statistically significant (at a 5 percent level at least). The same is, interestingly, true at the very end of the last period, just prior to year 2000. It would seem that the rather broad generalization namely, that "in the 1980s, there was a shift in world economy such that relatively poor countries began growing slower than the relatively rich countries"—has some validity. The world was exposed to the twin shock of the increased price of oil in 1979 and much higher real interest rates beginning in 1980. The first shock affected oil-importing countries both rich, middle-income and poor, but while the rich recovered after a few years, the middle-income and poor countries did not. It is very likely that the latter failed to recover because they had, in addition, to face sharply increased interest on their debt (for the discussion of the structural break, see Bairoch 1977, vol. 3; Rodrik 1999).

Now, whence does this increased unweighted inequality from the 1980s onward come? We have a number of candidates. Let us quickly dispose of a popular one: "increasing inequality among countries is due solely to the disastrous performance of African countries." While African "growth tragedy" did contribute to intercountry inequality, it was not its sole "engine" during the past two decades. This can be easily observed from the second line in figure 4.6, which shows Concept 1 inequality for the world without Africa. The increase is even sharper and begins earlier, in 1978 rather than in 1982. We need to look for other

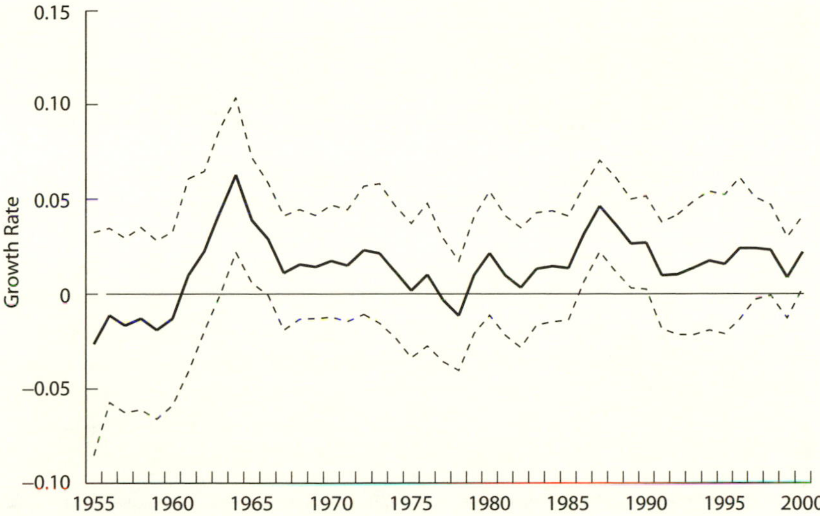


**Figure 4.7.** Coefficients of five-year average growth rate on initial GDP per capita. 95 percent confidence intervals shown in broken lines. Growth rate expressed in fractions: e.g., 0.05 is 5 percent per capita per annum.

candidates. For example, to Latin American countries, which are mostly in the middle of the international income distribution, and for whom the 1980s were the "lost decade." Or, to the transition economies that too were in the middle of the international income distribution, and for whom the 1980s were a decade of stagnation while the 1990s were not only a lost decade but also a decade of depression or, at best, severe recession.[29] When the middle of income distribution slides downward, overall inequality can easily creep up. Similarly, the performance of most African countries over the past two decades has been disastrous. In the year 2000, twenty-four African countries had a GDP per capita that was smaller than twenty years ago; for another five countries, the 2000 GDP per capita was less than its level ten years ago (see appendix 4). Most of the African countries started the 1960s and the 1970s with GDPs per capita in the lower middle or in the bottom of international distribution. When poor countries fall further behind, inequality of course rises.[30]

We look at these issues in figure 4.8. We divide the world in five regions: Africa; Asia; Latin America and the Caribbean; transition countries of Eastern Europe and the former USSR; and Western Europe, North America and (the rich) Oceania (WENAO). The last region is basically the club of rich countries. The bottom line in figure 4.8 shows the unweighted inequality between WENAO countries. We know from a number of studies

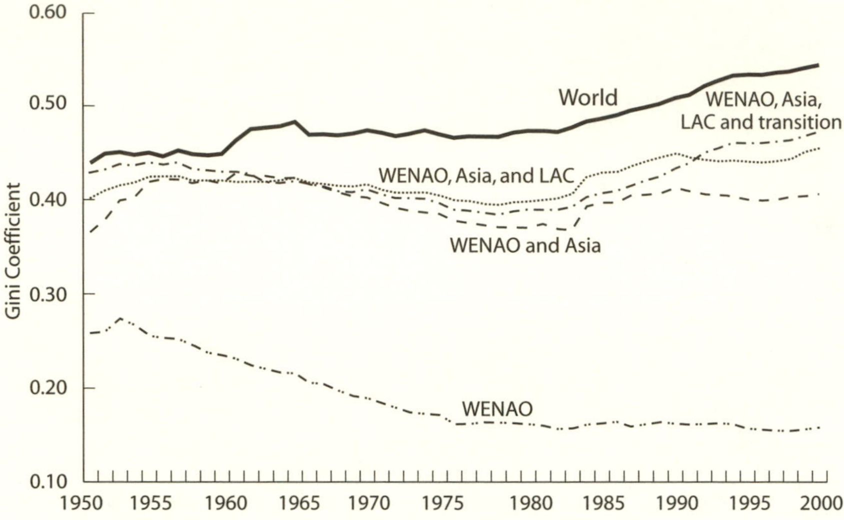


**Figure 4.8.** Unweighted international inequality II, 1950–2000.

(Dowrick and Nguyen 1989; Li and Papell 1999) that there was a GDP per capita convergence among the "club" of rich countries. This is what the Gini coefficient shows: while inequality among WENAO countries' GDPs per capita was in the range of 25–27 in the 1950s, it steadily declined throughout the 1960s, and has since remained at the level of about 15 Gini points.

Next, we combine all WENAO and Asian countries and find for the entire period a practically unchanged unweighted Gini varying within a narrow band between 37 and 42. For example, in 1953 the WENAO-plus-Asia Gini was 40.2; in 2000, it was 40.7. Note that since 1960, none of the Gini changes can be accounted for by the change in the sample composition because both WENAO and Asian countries that are included are the same. Thus, the remarkable stability in inequality of per capita GDPs among the WENAO and Asian countries combined is not an artifact. This, of course, does not imply that the relative positions of the countries have remained unchanged—witness the remarkable growth of Japan or South Korea—but that their climb, and contribution to lower unweighted inequality, was offset by other countries' relative declines (the Philippines, Jordan).

We now proceed by adding other regions, stacking, as it were, world income distribution, region by region.[31] When we add to the WENAO and Asian countries, the Latin American and Caribbean (LAC) countries, we find that the Gini increases very slightly, to over 40, but that it

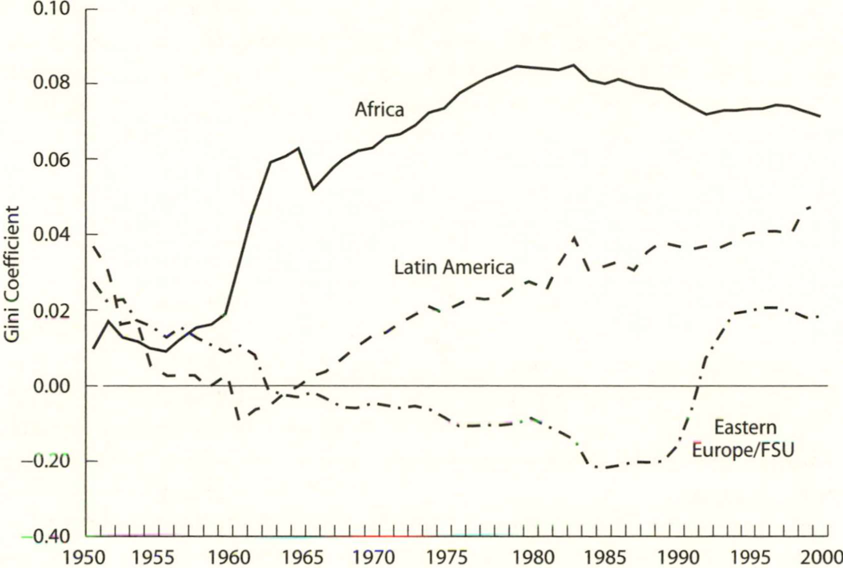


**Figure 4.9.** Gini point contributions to Concept 1 inequality, 1950–2000 (when the regions are stacked in the order explained in the text).

is both very stable and tracks what happens to the WENAO + Asia inequality until 1982. Then, as the Latin American countries enter their decade of stagnation, the Gini of WENAO + Asia + LAC begins its sharp increase reaching a plateau of 46 in 1990 (see the broken line in figure 4.8). Consequently, the Latin American crisis in the 1980s did contribute to the rising international inequality, as the relative position of the countries that were around the middle of international income distribution deteriorated.

We move even closer to an explanation once we add transition economies. This line too tracks very closely the previous two (WENAO + Asia and WENAO + Asia + LAC) until the mid-1980s. After that point, it begins to rise. By the early 1990s, "stacking" the transition countries on top of the other three regions adds to the overall inequality. From the early 1990s, the "locomotive" of increasing international inequality becomes the transition economies. They "take over" from Latin America. The steady increase in international inequality between the mid-1980s and the year 2000 is thus shown to have been driven first by the declining relative incomes of Latin American, and then (as that "source" began to wane somewhat) by the declining relative incomes of the transition countries.

The difference between "world" in figure 4.8 and "WENAO + Asia +

Latin America + transition" inequality is due to African countries. We see that this difference has been increasing from the 1960s until the early 1980s and has hence stabilized. Over the past twenty years, Africa's contribution to unweighted international inequality has been fairly constant.[32] This is also shown in figure 4.9. The figure also illustrates the continued growing importance of Latin America and the Caribbean in explaining Concept 1 inequality increase, and the sudden and dramatic shift in the role of the East European/Former Soviet Union (FSU) countries from an "inequality-reducing" world middle class to an "inequality-increasing" downwardly mobile group.

Summing up, inequality among countries was broadly constant in the 1960–82 period because the increasing contribution of Africa (due to its slow growth) was balanced by the shrinking international inequalities among the rich countries (WENAO) and the catching up by Eastern Europe/FSU and Latin America. In the next two decades, international inequality rose steadily, first due to GDP per capita stagnation and decline among the middle-income countries in Latin America, and then due to the same phenomenon—just more dramatic—among another set of middle-income countries in Eastern Europe and the former Soviet Union.

# 5

## Regional Convergence, Divergence, or . . . "Vergence"

IN THE MOVIE *Mr. Smith Goes to Washington*, the future Senator Smith is asked whether he is in favor of deflation or inflation. Aware that an affirmative answer to either is going to lead him into trouble, he declares himself to be in favor of . . . "flation."[33] Our analysis of unweighted international inequality has a direct bearing on two topics that have recently been very much present in economic literature: the issue of GDP per capita convergence or divergence (or lack of either: "vergence"), and the bimodality of international income distribution (the "twin peaks").

The idea of convergence derives from economic theory where through either international trade or movement of factors of production (migration of labor from poor to rich countries, and capital flows from rich to poor countries), and/or the spread of technology that allows the poor to catch up with the rich, poor countries are supposed to grow faster than the rich. There are at least three conventional types of convergence.[34] The unconditional convergence hypothesis posits that all countries' steady-state incomes will converge regardless of their initial levels. This means that all factors that determine steady-state income such as savings propensity, level of technology (the shift parameter in the neoclassical production function), technological progress, population growth, etc. will be the same across countries. The dispersion of countries' incomes measured by the standard deviation of their GDPs or the variance of logarithms would be decreasing over time. It is the so-called $\sigma$ convergence (Barro and Sala-i-Martin 1995).[35] This convergence is about *distribution* of countries' GDPs per capita—exactly the same thing as our Concept 1 inequality.[36]

A related $\beta$ convergence hypothesis is concerned with the relationship between growth rates and initial income levels. It starts from the assumption of diminishing marginal returns, which imply a higher marginal productivity of capital in capital-poor countries, and concludes that with the same savings propensities, income (and capital-) poor countries will tend to grow faster than rich countries. Then when we regress growth rates on initial income levels, we should expect to find a negative correlation between the two, that is, the $\beta$ coefficient in the regression would be less than zero. Unconditional $\beta$ convergence implies that all the relevant parameters that determine income will be the same across all countries, and that a simple regression of growth rate on initial income should yield a negative coefficient (as depicted in figure 4.7). Under the hypothesis of conditional β convergence, however, steady-state incomes are not the same for all countries, and since there may be differences in savings propensity, access to technology, investment in human capital, population growth, etc. between the countries, these variables need to be included explicitly on the right-hand side of the regression.[37] It is then said that conditional convergence exists if $\beta < 0$ in regressions such as $\ln y_t - \ln y_{t-1} = \alpha + \beta \ln y_{t-1} + \Sigma \gamma_i X_{ti}$, where $Xi$'s are a set of other controls.[38] The club convergence goes one step further in setting more restrictive criteria under which convergence would take place: in addition to countries' having to have the same structural characteristics, they also need to have the same initial conditions.[39]

The theory of convergence has led to a proliferation of econometric studies in the past two decades and has received confirmation—and here we mention only a small sample of studies—from the empirical findings pertaining to the industrialized countries over the hundred-year period beginning in 1870 (Baumol 1986; Baumol and Wolff 1988), individual U.S. states (Barro and Sala-i-Martin 1992), European regions (e.g., Cannon and Duck 2000, p. 418), African countries (Tsangarides 2001; Jones 2002), Spanish provinces (Goerlich and Mas 2001), units of the Russian federation (Yemtsov 2002) and OECD countries (e.g., Barro and Sala-i-Martin 1992 (p. 244); and, more recently, Maudos, Pastor, and Serrano 2000; Li and Papell 1999; Fuente 1999; Tsangarides 2001).[40] We have seen it here too in the fact that the unweighted Gini coefficient of per capita GDPs of WENAO countries has almost continuously declined since the early 1950s and is now only one-half of its 1950 value. However, once the debate shifted to other areas outside the rich world, and to a longer time horizon, analysts have observed divergence rather than convergence.

This fact has been, of course, well known and obvious to economic historians (Bairoch 1981; Maddison 1991; Abramovitz 1989; Pomeranz 2000), but it has not made sufficient mark among macroeconomists and growth theorists. There has been, however, a recent acknowledgment of divergence. Two well-known papers illustrate this shift: Pritchett's (1997) and Lucas (1998) show that over the past two centuries, per capita incomes of the countries of the world have diverged principally because today's rich world has been able to pull ahead of the rest. Maddison (1995, p. 22) shows that the ratio between the richest and the poorest country, expressed in international dollars, went up from 3 to 1 in 1820 to 72 to 1 in 1992.[41] Moreover, it is the regions that were (slightly) richer than the others in 1820 that also grew the fastest. Thus, the hierarchy of the regions stayed about the same since the time of Adam Smith, but income differences among them widened (Maddison 1995, pp. 20–22; 2001, pp. 46–47).[42] The story of divergence has an intuitive appeal in the observation (made by Pritchett 1997) that if the richest countries in the world, two centuries ago, were much poorer than today and if the poorest had at least to be at the subsistence level, then the differences in their income levels could not have been very large. Since a number of countries today is still at, or close to, the subsistence level of income while the rich are greatly above it, then the divergence of international incomes, rather than their convergence, must have been the story of the past two centuries. This incontestable evidence puts in doubt the workings of the standard growth theory, which postulates that through trade, migration, capital flows, or diffusion of technology incomes will converge. Moreover, the story of the divergence has been found to hold not only for the long period (Braudel's *longue durée*) of the past two centuries, but even for the more recent period of the past two decades (Easterly and Levine 2001)—a fact that we too have just noticed in the increase of our Concept 1 inequality.

These empirical facts that are difficult to square with economic theory have led to two reactions. First was endogenous growth theory, which holds that in addition to the "usual suspects" (improved education, increasing labor force, and capital accumulation), there are many other important factors that affect growth. They are either political (democracy, rule of law, social stability) or economic (inflation, fiscal deficit, openness). Allowing for these variables permits a number of authors to claim that conditional convergence holds—namely that after controlling for these variables, poor countries still grow faster than the rich.[43] But while "controlling" for other factors may make sense in a regression, it can hardly make sense in real life. If I am told that the Congo will grow faster than the United States or Singapore if it had the same institutions and the same quality of macroeconomic policy as the latter two, am I going to find this conclusion credible or even interesting? The truth is that these political and economic factors cannot be held constant—they are endogenous to the process of growth. In the words of Solimano (2001, p. 20), "[T]he usefulness of conditional convergence tests [is] rather limited since they impose by assumption the equality of factors whose disparity across countries has to be explained and [which] are at the core of differential growth performance across countries and international inequality."[44]

Another important departure from the conventional growth economics consists in the questioning of the constant returns to scale and thus the diminishing marginal productivity of the factors of production

(Krugman 1991; Easterly 2001; Easterly and Levine 2001). If divergence cannot be squared with the usual economics based on diminishing marginal returns to factors of production, then something else (such as technological progress, non-rival but excludable goods—see Romer 1990) that leads to increasing returns to scale, or perhaps complementarity between capital and highly skilled labor (Lucas 1990), must be the cause of divergence. Easterly and Levine (2001) support the idea of increasing returns to scale by pointing to large concentrations of skilled labor and capital, both within nations as well as internationally. If capital tends to flow to countries that are already capital-rich, and skilled labor to the countries that are skill-intensive, this must be because there are increasing returns to the concentration of people and capital. Technological progress is also faster when there is concentration of capital and labor. Under these conditions, it is very hard to speak of any kind of convergence of countries' incomes at all. As Islam (2003, p. 330) writes, "convergence under heterogeneity of both $A_0$ [technology level] and $g$ [technological progress] implies that economies are converging not only to different levels of per capita income but also to different growth rates. This may be termed as the Weak (notion of) Conditional Convergence (WCC), although some may wonder whether WCC is worth calling convergence at all."

Let us now consider *within-regional* income differences, or if we take the regions to be "clubs," the issue of club convergence. To do this, we look at unweighted regional Ginis. We observe (see table 5.1 and figure 5.1) that countries' income levels are strongly diverging in Africa, Asia, and, more recently, in Eastern Europe/former Soviet Union, while they are converging in the WENAO region and display no clear trend in Latin America.[45] Between 1960 and 2000, Asian unweighted Gini increased from 36 to 53, and is the highest of all the regions. This, of course, reflects a process of growing regional divergence where some

**TABLE 5.1.**
Unweighted Regional Ginis (Concept 1 inequality)

| | *1960* | *1978* | *2000* |
|---|---|---|---|
| Africa | 37.8 | 41.1 | 50.6 |
| Asia | 36.2 | 47.5 | 53.3 |
| LAC | 30.7 | 27.5 | 34.6 |
| Eastern Europe/FSU | 15.0 | 18.4 | 32.2 |
| WENAO | 23.1 | 16.3 | 15.8 |

*Note:* Asia does not include Kuwait.

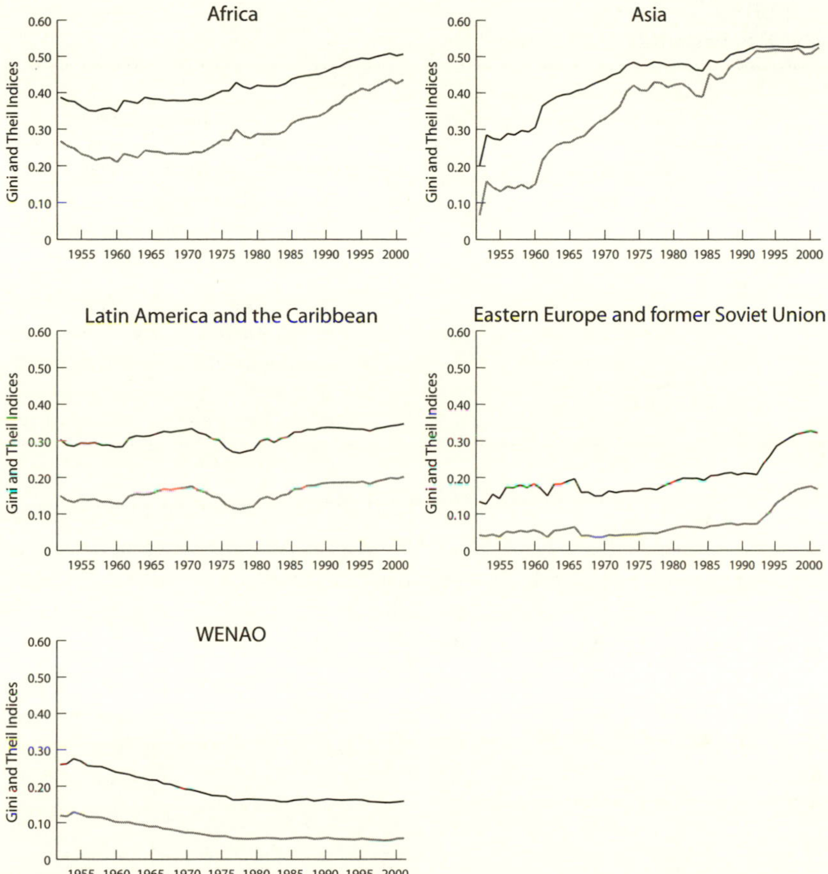


**Figure 5.1.** Regional convergence and divergence (Gini and Theil indices). Theil Entropy Index is always shown by the lower line.

countries (South Korea, Malaysia) have done very well while others (Laos, the Philippines, Bangladesh) have lagged. Very similar was the evolution of cross-country differences in Africa. This makes Asia and Africa by far the most heterogeneous regions. At the other end is the rich world (WENAO), where country differences are the smallest and have steadily decreased—leading to the phenomenon of convergence and giving rise to the extensive literature mentioned earlier.

A summary of the very different evolutions during the two periods 1960–78 and 1978–2000 is presented in table 5.2. The second period broadened *within*-regional divergence in economic performance everywhere (except in the rich world), and increased income differences *be-*

**TABLE 5.2.**
The Two Periods of International Growth

| *Period* | *Mean (unweighted) Incomes: "Rest against the West"* | *Regional Homogeneity* |
|---|---|---|
| 1960–78 | Rest catching-up | Strong divergence in Africa and Asia; mild divergence in Europe/FSU; mild convergence in WENAO and LAC. |
| 1978–2000 | All falling behind except Asia | Continued strong divergence in Africa, joined by Eastern Europe/FSU; mild divergence in Asia and LAC; continued convergence in WENAO only. |

*tween* regional mean incomes with the exception of Asia which continued to catch up with the rich. The rich world (WENAO) and a few other countries, most notably China and the "Asian tigers," pulled forward. Others, those around the middle of the international income ladder, fell behind—not only in relative but often in real terms too.[46]

# 6

# The Shape of International GDP Per Capita Distribution

## Looking at the Density Functions

Is the effect of pulling apart the countries also visible in the shape of the international distribution of GDPs per capita? Figure 6.1 gives a nonparametric estimate of the distribution of countries' GDPs per capita in 1960, 1978, and 2000. The values are normalized by the unweighted 1960 mean world GDP per capita so as to better capture growth of real incomes. Over both periods there is an "emptying out" of the poorest countries, as they move up in terms of income. The shaded part in 1960 moves up (is distributed) among different income levels, and the entire distribution to the right of 1 (= mean 1960 income) becomes thicker (top panel). The shape of the distribution curve changes between 1960 and 1978: the curve becomes much flatter and elongated. During the second period, the creeping up of incomes continues as the number of poor countries become fewer (notice that for all values less than 3, the curve for the year 2000 lies below the one for 1978), but the change in the shape of the distribution is much less dramatic. The distance between the rich and the poor pole increased: while the poor pole has remained in 2000 at the same income level as in 1978 (value of 1 on the horizontal axis), the rich pole has drifted rightward from about 5 to about 8. Thus the income distance between the two poles, which in 1978 was equal to about $PPP 13,000 (four times the mean 1960 GDP per capita) increased to about $PPP 20,000 (six times the mean).

The changing shape of the distribution between these three years is illustrated by the measures of asymmetry (skewness) and kurtosis (thickness of the tails; see table 6.1). Between 1960 and 1978, there was only a slight increase in inequality measured by the Gini and Theil (which we have already seen). The 1978 distribution of ln (GDP per capita) was left-skewed (longer left tail than right), and the thickness of the tails was reduced compared to 1960; in other words, there were fewer of both very rich and very poor countries. Over the past twenty years, however, the developments have been exactly the reverse: the distribution now exhibits a very strong right-skewness, and the number of countries at both tails went up. It is also notable that the median

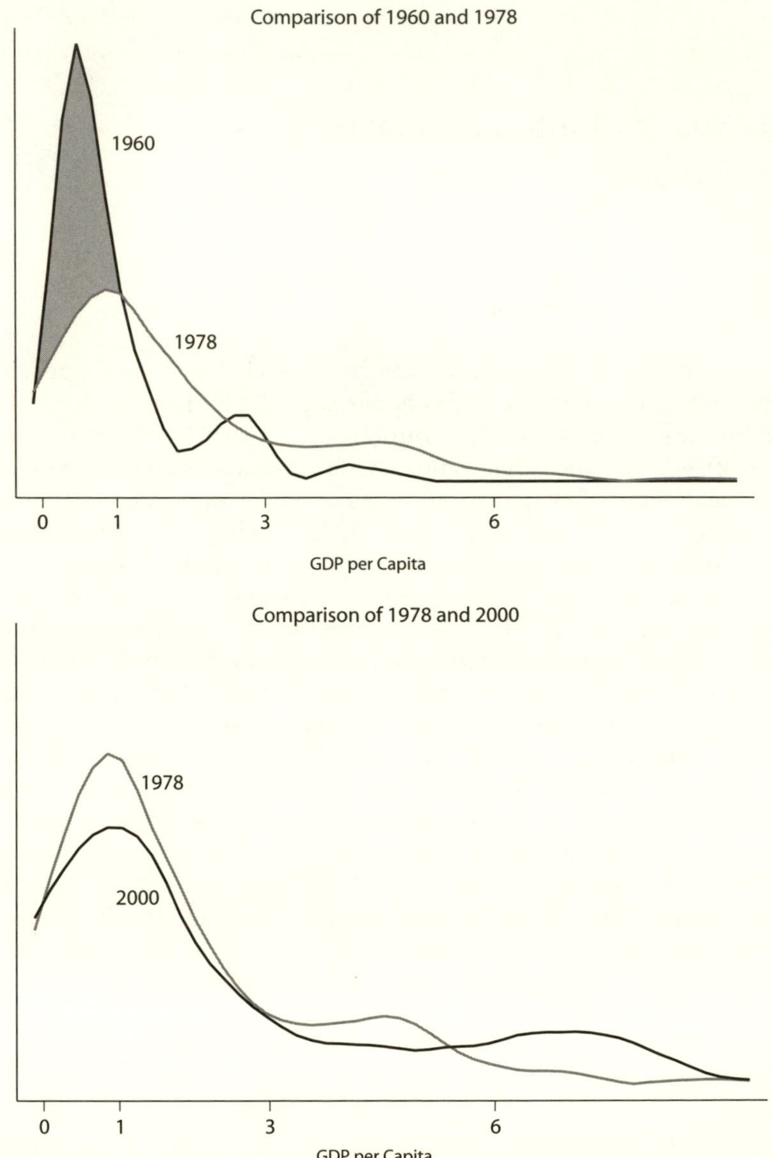


**Figure 6.1.** Distribution of countries by their per capita GDPs in 1960, 1978 and 2000 (normalized by unweighted world average 1960 GDP per capita). Non-parametric kernel density functions.

**TABLE 6.1.**
Characteristics of GDP Per Capita Distribution

| | *Skewness (asymmetry)* | *Kurtosis* | *Gini* | *Theil* | *Median Income* | *Mean Income* |
|---|---|---|---|---|---|---|
| 1960 | 0.22 | 5.96 | 46.3 | 36.2 | 0.65 | 1 |
| 1978 | –0.12 | 5.00 | 47.6 | 37.2 | 1.30 | 1.83 |
| 2000 | 1.99 | 5.41 | 54.3 | 49.8 | 1.24 | 2.43 |

*Note:* All GDP per capita values normalized by the 1960 mean GDP per capita. Skewness calculated over ln(GDP PPP): negative sign indicates left-skewness. Median and mean are unweighted.

income, which doubled over the 1960–78 period, went *down* during the past two decades.

The increasing right-skewness is also reflected in figure 6.2, where we plot the distance between GDP per capita of $n$-th country above the median and GDP per capita of $n$-th country below the median (all expressed in logs). When the distribution is normal (or symmetrical), the distances are the same and all the points fall along the 45-degree line. The top panel in figure 6.2, for the year 1978, shows a fairly close approximation to a symmetric distribution of (logarithms of) GDPs per capita. However, in 2000, the distribution becomes skewed to the right, and this tendency is present throughout.

## Analysis by Decile

We can look at what happened to the distribution by splitting the countries into deciles according to their GDP per capita. This means that approximately twelve to fifteen countries will be placed in each decile. Table 6.2 shows the mean unweighted GDP per capita for each decile in 1960, 1978, and 2000 with the deciles defined according to GDPs per capita for that particular year. Thus, for example, the countries belonging to the poorest decile in 1960 had, on average, GDP per capita of $PPP 572 (in 1995 prices); in 1978, the poorest decile's countries—not necessarily the same ones as in 1960—had, on average, GDP per capita of $PPP 748; in 2000, the bottom decile's mean GDP per capita was $PPP 727. The ratio between the top and the bottom deciles almost doubled during the 1960–2000 period: while in 1960 the richest decile's GDP per capita was 19 times greater than the average GDP per capita of the poorest countries, in 2000 the ratio was almost 37 to 1.

Growth rates by decile are shown in figure 6.3, top panel. All deciles, without exception, grew faster during the first period than during the

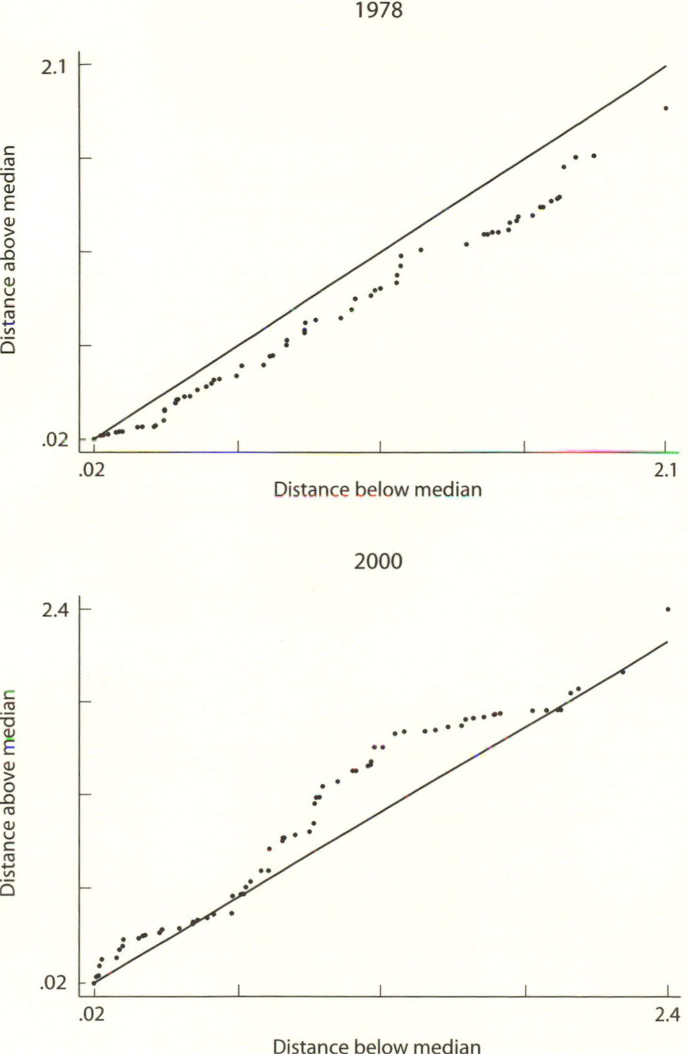


**Figure 6.2.** Symmetry of (log) GDP per capita distributions in 1978 and 2000.

second. This is not a surprising finding since we already know that growth decelerated significantly during the last two decades of the twentieth century. But it is the pattern of growth rates that is most interesting. In both periods there is a tendency for growth rates to increase with higher deciles,[47] but there are two differences: (i) in the second period, growth rates were negative or almost nil for the bottom six

**TABLE 6.2.**
Income Levels and Growth Rates by Decile of International Income Distribution (deciles formed according to GDP per capita of each year)

| | *1960* | *1978* | *Growth Rate 1960–78 (% p.a.)* | *2000* | *Growth Rate 1978–2000 (% p.a.)* |
|---|---|---|---|---|---|
| First | 572 | 748 | 1.5 | 727 | –0.1 |
| Second | 906 | 1161 | 1.4 | 1266 | 0.4 |
| Third | 1294 | 1864 | 2.0 | 1826 | –0.1 |
| Fourth | 1619 | 2805 | 3.1 | 2488 | –0.6 |
| Fifth | 1975 | 3637 | 3.5 | 3598 | –0.1 |
| Sixth | 2263 | 4617 | 4.0 | 5106 | 0.5 |
| Seventh | 2950 | 5787 | 3.8 | 6961 | 0.9 |
| Eighth | 3979 | 8179 | 4.1 | 11928 | 1.9 |
| Ninth | 6774 | 12552 | 3.5 | 19676 | 2.3 |
| Tenth | 10868 | 18369 | 3.0 | 27017 | 1.9 |
| Mean | 3277 | 5972 | 3.4 | 7970 | 1.5 |
| Tenth-to-first decile ratio | 19.0 | 24.6 | | 37.2 | |

*Note:* Decile means are unweighted.

deciles; in contrast, during 1960–78, growth rates were positive throughout; (ii) in the second period, growth rates peak for the three highest deciles; during 1960–78, the peak is reached around the middle of income distributions.

The negative or zero growth rate for the bottom six deciles between 1978 and 2000 means simply that the average income per decile was the same or less in 2000 than in 1978, not that the countries belonging to the bottom six deciles in 1978 had zero or negative growth rates. The reason is that the composition of each decile changes. For example, Botswana belonged to the bottom decile in 1960 and then improved so much as to reach the fourth decile in 1978. On the other hand, Zambia and Niger belonged in 1965 to the fourth decile but slipped to the second in 1978.

To see how countries belonging to a given decile have fared, we need to keep the composition of each decile unchanged. The results are shown in table 6.3 and the bottom panel of figure 6.3. There we see that between 1960 and 1978, all deciles (except for the second from the bottom and the very top) grew at a rate higher than 2.5 percent per capita per annum. That period was very good for most of the countries. It was particularly good for the countries that in 1960 were in the middle and upper-middle of the income distribution (from the third to the eighth decile); they grew at a rate of about 4 percent per person annually.

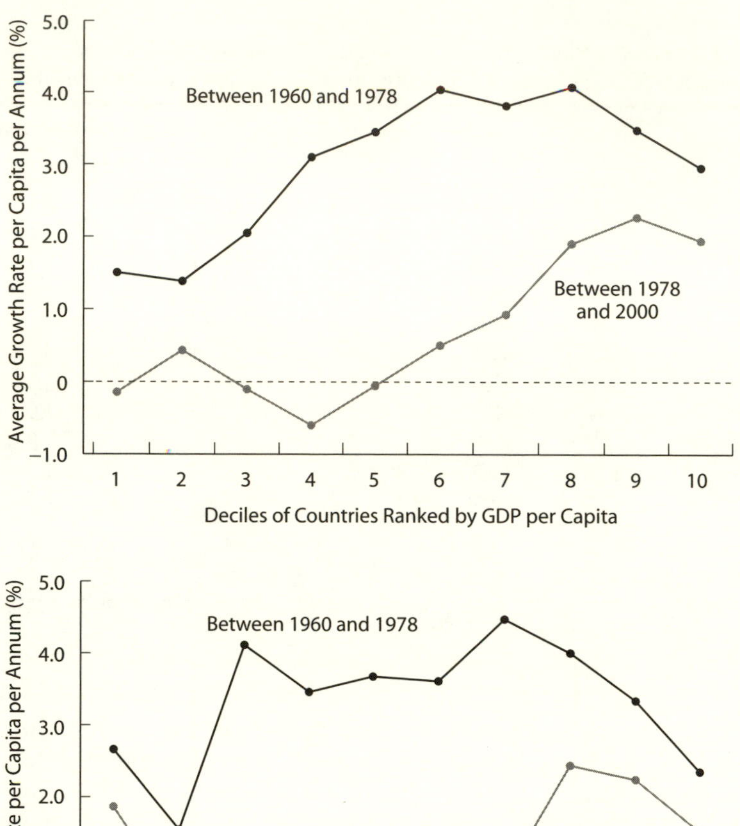


**Figure 6.3.** Growth by decile between 1960 and 2000 (per annum). Top panel: Deciles formed according to GDP per capita in each year. Bottom panel: Deciles formed according to GDP per capita in initial year.

About half of those that did the best—those in the seventh and eighth deciles—were Latin American and East European/FSU countries (13 out of 25 as shown in table 6.4).

The picture changes almost completely in the second period. Not

**TABLE 6.3.**
GDP Per Capita and Growth Rates by Decile of International Distribution (deciles formed according to GDP per capita in the initial year)

| | *1960* | *1978* | *Growth Rate 1960–78 (% p.a.)* | *1978* | *2000* | *Growth Rate 1978–2000 (% p.a.)* |
|---|---|---|---|---|---|---|
| First | 572 | 914 | 2.6 | 748 | 1079 | 1.8 |
| Second | 906 | 1191 | 1.5 | 1161 | 1278 | 0.5 |
| Third | 1294 | 2663 | 4.1 | 1864 | 2103 | 0.6 |
| Fourth | 1619 | 2975 | 3.4 | 2805 | 3673 | 1.4 |
| Fifth | 1975 | 3768 | 3.7 | 3637 | 4396 | 1.0 |
| Sixth | 2263 | 4272 | 3.6 | 4617 | 5337 | 0.7 |
| Seventh | 2950 | 6460 | 4.5 | 5787 | 6861 | 0.9 |
| Eighth | 3979 | 8039 | 4.0 | 8179 | 13216 | 2.4 |
| Ninth | 6774 | 12196 | 3.3 | 12552 | 19518 | 2.2 |
| Tenth | 10868 | 16482 | 2.3 | 18369 | 24794 | 1.5 |
| Mean | 3277 | 5831 | 3.3 | 5972 | 8234 | 1.6 |

*Note:* There are some, very small, differences between the overall mean levels and growth rates in the first and second periods as calculated in tables 6.2 and 6.3. This is due to the fact that in this table, the growth rates for the 1960–78 period are calculated across the countries included in the sample in 1960. Countries that were added in 1978 affect the calculations in table 6.2 but not those in table 6.3. The same is true for the 1978–2000 period. Decile means are unweighted.

only is the growth rate for each decile lower than in the first period, but countries from the top—eighth and ninth deciles (according to their 1978 income)—did better than everybody else (figure 6.3, bottom panel). In other words, while in 1960–78 it was the middle and upper-middle of the 1960 income distribution that did the best, in the latter period it was those that were initially among the richest that did the best—the middle of the 1978 income distribution did very poorly. The average growth rate of the middle deciles decelerated from about 4 percent per capita per annum to practically zero, with much greater variability of outcomes among the countries (compare standard deviations in tables 6.4 and 6.5).

Particularly striking is the contrast between the fortunes of various countries that belonged to the middle of the 1978 income distribution (sixth, seventh and eighth decile). Some of them were very successful; others declined precipitously (see figure 6.4, top panel). The variability of outcomes in the middle of income distribution was much greater than in the top, where all the countries, with the exception of the oil-

**TABLE 6.4.**
Composition of the 1960 Middle-Income Deciles and Average Annual Per Capita Growth Rate during the 1960–78 Period (in percent)

| *Seventh Decile* | *Growth Rate* | *Eighth Decile* | *Growth Rate* |
|---|---|---|---|
| Ukraine | 5.1 | Mexico | 3.2 |
| Singapore | 6.9 | Greece | 5.8 |
| Jamaica | 1.3 | Fiji | 1.9 |
| Iran | 5.2 | South Africa | 2.3 |
| Colombia | 2.7 | Slovenia | 6.7 |
| Panama | 3.4 | Trinidad & Tobago | 4.5 |
| Nicaragua | 2.3 | Seychelles | 3.2 |
| Hong Kong,China | 6.9 | Chile | 1.0 |
| Croatia | 5.5 | Algeria | 2.1 |
| Portugal | 5.2 | Mauritius | 3.3 |
| Costa Rica | 3.0 | Ireland | 3.7 |
| Puerto Rico | 4.7 | Barbados | 4.1 |
| | | Japan | 6.6 |
| Unweighted average | 4.4 | | 3.7 |
| Standard deviation | 1.8 | | 1.8 |
| Maximum | 6.9 | | 6.7 |
| Minimum | 1.3 | | 1.0 |

*Note:* Within each decile, countries are ranked by their 1960 GDP PPP per capita (in increasing order). The average unweighted growth rates calculated here differ from those given in table 6.3 for the following reason. The decile growth rate in table 6.3 is calculated from the ratio

$$\frac{(1/n)\sum_{i=1}^{n} y_{i,t}}{(1/n)\sum_{i=1}^{n} y_{i,t-5}}$$

where $y_{i,t}$ is GDP per capita of $i$-th country at time $t$, and $n$ = number of countries in a decile. (The countries in both years are the same.) The calculation in this table, however, is a simple arithmetic average of countries' growth rates. Thus, unlike in the other calculation, the size of country's per capita income does not matter.

exporting Kuwait and Saudi Arabia, grew at positive and very similar rates (notice the clustering of the dots in figure 6.4; bottom panel). But among the middle-decile countries in 1978, some like Singapore and Ireland moved up into the top decile while others—Moldova, Nicaragua, and Ukraine—dropped from the sixth into the third or fourth decile. In 1978, Malaysia and Moldova had almost the same income. But over the next twenty-two years, Malaysia grew at an average rate of

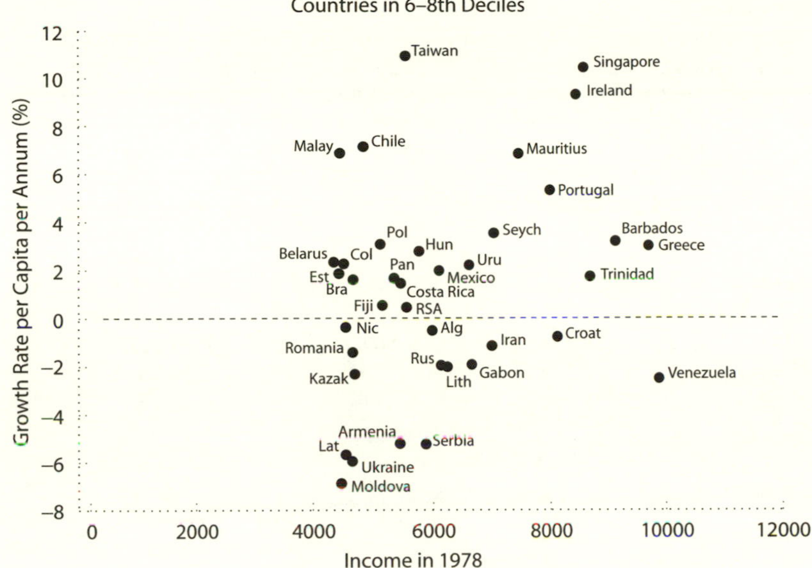


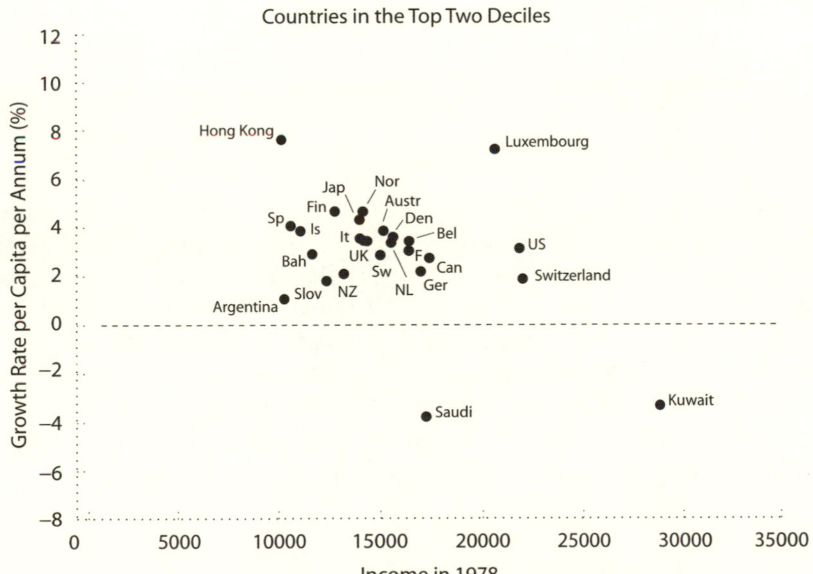


**Figure 6.4.** Growth rates (per capita, per annum) 1978–2000 against the initial income levels in 1978. Deciles formed according to 1978 income levels.

**TABLE 6.5.**
Composition of the 1978 Middle-Income Deciles and Average Annual Per Capita Growth Rate during the 1978–2000 Period (in percent)

| *Sixth Decile* | *Growth Rate* | *Seventh Decile* | *Growth Rate* | *Eighth Decile* | *Growth Rate* |
|---|---|---|---|---|---|
| Belarus | 2.3 | Fiji | 0.5 | Gabon | –1.9 |
| Estonia | 1.9 | Panama | 1.7 | Iran | –1.2 |
| Malaysia | 6.9 | Armenia | –5.2 | Seychelles | 3.5 |
| Moldova | –6.9 | Costa Rica | 1.4 | Mauritius | 6.8 |
| Colombia | 2.3 | Taiwan | 10.9 | Puerto Rico | n.a. |
| Latvia | –0.4 | South Africa | 0.4 | Portugal | 5.3 |
| Nicaragua | –5.7 | Hungary | 2.8 | Croatia | –0.8 |
| Ukraine | –6.0 | Serbia/MN | –5.2 | Ireland | 9.3 |
| Romania | –1.4 | Algeria | –0.5 | Singapore | 10.4 |
| Brazil | 1.6 | Mexico | 2.0 | Trinidad & Tobago | 1.7 |
| Kazakhstan | –2.3 | Russia | –2.0 | Barbados | 3.2 |
| Chile | 7.1 | Lithuania | –2.0 | Greece | 3.0 |
| Poland | 3.1 | Uruguay | 2.2 | Venezuela | –2.5 |
| Unweighted average | 0.2 | | 0.5 | | 3.1 |
| Standard deviation | 4.5 | | 4.1 | | 4.3 |
| Maximum | 6.9 | | 10.9 | | 10.4 |
| Minimum | –6.9 | | –5.2 | | –2.5 |

*Note:* Within each decile, countries are ranked by their 1978 GDP PPP per capita (in increasing order). See note to table 6.4.

6.9 percent per capita per annum, while Moldova declined at the same rate (table 6.5). In 2000, the income ratio between them was 5 to 1. Very similar are the stories of other countries belonging to the middle deciles in 1978: Taiwan (average growth 10.9 percent per annum) vs. Serbia and Montenegro or Armenia (–5.2 percent), or Singapore (10.4) vs. Venezuela (–2.5). Overall, 14 out of 39 countries shown in table 6.5 declined, while seven had an average per capita growth rate in excess of 5 percent per annum. This was a stark example of the bifurcation of the Third World—a topic to which we shall return.

# 7

## Winners and Losers: Increasing Dominance of the West

> The waning of economic prosperity of Latin America during [the] closing decades of the century has been additionally disappointing because it contrasts so starkly with its earlier promise.
>
> —Claudio Veliz, quoted in Felipe Fernandez-Armesto, *The Americas: A Hemispheric History* (2003), p. 187

### If You Are Not Western, Can You Be Rich?

The emptying out of the middle of income distribution had the following two consequences. It reinforced the already strong domination of Western countries at the very top of the income distribution, and it reduced the number of possible contenders for positions in the top of income distribution. In other words, Western countries have pulled ahead of the rest of the world, and in only a few exceptional cases have non-Western countries been able to catch up.[48]

We define GDP per capita of the poorest WENAO country (excluding Turkey) as the cut-off point between the rich and those immediately behind them, "the contenders." In 1960 and 1978, the poorest WENAO country was Portugal, with GDP per capita of respectively $PPP 3205 and $PPP 7993.[49] In 2000, the poorest WENAO country was Greece, with GDP per capita of $PPP 13, 821. All countries above that level are deemed rich. The countries whose GDP per capita is no more than one-third below that of the poorest WENAO country are called "contenders." In principle, they are within striking distance of catching up and joining the rich. For example, if the poorest WENAO country (on the cut-off point between the rich and the rest of the world) grows by 2 percent per annum per capita, the contender, which is as far as one-third below the cut-off point, needs to maintain an average annual growth of 3.4 percent per capita to join the club of the rich after one generation (twenty years). Basically, a contender country has a fairly reasonable chance of catching up within a generation or two.

The third group of countries are those with GDP per capita levels between one- and two-thirds of the poorest WENAO country. These countries can be viewed as the Third World: they are not within striking distance of the rich since their incomes would on average be only about one-half of the poorest WENAO country. Finally, the fourth group is composed of countries whose GDPs are less than a third of the GDP per capita of the poorest Western country. We thus have four groups of countries: the rich, the contenders, the Third and the Fourth (very poor) worlds. Note that unlike in the analysis where we dealt with the distribution of countries into deciles according to their GDP per capita, here not only are the sizes of the four groups not given, but there is nothing in principle that precludes the entire world into squeezing into the rich world, or into the first two or three groups. Very simply, if those poorest grow sufficiently fast as not to remain at less than one-third of the poorest WENAO country's income, the Fourth World would empty out. The same holds for the Third World and so on. In other words, the changing sizes of these four worlds will tell us something about the catch-up or lack thereof between the West and the Rest.

We divided the world into four groups of countries in the years 1960, 1978, and 2000. In 1960, the rich world was composed of forty-one countries. Twenty-two of them were WENAO countries. There were therefore nineteen non-WENAO countries among the rich: in Latin America and the Caribbean (by increasing order of income)—Costa Rica, Puerto Rico, Mexico, Trinidad and Tobago, Chile, Barbados, Uruguay, Argentina, Venezuela, and the Bahamas; in Eastern Europe—Slovenia;[50] in Asia—Fiji, Japan, and Saudi Arabia; in Africa—South Africa, Seychelles, Algeria, Mauritius, and Angola.[51] Now, consider the fate of these nineteen rich non-WENAO countries. By 1978, eight of them have slipped to the list of contenders and three even further into the Third World (see table 7.1). By 2000, the "purge" of the non-WENAO countries from among the rich continues. An additional five countries (Argentina, Barbados, Saudi Arabia, Trinidad and Tobago, and Venezuela) slip into the second and third groups. Mauritius rejoins the rich. All in all, out of the nineteen non-Western countries that belonged to the rich club in 1960, only four remained there (the Bahamas, Japan, Mauritius, and Slovenia). In the meantime, however, four new non-Western countries joined the rich: Singapore and Hong Kong already in 1978, and Taiwan and South Korea by 2000.

The net result was a dramatic decline in the number of rich countries and an increase in the share of Western countries among the rich. While

**TABLE 7.1.**
Transition Matrix between 1960 and 1978

| | 1978 | | | |
|---|---|---|---|---|
| *1960* | *Rich* | *Contenders* | *Third World* | *Fourth World* |
| Rich | Argentina<br>Australia<br>Austria<br>Bahamas<br>Barbados<br>Belgium<br>Canada<br>Denmark<br>Finland<br>France<br>Germany<br>Greece<br>Ireland<br>Israel<br>Italy<br>Japan<br>Luxembourg<br>Netherlands<br>New Zealand<br>Norway<br>Portugal<br>Saudi Arabia<br>Slovenia<br>Spain<br>Sweden<br>Switzerland<br>Trinidad & Tobago<br>United Kingdom<br>United States<br>Venezuela | Algeria<br>Costa Rica<br>Mauritius<br>Mexico<br>Puerto Rico<br>Seychelles<br>South Africa<br>Uruguay | Angola<br>Fiji<br>Chile | |
| Contenders | Singapore<br>Hong Kong<br>Croatia | Lithuania<br>Serbia/MN<br>Hungary<br>Gabon<br>Russia<br>Iran<br>Panama | Colombia<br>Guyana<br>Jamaica<br>Kazakhstan<br>Nicaragua<br>Poland<br>Turkey<br>Ukraine | Congo<br>Ghana<br>Haiti<br>Senegal |

**TABLE 7.1.** (*cont.*)

| | *1978* | | | |
|---|---|---|---|---|
| *1960* | *Rich* | *Contenders* | *Third World* | *Fourth World* |
| Third World | | Taiwan | Belarus | Nigeria |
| | | Armenia | Bolivia | Chad |
| | | Brazil | Guinea | |
| | | Bulgaria | Cote d'Ivoire | |
| | | Dominican Rep. | Sri Lanka | |
| | | Ecuador | Papua New Guinea | |
| | | El Salvador | Egypt | |
| | | Estonia | Honduras | |
| | | Guatemala | Central African Rep. | |
| | | Jordan | Zambia | |
| | | South Korea | Zimbabwe | |
| | | Kyrghyz Republic | Niger | |
| | | Latvia | Uganda | |
| | | Malaysia | Cameroon | |
| | | Moldova | | |
| | | Morocco | | |
| | | Paraguay | | |
| | | Peru | | |
| | | Philippines | | |
| | | Romania | | |
| | | Thailand | | |
| | | Turkmenistan | | |
| | | Uzbekistan | | |
| Fourth World | | | | Ethiopia |
| | | | | Tanzania |
| | | | | China |
| | | | | Malawi |
| | | | | Burkina Faso |
| | | | | Guinea-Bissau |
| | | | | Botswana |
| | | | | Lesotho |
| | | | | Congo, D.R. |
| | | | | India |
| | | | | Mali |
| | | | | Rwanda |
| | | | | Sierra Leone |
| | | | | Gambia |
| | | | | Pakistan |
| | | | | Benin |

TABLE 7.1. *(cont.)*

| | 1978 | | | |
|---|---|---|---|---|
| *1960* | *Rich* | *Contenders* | *Third World* | *Fourth World* |
| | | | | Kenya<br>Nepal<br>Mozambique<br>Sudan<br>Indonesia<br>Bangladesh<br>Mauritania<br>Togo<br>Madagascar |

*Note:* The GDP per capita limits dividing the four worlds were in 1960, $PPP 3205, 2135 and 1067; and in 1978, $PPP 7993, 5323, and 2662 (all in 1995 international prices).

in the year 1960, there were, as we have seen, forty-one rich countries—nineteen of them being non-Western—in 2000, there were only thirty-one rich countries, and only nine of them were non-Western. None of the African countries (except for Mauritius) and none of the Latin American and the Caribbean countries (expect for the Bahamas) were left among the rich. Latin America and the Caribbean, probably for the first time in 200 years, had no country that was richer than the poorest West European country.[52]

Tables 7.1 and 7.2 display the mobility matrices respectively between 1960 and 1978, and 1978 and 2000. We have already looked at what happened among the rich. Let us consider now the changes among the three other groups.

## A Downwardly Mobile World

Let us look first at the "contenders" in 1960. They were an interesting group. As we would expect, Eastern European and Latin American countries predominated. From Eastern Europe/FSU, there were (again, in increasing order of GDP per capita) Lithuania, Serbia and Montenegro, Hungary, Kazakhstan, Poland, Russia, Ukraine, and Croatia. From Latin America and the Caribbean, there were Haiti, Guyana, Jamaica, Colombia, Panama, and Nicaragua. There were also four African countries: the Congo, Senegal, Gabon, and Ghana; and three from Asia: Singapore, Iran, and Hong Kong. All of these countries could look forward to joining the club of the rich. For example, Croatia, Nicaragua,

**TABLE 7.2.**
Transition Matrix between 1978 and 2000

| | *2000* | | | |
|---|---|---|---|---|
| *1978* | *Rich* | *Contenders* | *Third World* | *Fourth World* |
| Rich | Australia<br>Austria<br>Bahamas<br>Belgium<br>Canada<br>Denmark<br>Finland<br>France<br>Germany<br>Greece<br>Hong Kong, China<br>Ireland<br>Israel<br>Italy<br>Japan<br>Kuwait<br>Luxembourg<br>Netherlands<br>New Zealand<br>Norway<br>Portugal<br>Singapore<br>Slovenia<br>Spain<br>Sweden<br>Switzerland<br>United Kingdom<br>United States | Argentina<br>Barbados<br>Saudi Arabia<br>Trinidad & Tobago | Croatia<br>Venezuela | |
| Contenders | Mauritius<br>Taiwan | Seychelles | Algeria<br>Costa Rica<br>Gabon<br>Hungary<br>Iran<br>Mexico<br>Panama<br>South Africa<br>Lithuania<br>Russia<br>Uruguay | Armenia<br>Serbia/MN |
| Third World | South Korea | Chile<br>Malaysia | Brazil<br>Colombia<br>Fiji<br>Poland | Angola<br>Bolivia<br>Bulgaria<br>Djibouti |

**TABLE 7.2.** (*cont.*)

| *1978* | *2000* | | | |
|---|---|---|---|---|
| | *Rich* | *Contenders* | *Third World* | *Fourth World* |
| | | | Tunisia | Ecuador |
| | | | Turkey | El Salvador |
| | | | Belarus | Guatemala |
| | | | Dominican Rep. | Guyana |
| | | | Estonia | Jamaica |
| | | | Thailand | Jordan |
| | | | | Kazakhstan |
| | | | | Kyrghyz Rep. |
| | | | | Latvia |
| | | | | Moldova |
| | | | | Morocco |
| | | | | Nicaragua |
| | | | | Paraguay |
| | | | | Peru |
| | | | | Philippines |
| | | | | Romania |
| | | | | Turkmenistan |
| | | | | Ukraine |
| | | | | Uzbekistan |
| Fourth World | | | Botswana | Bangladesh |
| | | | Egypt | Benin |
| | | | | Burkina Faso |
| | | | | Central African Rep. |
| | | | | Chad |
| | | | | China |
| | | | | Cote d'Ivoire |
| | | | | Cameroon |
| | | | | Congo. |
| | | | | Ethiopia |
| | | | | Ghana |
| | | | | Guinea |
| | | | | Gambia |
| | | | | Guinea-Bissau |
| | | | | Honduras |
| | | | | Haiti |
| | | | | Indonesia |
| | | | | India |
| | | | | Kenya |
| | | | | Sri Lanka |
| | | | | Lesotho |
| | | | | Madagascar |
| | | | | Mali |
| | | | | Mozambique |
| | | | | Mauritania |
| | | | | Malawi |

**TABLE 7.2.** (*cont.*)

| | 2000 | | | |
|---|---|---|---|---|
| *1978* | *Rich* | *Contenders* | *Third World* | *Fourth World* |
| | | | | Niger<br>Nigeria<br>Nepal<br>Pakistan<br>Papua New Guinea<br>Rwanda<br>Sudan<br>Senegal<br>Sierra Leone<br>Togo<br>Turkmenistan<br>Tanzania<br>Uganda<br>Congo, DR<br>Zambia<br>Zimbabwe |

*Note:* The GDP per capita limits dividing the four worlds were in 1978, $PPP 7993, 5323, and 2662; and in 2000, $PPP 13,821, 9205, and 4602 (all at 1995 prices).

Panama, and Colombia had GDPs per capita that were only marginally below Portugal's. However, by 1978, eight contenders had slipped into the Third World, and three into the Fourth. By 2000, no fewer than 20 out of the 22 original contenders were either in the Third or the Fourth World. The most extraordinary thing, therefore, is that out of the twenty-two countries that, in 1960, were within the striking distance of joining the club of the rich, only two—Singapore and Hong Kong—succeeded while all the others not merely failed but slipped into the lower categories. Moreover, as we have seen, almost all of the non-Western countries that were rich in 1960 lost out too. The less unsuccessful among them (Argentina, Barbados, etc.) slipped into the ranks of the contenders, while others went even further down. Thus, in a remarkable development, today's contenders are basically the 1960s *rich* non-Western countries, while the 1960s non-Western contenders are languishing in the Third or the Fourth World.

Tables 7.3 and 7.4 give the four worlds transition matrices for the two periods. Two conclusions can be made. First, there was more stability at the extremes, among the rich and particularly among the poor. All of the poorest countries stayed in the bottom between 1960 and 1978, and 95 percent did the same during the later period. Second, the churning among the contenders and the Third World was largely

**TABLE 7.3.**
Transition Matrices 1960–78 and 1978–2000 (in percentages)

| | *Rich* | *Contenders* | *Third World* | *Fourth World* | *Total* |
|---|---|---|---|---|---|
| 1960–78 | | | | | |
| Rich | 73 | 20 | 7 | 0 | 100 |
| Contenders | 14 | 32 | 36 | 18 | 100 |
| Third World | 0 | 5 | 59 | 36 | 100 |
| Fourth World | 0 | 0 | 0 | 100 | 100 |
| 1978–2000 | | | | | |
| Rich | 82 | 12 | 6 | 0 | 100 |
| Contenders | 13 | 6 | 69 | 13 | 100 |
| Third World | 3 | 6 | 28 | 64 | 100 |
| Fourth World | 0 | 0 | 5 | 95 | 100 |

downward. Among the contenders, the number of downwardly vs. upwardly mobile countries was 12 to 3 in the first period, and 13 to 2 in the second. Regarding the Third World countries, almost two-thirds of the them slipped into the Fourth World during the 1978–2000 period. Overall upward mobility was 4 and 3 percent in the two periods respectively; overall downward mobility was, in contrast, 24 and 29 percent (figure 7.1).

Stability on the bottom, combined with downward mobility of the

**TABLE 7.4.**
Transition Matrices 1960–78 and 1978–2000 (number of countries)

| | *Rich* | *Contenders* | *Third World* | *Fourth World* | *Number of Countries* |
|---|---|---|---|---|---|
| 1960–78 | | | | | |
| Rich | 30 | 8 | 3 | 0 | 41 |
| Contenders | 3 | 7 | 8 | 4 | 22 |
| Third World | 0 | 2 | 23 | 14 | 39 |
| Fourth World | 0 | 0 | 0 | 25 | 25 |
| 1978–2000 | | | | | |
| Rich | 28 | 4 | 2 | 0 | 34 |
| Contenders | 2 | 1 | 11 | 2 | 16 |
| Third World | 1 | 2 | 10 | 23 | 36 |
| Fourth World | 0 | 0 | 2 | 42 | 44 |

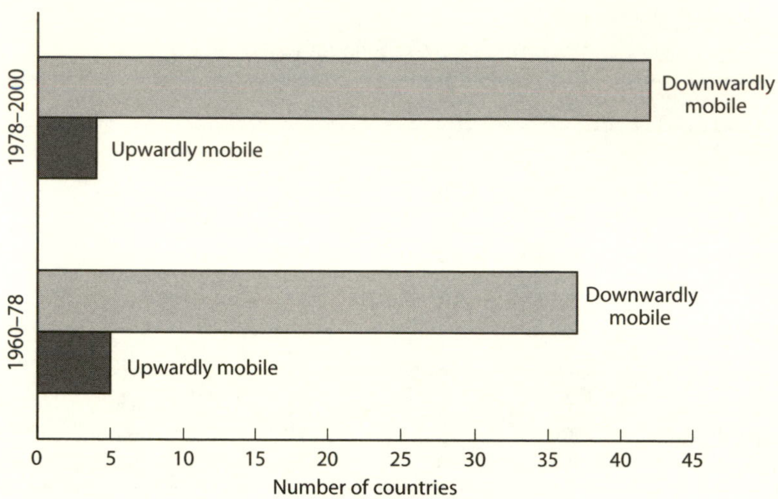


**Figure 7.1.** Overall upward and downward mobility: (1960–78 and 1978–2000; number of countries).

contenders and the Third World countries, resulted in the remarkable fact that once a country became part of the poorest group, it found it almost impossible to escape from (relative) poverty. During the past forty years, only two countries (Botswana and Egypt) escaped from the trap of the Fourth World. This fact bodes ill for the slew of countries from Eastern Europe and Latin America who in the past two decades have dropped into the Fourth World. Unless there is a remarkable discontinuity with the patterns of development that had lasted during the past half century (and possibly longer), the likelihood of escaping from the bottom rung is almost negligible.

The swelling of the Fourth World (as the number of the countries that belong to the poorest category increased from 25 in 1960 to 43 in 1978 to 71 in 2000; see figure 7.2) was also a process whereby most African countries ended up among the poorest. Four out of each five African countries are now part of the Fourth World. Being an African country virtually guarantees membership in the poorest group. At one end, there is the "Africanization" of poverty, at the other end, the "Westernization" of wealth. By 2000, there was practically no "intersection" between African and WENAO countries.[53] While in 1960 Africa had five "representants" among the rich and three among the contenders, by 2000 the highest placed African countries were those in the Third World—save for the lonely and tiny Mauritius and Seychelles. Even the Third World has become increasingly out of reach for Africa. The only

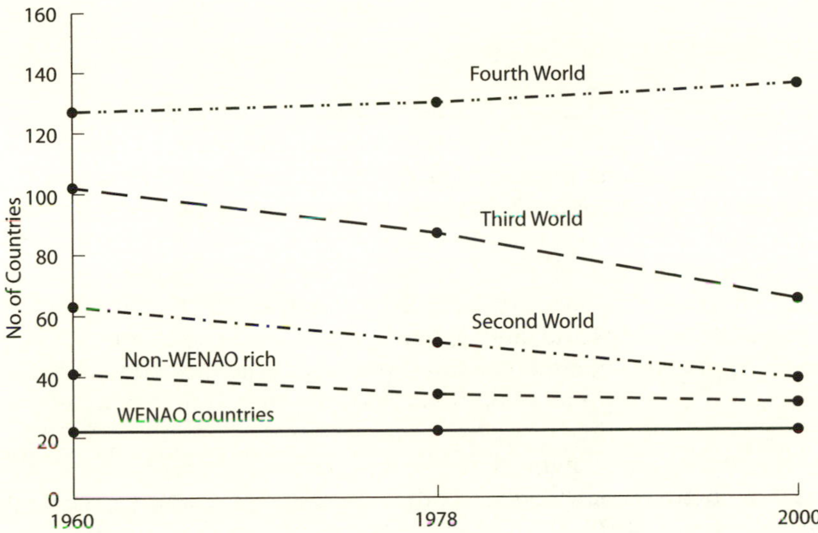


**Figure 7.2.** The four "worlds" in 1960, 1978, and 2000 (number of countries).

African countries there in 2000 were those that were well-off in the past (Algeria, South Africa, and Gabon) and the two African success cases (Egypt and Botswana).[54] The African growth tragedy is thus well illustrated by the unremitting downward mobility of the entire continent.

Similarly to Africa, the position of Latin America and the Caribbean (LAC) deteriorated severely. In 1960, Latin American countries were about evenly distributed among the rich, the contenders, and the Third World. None was in the poorest group. But in 2000, almost one-half of Latin American countries were in the Fourth World, and only one (compared to ten in 1960) was rich. The changes in Eastern Europe/FSU mirrored those in Latin America. While in 1960 almost all of these countries were either among the contenders or the Third World (and none was among the poorest), in 2000 more than a half were part of the Fourth World.

A different way to look at this striking downward mobility is to compare the sizes of the four groups in 1960 and 2000 (figure 7.2). While in 1960 there were only twenty-five countries belonging to the Fourth World, in 2000, there were almost three times as many. Being part of the Fourth World is now the most common category for all regions (except for the West): between 50 and 60 percent of Asian, LAC, and East European/FSU countries belong to the poorest category, as do no fewer than 80 percent of African countries.

## The Contenders That Failed

It is the failure of a number of non-Western economies to catch up, or to maintain their relative position in the last quarter of the twentieth century, that lies behind the emptying out of the middle of the income distribution shown in figure 7.2. It is therefore important to consider what happened to those countries that held a promise of catching up in the 1960s, but that slipped into the Third or the Fourth World. There are thirty-three such downwardly mobile countries (13 that in 1960 belonged to the rich world, and 20 that were contenders). About a half of them display two common features: political instability punctuated by wars, insurgencies, and revolutions; and transition from a planned to a market economy which resulted in massive real income declines.

Nicaragua, Iran, Angola, Croatia, and Serbia and Montenegro faced civil or international wars or both. Consider, for example, what the decade of wars, 1977–88, did to the incomes of Iran and Nicaragua (figure 7.3). Both countries reached their peak income in 1976–77. Then, for both, the period 1977–88 (marked in the graph) was a decade of revolutions and internal and external wars. At the end of the period, Nicaragua's GDP per capita was reduced by more than a half (from $PPP 5,000 in 1977 to $PPP 2,300 in 1988) and Iran's GDP per capita by almost as much (from $PPP 7,900 to $PPP 4,300).[55] It is a scant surprise that these countries could no longer count themselves among the contenders to joining the club of the rich.[56]

Algeria, Colombia, Haiti, Fiji, Panama, and South Africa faced massive domestic insurgencies or conflicts during the period 1960–2000. Political instability appears to have been one of the main, and possibly the main, reason why the promise of development went unfulfilled. Russia, Ukraine, Hungary, Poland, Kazakhstan, and Lithuania were affected by the stagnation in the 1980s and then by moderate to large losses during the transition from planned to market economy. Finally, Saudi Arabia and Gabon declined on lower oil prices.

That leaves us with thirteen countries whose cause of decline we cannot easily identify. Four of them (Argentina, Barbados, Trinidad and Tobago, and Seychelles) slipped from the rich into the contenders. A few went all the way from being rich in 1960 to joining the Third World at the end of the century (Costa Rica, Mexico, Venezuela, and Uruguay). Others (Turkey, Jamaica, Guyana, Senegal, and Ghana) went from being contenders to the Third or the Fourth World. One can then ask, what were the factors or policy elements that distinguish these failed contenders from the seven upwardly mobile countries: Singapore, Hong Kong, Taiwan, South Korea, Malaysia, Botswana and Egypt, plus

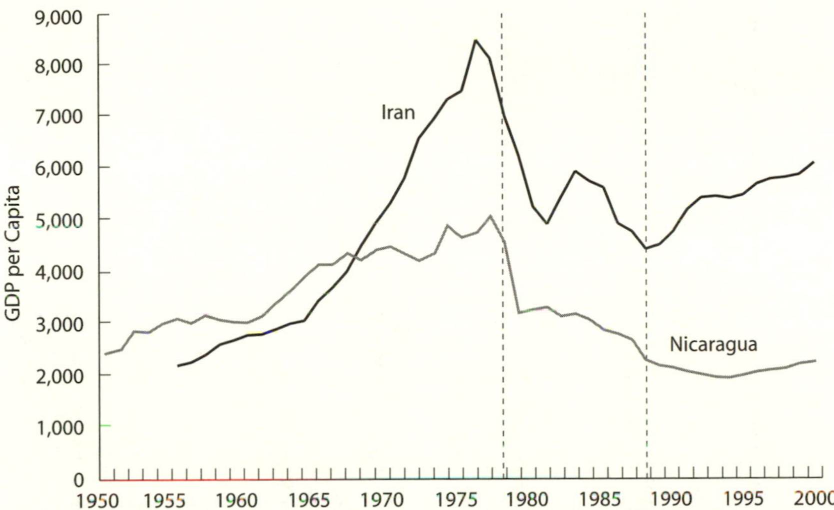


**Figure 7.3.** Iran and Nicaragua: GDP per capita, 1950–2000. GDP per capita in $PPP at 1995 international prices.

Chile and Mauritius, which at first lost some ground and then recovered it. If we eliminate the two entrepôt economies (Singapore and Hong Kong), and add to the list of successes Thailand and China, which were among the ten most successful economies during the 1960–2000 period, we are left with a total of seven success cases and thirteen failures.[57]

In table 7.5, we select several institutional and political features of each country, and look at the counties' initial conditions in the early 1960s. Two variables can be considered exogenous: colonial heritage and ethnolinguistic fractionalization of the country. Levels of inequality, democracy, and type of political system are more political than economic variables reflecting the institutional set-up of the country, preferences of the population, and historical heritage. There is only one clear economic policy variable—average tariff rate—that denotes the level of disconnect with (or conversely, the level of openness to) the rest of the world.

Consider the differences in initial conditions between the failed and successful contenders. Table 7.6 shows that in the early 1960s there were two salient differences: the future successful countries had significantly lower inequality and were less democratic. Ethnic fractionalization was almost the same in both groups. The average number of years of schooling was only marginally greater in the future success cases. There were only very small differences in political systems,[58] mostly

**TABLE 7.5.**
Comparison of Failed and Successful Contenders, 1960–2000

| | *Gini Coefficients* | | | *Democracy* | | | | | | *Average Tariff Rate (in %)* | |
|---|---|---|---|---|---|---|---|---|---|---|---|
| | *~1960* | *~1978* | *~2000* | *~1960* | *~1978* | *~2000* | *Political System* | *Ethnic Fraction* | *Colonial Power* | *~1980* | *~2000* |
| Argentina[a] | — | — | 47 | 3 | 0 | 8 | Direct presidential | 0.41 | Spain | 28 | 13 |
| Barbados | — | 49 | 39 | — | — | — | Parliamentary | 0.20 | UK | — | 10 |
| Costa Rica | 50 | 50 | 47 | 10 | 10 | 10 | Direct presidential | 0.24 | Spain | — | 8 |
| Ghana | — | — | 33 | 0 | 6 | 3 | Direct presidential | 0.73 | UK | 43 | 8 |
| Guyana | 56 | — | 43 | — | 3 | 6 | Parliamentary; since 1981 strong presidential | 0.63 | UK | — | 10 |
| Jamaica | — | 45 | 40 | 10 | 10 | 9 | Parliamentary | 0.35 | UK | 16 | 10 |
| Mexico | 58 | 58 | 57 | 0 | 1 | 8 | Direct presidential | 0.59 | Spain | 27 | 10 |
| Panama | 57 | 49 | — | 5 | 0 | 9 | Direct presidential (parliamentary between 1979 and 1984) | 0.60 | Spain | — | 9 |
| Senegal | 56 | — | — | 3 | 2 | 8 | Direct presidential | 0.81 | France | — | 12 |
| Seychelles | — | 46 | — | — | — | — | Parliamentary | 0.08 | France/UK | — | |
| Trinindad | 46 | 42 | — | 8 | 8 | 10 | Parliamentary | 0.66 | UK | — | 9 |
| Turkey | — | 51 | 49 | 10 | 9 | 8 | Parliamentary (except 1980–83 directly elected president) | 0.19 | — | 40 | 13 |
| Uruguay[a] | — | — | 43 | 8 | 0 | 10 | Direct presidential | 0.26 | Spain | 47 | 12 |
| Venezuela | 42 | 41 | 47 | 7 | 9 | 7 | Direct presidential | 0.54 | Spain | 28 | 12 |

| | | | | | | | | | | | |
|---|---|---|---|---|---|---|---|---|---|---|---|
| Chile | 46 | 53 | 50 | 5 | 0 | 9 | Direct presidential | 0.43 | Spain | 35 | 11 |
| South Korea | 34 | 38 | 29 | 0 | 3 | 8 | Strong presidential until 1988, directly elected president since | 0 | Japan | 24 | 11 |
| Malaysia | 48 | 51 | 49 | 10 | 8 | 4 | Parliamentary | 0.70 | UK | 11 | 7 |
| Thailand | 41 | 42 | 41 | 0 | 3 | 9 | Parliamentary (except 1977–79 direct presidential) | 0.63 | — | 32 | 17 |
| China | 31 | 32 | 44 | 0 | 0 | 0 | Strong presidential | 0.60 | — | 50 | 17 |
| Mauritius | — | 46 | — | — | 9 | 10 | Parliamentary | 0.48 | France/UK | 35 | 19 |
| Botswana | — | — | 54 | — | 10 | 9 | Parliamentary | 0.48 | UK | — | 11 |
| Egypt | 42 | 38 | — | 0 | 0 | 0 | Strong presidential | 0.25 | — | 47 | 21 |
| Taiwan | 32 | 29 | 32 | 0 | 0 | 9 | Strong presidential until 1997, direct presidential after | — | Japan | 31 | 9 |

*Sources:* Ginis from WIDER database and World Income Distribution (WYD) database created by B. Milanovic (available at www.worldbank.org/research/inequality/data.htm.). Democracy is approximated by the DEMOC variable from *Polity98D* (November 2000) and *Polity IV* (November 2001). It is defined as an index of "general openness of political institutions" ranging from 0 (most repressive) to 10 (most open). Data are available at http://weber.ucsd.edu/~kgledits/Polity.html. Political system is from *Database of Political Institutions*, see Beck et al. (2000). The political system defines the way of electing and the powers of the chief executive. It takes three values: if the chief executive depends on parliamentary majority, the system is parliamentary; if the chief executive is elected by a popular vote or is unelected, the system is "direct presidential." Finally, the systems where chief executive is elected by an electoral college (or national parliament) and that assembly cannot easily recall, are called "strong presidential." Index of ethnolinguistic heterogeneity is calculated by Barrett (1982) (data kindly provided by Anthony Annett from the IMF). Unweighted average tariff rate from www.worldbank.org/research/trade (calculated and kindly provided by Francis Ng from the World Bank).

[a]Urban areas only (from Szekely and Hilgert 1999, p. 47).

due to the higher percentage of directly elected presidents in the failed contenders. Colonial heritage is also not very different between the two groups: all major metropolises are represented in both (Japan's former colonies are only among the success cases, however). There were no obvious differences in average tariff rates: in the early 1980s, the average tariff rate was 33 percent in both groups; by the end of the century it went down to 10 percent for the failed contenders, and 14 percent for the successful countries.[59]

Now, the observed differences in inequality levels and democracy between the two groups may be seemingly explained by the difference in the regional composition of the groups. Two-thirds of the failed contenders are Latin American and Caribbean countries, and one-half of the success cases are located in Asia. It is commonly held that Asian countries are characterized by relatively low income-inequality (due to land reforms and widely spread primary education) and repressive albeit "developmentalist" regimes. On the other hand, Latin American countries traditionally display high inequality, as well as democratic ups and down. We thus seem, to some extent, to be "rediscovering" the key features of each continent, not the differences between the two groups of failures and successes.

**TABLE 7.6.**
Differences in Initial Conditions between the Failed and Successful Contenders

| | *Failed Contenders (number of observations)* | *Successful Countries (number of observations)* | *t (p) Values* |
|---|---|---|---|
| Gini prior to 1965 | 49.8 (14) | 39.4 (7) | 3.29 (0.00) |
| Democracy prior to 1965 | 5.09 (131) | 1.95 (104) | 6.63 (0.00) |
| Ethnic fractionalization | 0.45 (14) | 0.45 (8) | 0.03 (0.98) |
| Average number of years of schooling (prior to 1965) | 3.78 (27) | 4.02 (14) | 0.48 (0.63) |
| Political system (1975–80) | | | |
| Direct presidential and strong presidential (%) | 60 | 57.5 | |
| Parliamentary (%) | 40 | 42.5 | |
| Number of observations | 65 | 40 | |

*Sources:* See note to table 7.5. Average years of education from Thomas, Fan, and Wang (2001).

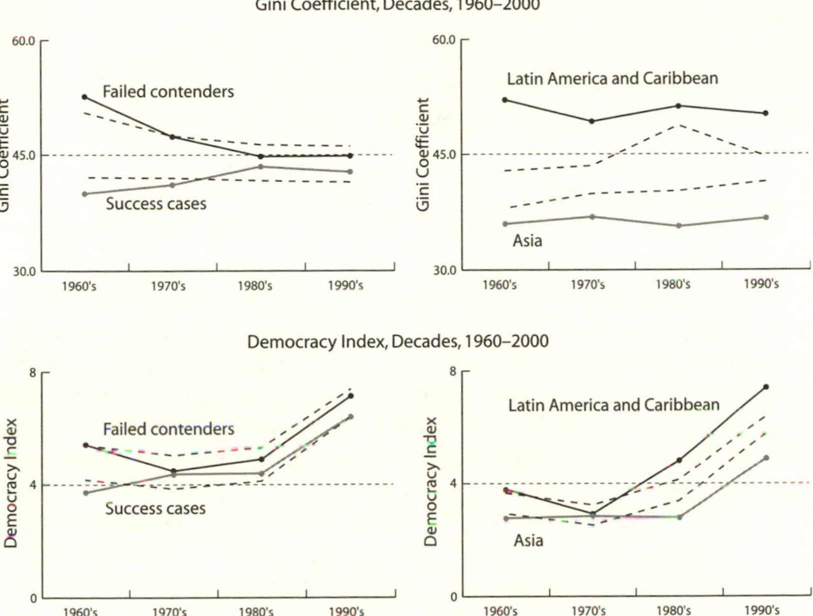


**Figure 7.4.** Failed contenders vs. success cases; and Latin America vs. Asia. The broken lines show the 95 percent confidence intervals for the hypothesis that the two means are the same. The democracy index is the same as that used in table 7.5.

However, this impression is not correct: it would be wrong to ascribe the differences in features between the failed contenders and the success cases respectively to Latin American and Asian characteristics as such. This can be seen from Figure 7.4. The failed and successful countries (shown in the two left panels) have since the early 1960s converged *both* in terms of inequality levels and democracy so much that the differences between them have during the past twenty years become statistically insignificant. But—and this is crucial—Latin America and Asia as continents (shown in the two right panels) have not converged at all. Latin American countries still have (on average) statistically significantly greater inequality, and are (on average) more democratic than Asian countries. While, for instance, democracy has progressed in both continents in the 1990s, the differences have not lessened. Thus the convergence in characteristics between the failed contenders and success cases is proper to these two groups, and does not extend to Latin America and Asia as a whole.

## A Summary

The developments over the past two decades of the twentieth century are remarkable for a following set of reasons.

1. They have reinforced the position of the West as the club of the rich. Not only because at the end of the century there are only nine non-Western countries that are rich (compared to nineteen in 1960), but because the "threat" of non-Western contenders joining the club has all but disappeared.

2. The hope of non-Western countries catching up has effectively been dashed over the past quarter of a century. While in 1960, there were forty-one non-Western countries that were either rich or had a good chance of joining the rich within a generation (sixteen of which were Latin American), at the end of the century there were only seventeen such countries (five of which are from Latin America and the Caribbean). Most of today's contenders are in effect the "fallen" rich, that is, countries like Argentina, the Czech republic, or Barbados, who once (in 1960) belonged to the club of the rich but have since declined.

3. While the West reinforced its control of the top, being an African country became synonymous with being very poor, much more so than probably ever in history.[60] There was an uninterrupted slide downward: African countries that were contenders in 1960 joined the Third World, and *all* African countries that were part of the Third World dropped to the level of the Fourth. At the end of the century, the likelihood of being very poor while African was about 80 percent.

4. The downward mobility of the countries—of which Africa is the most striking example—is reflected in the fact that while the number of the rich countries and contenders decreased between 1960 and 1998, the ranks of the Third and the Fourth World swelled.

5. Almost the only successes—upwardly mobile countries—are to be found in Asia. Taiwan moved from the Third World in 1960 to be among the rich at the end of the century. Similarly, Singapore, Hong Kong, South Korea, and Malaysia made it to the rich or contenders from "below." Add to that Botswana and Egypt, who moved from the Fourth to the Third World. And that is all.

## Conclusion: The Watershed Years and the Bifurcation of the Third World

The periodization we used here shows that something dramatic—reflected both in the growth rate of world income and the distribution of growth rates among countries—occurred at the very end of the

1970s. Arrighi (2002), Galbraith (2002), Easterly (2001), and, as we have seen, Paul Bairoch (1997) point out that economically and politically the years 1979–80 represented a watershed between the two epochs. In Arrighi's view, the watershed occurred because the United States, which, up to then, was a major capital exporter, suddenly became a major importer of capital in order to finance its current account and budget deficits. This had two dramatic effects: it reduced capital flows to the less developed countries and increased real interest rates, thus leading to the debt crisis of the 1980s. Moreover, in Arrighi's view, this "tectonic" change had a very different effect on different developing countries, and it brought about a bifurcation in their performance, a fact highlighted in the previous section. To quote Arrighi (2002), "there were those [countries] . . . that for historical and geographical reasons, had a strong advantage in competing for a share of the expanding North American demand for cheap industrial products. . . . On the other hand, there were regions that, for historical and geographic reasons, were particularly disadvantaged in competing for a share of the North American demand. These [second] areas tended to run into balance-of-payments difficulties that put them into a hopeless position of having to compete [for capital] directly with the United States in world financial markets."[61]

These economic effects had their political counterparts or even political roots. The redirection of capital flows toward the United States, and the world-wide increase in real interest rates were driven by the political and military facts of the massive U.S. rearmament and the intensification of the Cold War. This, coupled with Reagan's tax cuts, created large U.S. current account and budget deficits. Thus, the chain of events was from a political decision to rearm and outspend the Soviet Union, to its economic implication of large budget deficits and the need for capital inflows, to the rising interest rates that suffocated less developed countries unable to compete in international markets.

According to Easterly (2001), the changes that occurred around 1978–80, namely "the increase in world interest rates, the increased debt burden of developing countries, the growth slowdown in the industrial world, and skill-biased technological change may have contributed to the developing countries' stagnation" and to the bifurcation of the developing world. One (smaller) group of developing countries managed to move to a Rostovian self-sustained long-term growth, thanks to the presence of the four conditions listed by Arrighi: (i) the abundance of cheap labor, (ii) entrepreneurial talent, exemplified in the Chinese Asian diaspora, (iii) strong state, and (iv) privileged access to the U.S. market. The other (larger) group, most notably the countries of Africa, where only the first of the four conditions was present, fell further behind. Thus, the former Third World splintered. Africa, as Arrighi points out, did particularly badly on the four conditions: it was never characterized by the relative abundance of labor; it had very few entrepreneurs, not the least because domestic entrepreneurship was discouraged by colonialists; it had no diaspora that could bring in technical know-how and capital; and, unlike Northern Asian countries, which, after the Korean war and in order to counteract the Chinese and Soviet influence, were granted a preferential treatment to the U.S. market, Africa never loomed much on the political horizon.

The same view is held by Bairoch (1997, 3:997–1000). According to him, the "watershed years," 1978–80, opened up an entirely new (third) phase in the development of the Third World. The first phase covers the period up to the end of World War II and is characterized by slow and erratic growth. According to Bairoch's estimates, the average annual growth rate of Third World countries was only 0.3 percent per capita. The second phase, from the end of the World War II up to 1978, witnessed an acceleration of growth—with average Third World growth being about 2.2 percent per capita. This entire period is deemed by Bairoch to have been both "a relative success" as the Third World countries grew faster than the rich world (when the rich world was at that level of development), and a "relative failure" as the Third World still failed to reduce the distance that separated it from the advanced countries. But, "from 1978–1980 commences the third phase which for many market-oriented Third World countries is characterized by a total failure of economic growth" (Bairoch 1997, 3:999; my translation). Galbraith (2002) and Galbraith and Kum (2002) observe the same discontinuity and focus on the role of interest rates: "the rise in interest rates produced dramatic and continuing cuts in imports [of the Third World countries] with devastating results for the development prospects of poorer countries. Many of them never recovered" (Galbraith 2002, p. 23).

Thus, the late 1970s/early 1980s were indeed the turning point for many countries. Those buffeted by the twin shocks of rising oil prices and higher real interest rates saw their growth rates plummet and, in some cases, turn negative. Many of these countries have yet to regain their end-1970s income levels (see appendix 3).[62] In addition, the changed political climate in the 1990s, brought about by the end of the Cold War, further reduced the political importance of a number of Third World countries—most dramatically those in Africa (but not only them, as Argentina was soon to discover)—and concessional capital flows dried out.[63] The most recent debt forgiveness initiatives are a simple acknowledgment of the fact that the debt burden has become unsustainable for many countries, and that writing it off is better both from the debtor's and creditor's perspective—since these loans are unlikely ever to be repaid in full. The number of countries that had gone or are going through the debt write-off exercise (forty-three heavily indebted poor countries have been identified as eligible; see Birdsall and Williamson 2002, p. 28) is itself a testimony to the widespread nature of the problem. But the write-off alone will do little to launch these countries on a growth path. Foreign capital flows will remain scarce, substantial domestic capital accumulation is unlikely, and the rules of the game—rewritten during the past two decades—are now much more inimical to the poor countries than they were in the 1960s.[64]

The main sources of the anti-poor biases in the international rules concern protectionism and subsidization of the goods where the rich have a hard time competing (no trade liberalization on textiles, continued subsidies of food), combined with a very tough stance in the areas where the rich countries have an advantage (protection of intellectual property rights, liberalization of financial services). In the words of Nayyar (1997, p. 28), "[N]ational borders should not matter for trade flows and capital flows but should be clearly demarcated for technology flows and labor flows. It follows that the developing countries would provide access to their markets without a corresponding access to technology and would accept capital mobility without a corresponding provision for labor mobility." In addition, the dispute settlement system introduced by WTO is exorbitantly expensive and complex, putting the less-developed countries at a clear disadvantage.[65]

We should not, therefore, be surprised if marginalization of many countries, and of the whole African continent, deepens. Like some social or ethnic groups in affluent countries, they would be "excluded" from progress.[66] At some regular intervals, debt would be forgiven, but, since the Roman times, we know that debt forgiveness is simply a palliative solution, and—unless the structural conditions are changed—one debt forgiveness only follows upon another. In the long term, it solves little.

# Part III

GLOBAL INEQUALITY

# 8

## Concept 2 Inequality: Decreasing in the Past Twenty Years

FIGURE 8.1 shows population-weighted international inequality calculated for the same period and same countries as before (see chapter 4 on unweighted international inequality). After a significant jump in 1952 when China was added to the sample, and then in 1960 when African countries were included, the weighted international inequality almost constantly slides down, and the decline accelerates in the decade of the 1990s. Between 1965 and 2000, across a practically constant sample of countries, the weighted international inequality decreased from a Gini of 55.7 to 50.5—a 10 percent drop. The decline of the Theil index was even steeper.

What drives the change in the population-weighted Gini? Is it that per capita GDPs in poor and populous countries like China and India grow faster than in rich countries, or perhaps that population growth in rich and middle-income countries is higher even if GDPs per capita grow at the same rate? Or perhaps both? Results shown in figure 8.2 allow us to dispense with one possible explanation: that it is the changing population shares between poor and the rich countries that push population-weighted international inequality down. As figure 8.2 shows, the downward trend in the Gini coefficient is unchanged whether we use the current population shares for each year, or the 1960 or 2000 population shares. There are only very small differences. The Gini coefficients calculated with the 2000 and the current population shares are consistently higher since the mid-1960s than the Ginis obtained using the 1960 population shares—indicating that uneven population growth (that is, faster population growth in poorer countries) increased the *level* of inequality. Yet it also contributed to its faster decline. This can be seen from the fact that the gap between the Ginis calculated using the 2000 and 1960 weights, which widened in the 1970s and 1980s, gradually diminished afterward. In other words, the current-year- and the 2000-population weighted Ginis both decline faster than the 1960-population weighted Gini. However, the gap between the various Ginis is hardly significant: at the most, it is a little over one Gini point.

Let us now try to look at other causes behind the decline in weighted

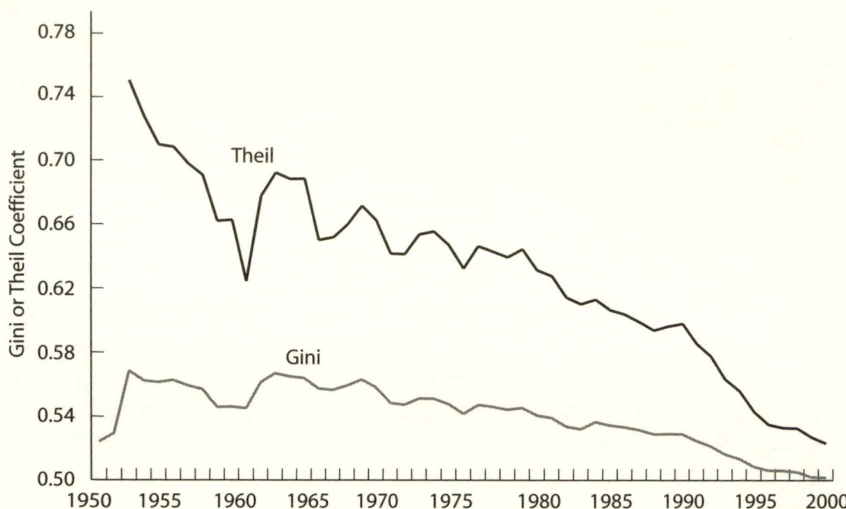


**Figure 8.1.** Concept 2 inequality: Weighted international inequality, 1950–2000.

international inequality. Figure 8.3 shows weighted international inequality but excludes India and China. Two important things can be seen. First, when China alone is excluded, weighted international inequality does not show a trend, or rather it shows mild *increasing* trend from the early 1980s onward. Thus, the inclusion or exclusion of China

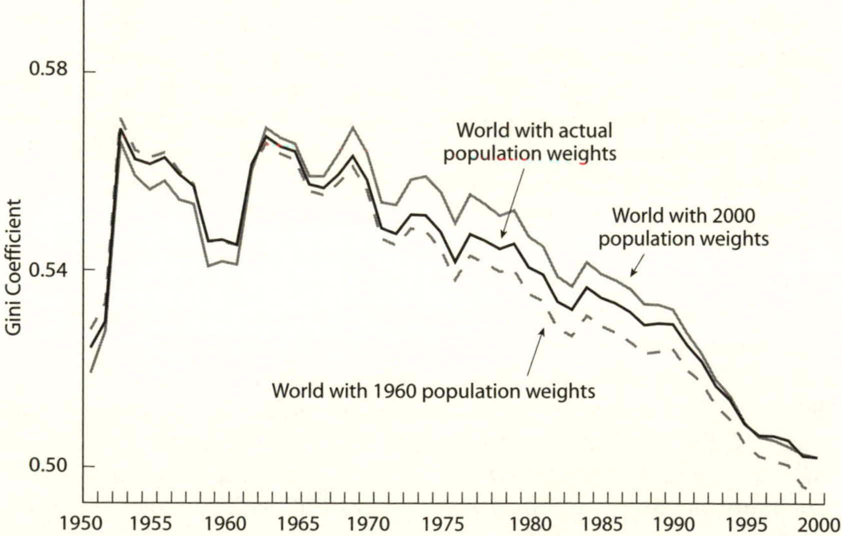


**Figure 8.2.** International weighted inequality (with different population weights).

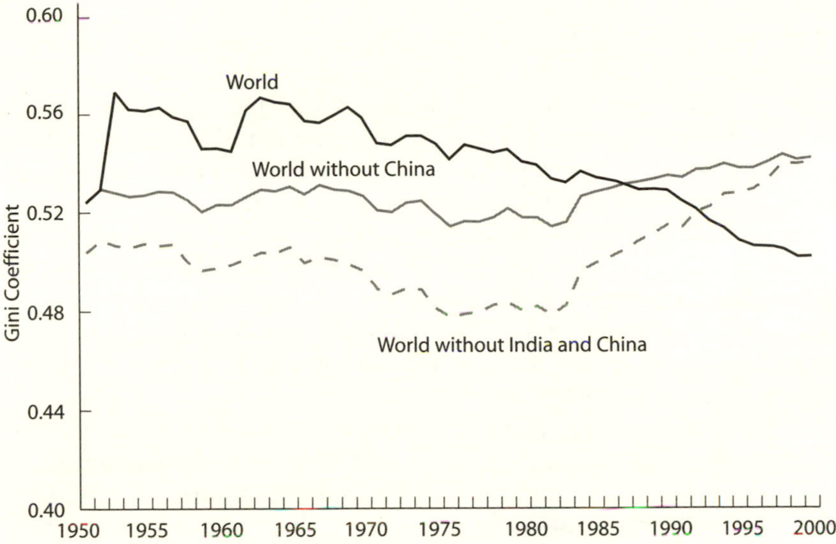


**Figure 8.3.** Weighted international inequality without China and India.

alone makes a huge difference, replacing the strongly decreasing trend of Concept 2 inequality with a mildly increasing one. Second, when we exclude both India and China, we note an increase in inequality that begins, as in the case of unweighted international inequality, around the mid-1980s. Consequently, it is India's and China's faster growth compared to that of the rich countries at the other pole of income distribution (Western Europe, North America, and Oceania) that is responsible for decreasing weighted international inequality and therefore for the difference in trends between concepts 1 and 2—that is, for what we dubbed at the beginning "the mother of all inequality disputes."

Two additional interesting facts are revealed in figure 8.3.[67] First, that Concept 2 inequality without China (or without China and India) is, during the past decade, greater than when these two countries are included. In other words, the inclusion of China and India *reduces* weighted international inequality today in contrast to the situation throughout the previous decades. This clearly illustrates the countries' upward movement through income distribution: they are no longer very poor countries. Second, during the recent period, the inclusion or not of India does not seem to make a difference to Concept 2 inequality. We notice that at the end of the 1990s the population-weighted Gini is practically the same whether we exclude China only, or exclude both China and India. This implies that the presence of China is currently inequality-reducing (for Concept 2 inequality), while the inclusion of India is neutral.[68]

## The "Triangle" That Matters: China, India, and the United States

Let us thus consider the "triangle" of China, India, and the United States—the natural candidates for an explanation of the Concept 2 declining trend. At the end of the second millennium, these three countries account for about 45 percent of world population, a little over 40 percent of world (PPP) income, and about one-half of Concept 2 inequality. China has experienced tremendously fast growth since the reforms started in the late 1970s; India has too, even if less impressively, and both must have reduced their distance with respect to the United States. Hence, they should have contributed significantly to the reduction in world inequality.

Table 8.1 shows three countries' GDP per capita in $PPP terms, their GDPs per capita "normalized" by world (population-weighted) mean GDP per capita, and the distance between such normalized GDPs. Looking at the numbers in the first three columns, we see that China registered fast growth, increasing its GDP per capita by more than one-half between 1965 and 1980, and then quintupling it between 1978 and 2000.[69] China's GDP per capita increased from being equal to 13 percent of the world mean to 60 percent of the world mean.[70]

However, much less impressive—and this is key for the Gini contributions—was the reduction in the world mean-normalized gap between the United States and China: the gap was equal to 4.47 times the mean world GDP per capita in 1965 (16527 – 472 divided by 3589), and despite massive Chinese growth was still 4 times in 2000. This was, of course, due to the significant growth of the United States itself, which, starting from a much higher base, had to grow less in percentage terms in order to maintain the normalized gap unchanged. But since it is the gap that matters in the calculation of the Gini, we can already see that the contribution of the United States-China shrinking gap was much less than it seemed at first. Notice, moreover, that the gap between the United States and India actually *increased* over the recent period (1978 to 2000), and similarly that the gap between India and China also increased (after "changing sign" around 1980 when China overtook India).

But to get the exact contributions of these three countries to the weighted international Gini, we need to weigh the gaps shown in the last three columns of table 8.1 by the countries' population shares. The first three columns of table 8.2 give the population shares of China, India, and the United States; the next three, the calculated values of the intercountry terms (ICT) that enter in the calculation of the Gini. The importance of the "triangle" was the greatest in 1965; it decreased significantly between then and 1978, and has stayed since at about the

**TABLE 8.1.**
China, India, and the United States in 1965, 1978, and 2000

| | *GDP Per Capita (in $PPP)* | | | *GDP Per Capita ("normalized" by world GDP per capita)* | | | | *"Normalized" Gap Between the Triangle Countries* | | |
|---|---|---|---|---|---|---|---|---|---|---|
| | *1965* | *1978* | *2000* | *1965* | *1978* | *2000* | | *1965* | *1978* | *2000* |
| China | 472 | 754 | 4144 | 0.13 | 0.15 | 0.60 | China-India | 0.063 | 0.021 | 0.356 |
| India | 698 | 857 | 1693 | 0.19 | 0.17 | 0.25 | India-USA | 4.410 | 4.237 | 4.333 |
| USA | 16527 | 21790 | 31519 | 4.60 | 4.41 | 4.58 | China-USA | 4.473 | 4.258 | 3.977 |
| World | 3589 | 4940 | 6883 | 1.00 | 1.00 | 1.00 | | — | — | — |

*Note:* "Normalized" gap is calculated as the difference between the countries' per capita GDPs divided by the world's mean per capita GDP (all in $PPP terms). World mean income is population-weighted.

same level. In both 1978 and 2000, the "triangle" contributed over 9 Gini points to total Concept 2 inequality.[71] It is easy to see why the importance of the interactions among the three most important countries did not change much during the past two decades: the mean-normalized distance between India and the United States went up slightly, the distance between China and the United States decreased, but, by exactly as much, the distance between China and India—which was practically nil in 1978—increased. This last point illustrates the ambivalence of China's growth "through the ranks" of world income distribution: as its distance from the West diminishes and inequality is thus reduced, it

**TABLE 8.2.**
China, India, the United States: Population Shares and Gini Contributions

| | *Population Shares* | | | | *Gini Points (ICT)* | | |
|---|---|---|---|---|---|---|---|
| | *1965* | *1978* | *2000* | | *1965* | *1978* | *2000* |
| China | 0.228 | 0.236 | 0.218 | China-India | 0.22 | 0.08 | 1.37 |
| India | 0.155 | 0.162 | 0.177 | India-US | 4.24 | 3.79 | 3.72 |
| USA | 0.062 | 0.055 | 0.049 | China-US | 6.32 | 5.54 | 4.20 |
| Total triangle | 0.445 | 0.454 | 0.443 | Total triangle | 10.78 | 9.40 | 9.29 |
| | | | | Change | — | –1.38 | –0.11 |
| | | | | World Gini | 55.7 | 54.4 | 50.1 |
| | | | | Change | — | –1.3 | –4.3 |

*Note:* Each ICT, for the country pair ($j$ and $i$) such that $y_j > y_i$, is equal to $\frac{1}{\mu}(y_j - y_i)p_i p_j$.

opens up the distance between China and the slower-growing (or stagnating) poor countries and thus contributes to world inequality.

A glance at table 8.2 shows that the changes within the triangle explained the entire decrease in the Concept 2 inequality between 1965 and 1978. The weighted international inequality decreased between these two years by 1.3 Gini points (from 55.7 to 54.4), while the triangle's contribution was reduced by 1.38 Gini points. Thus, our hypothesis that the interaction within the China-India-United States triangle was crucial is confirmed for the period 1965–78.

However, it is not confirmed for the second period (1978–2000). As we have seen, the contribution of the triangle remained practically unchanged in face of a huge decrease of Concept 2 inequality. Between these two years, weighted international inequality went down from a Gini of 54.4 to 50.1. Clearly the explanation for that decline must be sought elsewhere.

Before we move to that search, consider disentangling the effect of changing *income* gaps within the triangle from the effect of changing *population* shares. If we apply the 1965 population shares to the actual income gaps, we obtain the values in the first four rows of table 8.3. We see that between 1965 and 1978, the shrinking of the income gaps between the members of the triangle shaved off 0.62 Gini points of weighted international inequality (10.78 minus 10.16). Since the overall international inequality decreased over the same period by 1.29 Gini points, we conclude that almost one-half of the decrease was due to the shrinking income gaps among the triangle. And as the populations also moved in the "right" direction, the triangle was responsible for more than 100 percent of the overall decrease in international inequality between 1965 and 1978.

But then the situation radically changes. The absolute triangle's contribution to international inequality in 2000 was only 0.11 Gini points less than in 1978 (see line 5 in table 8.3). This explains 2 percent of the overall Gini decrease between 1978 and 2000, or, in other words, this contribution is negligible. Moreover, the income gaps between China, India, and the United States did not shrink—they *increased*, thus adding to inequality. It is only because population shares of all three countries went down in 2000 compared to 1978 that the triangle's contribution to international inequality stayed almost unchanged.

So, we need to expand our search for the cause of the decline in weighted international inequality between 1978 and 2000 to countries other than those in the triangle. As we have seen, between 1978 and 2000, weighted international inequality decreased by 4.3 Gini points. China's rapid growth was the key explanatory factor: as China's distance with respect to all richer and populous countries decreased, it re-

**TABLE 8.3.**
Income and Population Contributions of the Triangle to World Inequality

| | *Gini Point Contributions with 1965 Population Shares* | | |
|---|---|---|---|
| | *1965* | *1978* | *2000* |
| (1) China-India | 0.22 | 0.07 | 1.26 |
| (2) India-USA | 4.24 | 4.08 | 4.17 |
| (3) China-USA | 6.32 | 6.01 | 5.62 |
| (4) Total triangle | 10.78 | 10.16 | 11.05 |
| Difference | | –0.62 | +0.89 |
| | | *1965–78* | *1978–2000* |
| (5) Total change in triangle contribution (from table 8.2) | | –1.38 | –0.11 |
| (6) Due to income | | –0.62 | +0.89 |
| (7) Due to population (and interaction term) | | –0.76 | –0.99 |
| (8) Overall Concept 2 Gini change (from table 8.2) | | –1.29 | –4.33 |
| Percentage breakdown of triangle contribution | | | |
| Due to the triangle (5) : (8) | | 107.1 | 2.5 |
| Due to income gaps in the triangle (6) : (8) | | 48.0 | –20.5 |

duced the Gini in turn. (However, it should be noticed that China's pulling ahead of India, Bangladesh, and Pakistan *added* to world inequality.) This is depicted in figure 8.4. Since all the values are normalized by current mean world income, the distance between the lines is the term that (weighted by the population shares) enters into the Gini calculation. Between 1978 and 2000, the distances among the three rich countries, and between each of them and India, remained about the same.[72] It is only the distance between China (on the one hand), and the United States, Japan, and Germany, on the other, that shrunk—while the distance between China and India increased.

The reduced income distance between China and the six large OECD countries (United States, Japan, Germany, France, United Kingdom, and Italy) lowered the weighted international Gini by a whopping 3.5 Gini points, which is 80 percent of the overall Gini decline between 1978 and 2000 (table 8.4). When we add the decreasing distance between China and the three large middle-income countries (Brazil, Mexico, and Russia), we end up with more than a full accounting for the Gini decline. The last line of table 8.4 shows the interaction between China and the large and poor Third World countries (Pakistan, Bang-

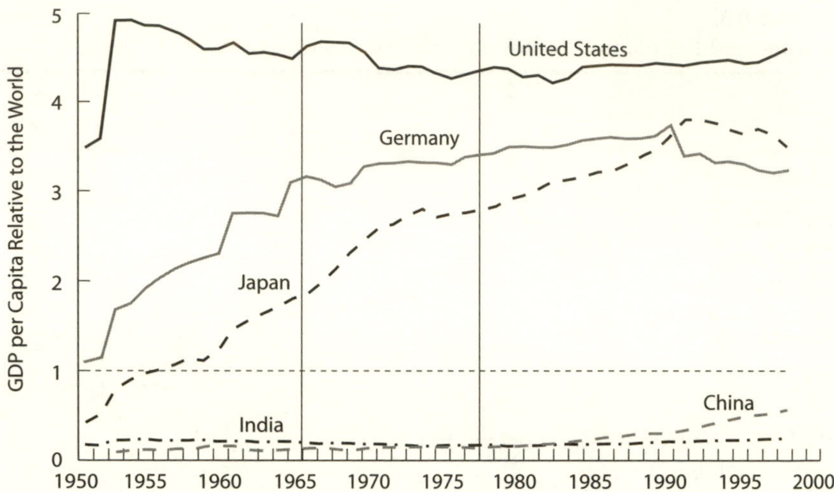


**Figure 8.4.** GDP per capita (normalized by current mean world GDP per capita) for five countries. The sharp increase of countries' normalized income in 1952 is due to the addition of (a very poor) China to the sample.

ladesh, Indonesia, and Nigeria). There, as in the interaction between China and India, we see the other side of the coin of China's rapid advance: a contribution to world inequality. Now, of course, assuming that China's advance continues, the positive (inequality-reducing) effects will continue to dominate for quite some time. Yet a point may be reached where the lack of (sufficient) progress in the poor countries and

**TABLE 8.4.**
Gini Points (ICTs): China and the Rest of the World, 1978 and 2000

| | *1978* | *2000* | *Change* |
|---|---|---|---|
| China-United States | 5.5 | 4.2 | –1.3 |
| China-Japan | 1.8 | 1.3 | –0.5 |
| China-Germany | 1.5 | 0.8 | –0.7 |
| China-other large OECD countries | 2.7 | 1.7 | –1.0 |
| China-(Brazil,Mexico,Russia) | 1.8 | 0.4 | –1.4 |
| Total | 13.3 | 8.4 | –4.9 |
| World Gini | 54.4 | 50.1 | –4.3 |
| China-(poor large Third World countries) | 0.27 | 0.58 | +0.34 |

*Note:* Other large OECD countries = France, Italy and United Kingdom. Poor large Third World countries are Pakistan, Bangladesh, Indonesia, and Nigeria.

their increasing distance from China may offset (in terms of Concept 2 inequality) the gains from China's greater proximity to the rich world.

To sum up. For the period 1965–78, the main explanation of the decline in weighted international inequality was the decreasing income gap between the three most important countries (China, India, and the United States). In the second period, however, the entire decrease in weighted international inequality was driven by China's growth relative to the rich part of the world.

## How Many Peaks?

We have looked above at the distribution of countries according to their GDP per capita. Once we introduce population, we can look at the distribution of the population—not according to their "true" income, this is the topic of Concept 3 inequality—but according to the average income (GDP per capita) of the country where they live. This is done in figure 8.5, which illustrates three facts: (i) growth of incomes shown in the rightward shift of the distribution, (ii) the "unsticking" of the very poorest as some of them (China) have pooled ahead of the rest, and (iii) the continuous emptiness in the middle levels of income distribution, that is, the absence of world middle class. To illustrate the first point, consider that in 1960, slightly more than one-half of world population lived in countries whose GDP per capita was less than $PPP 1,200, and 82 percent lived in countries whose GDP per capita was less than $PPP 5,500. In 1978, these values have dropped to 46 and 72 percent, and in 2000—as China and India pulled ahead—they were only 7 percent (for under $PPP 1,200), and 70 percent (for under $PPP 5,500).[73] Thus, over the past two decades, the progress was quite remarkable in poor and populous countries (that is, India and China) but not nearly as impressive in the rest of the world. The world middle class, as we shall see in chapter 10, has remained very small.

## Alternative Chinese GDP Data

As we have seen, the conclusion about the decrease in Concept 2 inequality during the last twenty years of the century entirely depends on China's GDP. The problem, however, is that Chinese GDP data are widely considered unreliable. This pertains to the Chinese economic performance during both the Maoist and Dengist periods as well as afterwards and it poses essentially two interrelated accounting problems. First, whether or not to believe the official growth rates and therefore

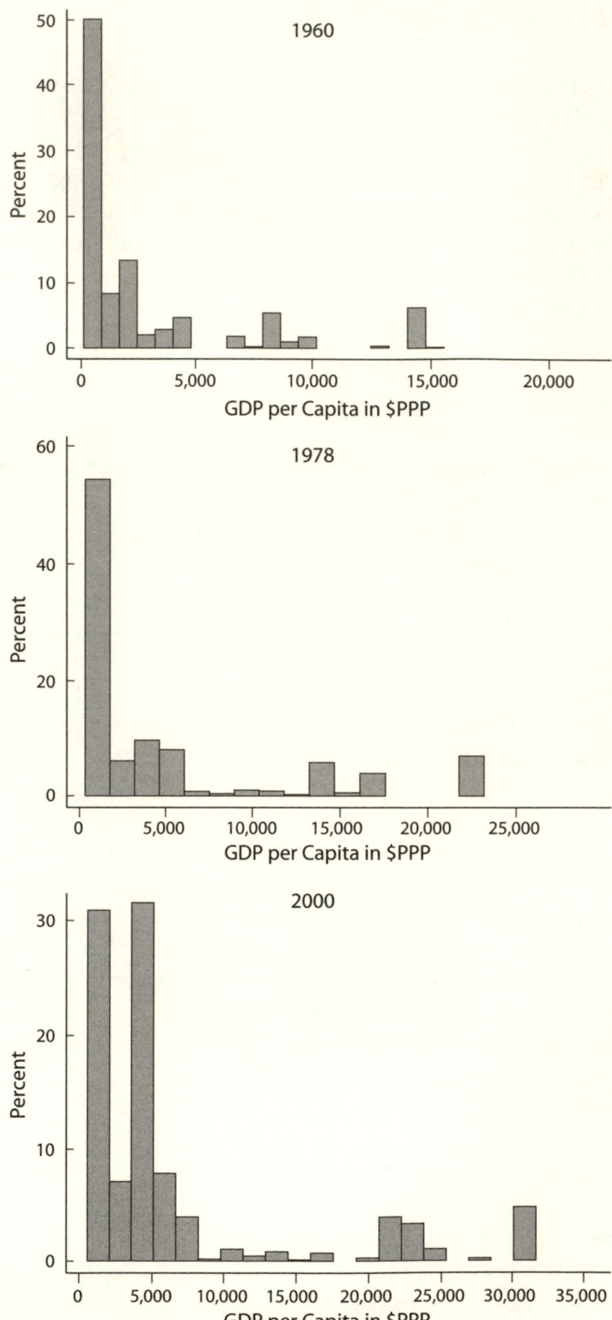


**Figure 8.5.** Distribution of people according to GDP per capita of the country where they live in 1960, 1978, and 2000. Horizontal axis: GDP per capita in 1995 international prices. Vertical axis: Share of world population.

**TABLE 8.5.**
Implied Growth Rates of China's Real GDP Per Capita according to Different Sources

| | *Official* | *PWT 6.1* | *Maddison (2001)* | *World Bank* |
|---|---|---|---|---|
| 1952–78 | 4.0 | 1.8 | 2.3 | 4.1 |
| 1978–99 | 8.1 | 6.4 | 5.9 | 8.1 |
| 1952–99 | 5.8 | 3.8 | 3.9 | 5.9 |

*Note:* Rates calculated as simple geometric averages. *Sources:* Official data: 1952–78, real national income from Chinese Statistical Yearbook 1985, p. 34; 1978–99, real GDP from Chinese Statistical Yearbook 2002, p. 58. World Bank from SIMA database (World Development Indicators). Maddison (2001, p. 304). Penn World Tables 6. 1 downloaded from http://pwt.econ.upenn.edu/ (the variable RGDPCH). Maddison's data expressed in 1990 Geary-Khamis international dollars; PWT6.1 data expressed in 1996 international dollars. Official data expressed at "comparable" prices. World Bank data in 1995 international prices.

how to judge China's overall performance as well as how to compare the results during the different subperiods (the Cultural Revolution, post-1978 reforms, etc). Second, depending on our decision regarding the 1952–2000 growth rates,[74] the *levels* of GDP in the early years, that is, in the 1950s and 1960s, will be higher or lower. The reason is that these levels are calculated backward, namely, one starts with the current level of GDP (on which there is more or less an agreement) and applies to it growth rates of all the intervening years. If we believe the official (higher) growth rates, then the pre-1952 level must have been very low; if we reduce growth rates, then the 1952 level turns out significantly higher. The second point has important implications for the calculation of our Concept 2 inequality over the 1950–2000 period, as well as for the long-run evolution of global inequality, a topic that we shall briefly address in chapter 11.

In the analysis so far, we have used the World Bank data, which almost fully track the official Chinese statistics (see table 8.5). However, the two alternative sources, Maddison (2001) and the Penn World Tables (PWT) 6.1 give much lower growth rates for both the pre-reform and post-reform periods. Thus, while all three sources do agree (within 16 percent) on China's current level of GDP per capita (see table 8.6), the differences in the initial levels of GDP per capita are very wide. Maddison's data give China's 1952 per capita GDP as 2.4 times greater than the one implied by the World Bank data.[75] PWT 6.1 is generally closer to Maddison's data (which is not surprising as the authors have followed, albeit with some adjustments [see Heston 2001], Maddison's calculations).

Now, these alternative calculations of the Chinese GDP per capita

**TABLE 8.6.**
Implied China's GDP Per Capita in Different Years according to Different Sources (in 1995 international prices)

| | *PWT 6.1* | *Maddison (2001)* | *World Bank* |
|---|---|---|---|
| 1952 | 568 | 627 | 262 |
| 1960 | 662 | 785 | 497 |
| 1966 | 773 | 879 | 534 |
| 1978 | 899 | 1142 | 754 |
| 1988 | 1703 | 2119 | 1676 |
| 1999 | 3319 | 3803 | 3867 |
| 2000 | 3642 | na | 4144 |

*Sources:* See sources in table 8.5. Conversion into 1995 international dollars done by multiplying Maddison's data by 1.167, and PWT6.1 data by 0.97 (changes in the US CPI between the relevant years). The official Chinese data have not been expressed in international prices.

must, as one can immediately see, have the following implications for the Concept 2 inequality. Higher initial levels of GDP per capita will reduce the early levels of international inequality (as China is now shown to have been less poor), while lower subsequent growth rates will lead to a smaller decrease in Concept 2 inequality (as the Chinese are now shown not to have caught up with the rich countries as much as we previously assumed). Therefore, both the level and the change in Concept 2 inequality will be less. And this is indeed what we observe in the new calculations shown in figure 8.6. Maddison's data give consistently the lowest inequality level, and the lowest decrease in it. For example, while the World Bank data imply an almost 4-Gini-point decline in international weighted inequality between 1978 and 2000, Maddison's data over the same period show a decline of only 2.7 Gini points, and Penn World Tables 6.1, 3 Gini points. The differences are even greater with the Theil index (not shown here): 7 to 8 Theil points according to the two alternative measures, and almost 12 Gini points according to the World Bank data.

## Breaking China and India into Provinces and States

Because of the overwhelming importance of China and India—both due to their sizes and high growth rates during the past two decades—an improvement in the estimates of Concept 2 inequality can be gained by breaking up these two countries into their regional units—states in the case of India, provinces for China. We have annual data on GDP per

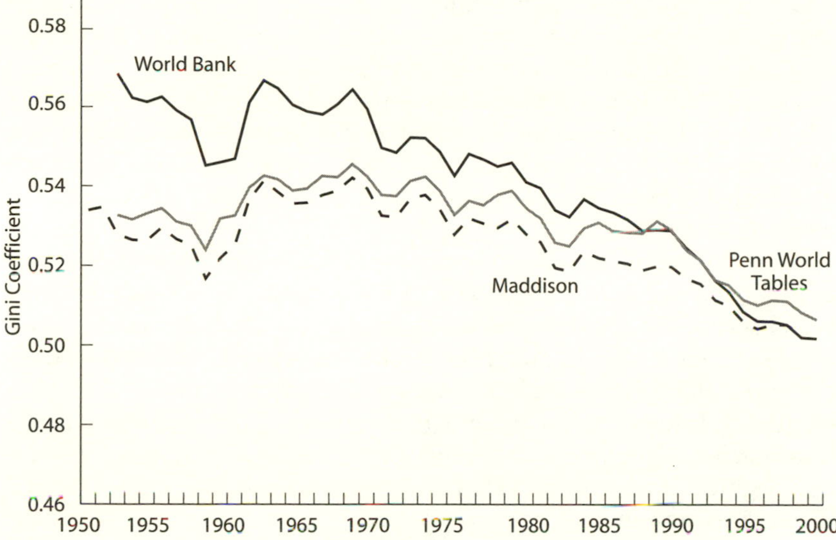


**Figure 8.6.** International population-weighted inequality (Gini) with alternative estimates of China's GDP per capita. *Source:* See sources in table 8.5.

capita levels for twenty-nine provinces in China from 1978 to 2000 (accounting for 99 percent of China's population in 2000), and for fourteen states in India from 1980 to 2000 (accounting for 93 percent of India's 2000 population).[76] Starting from 1980, we therefore replace China and India by their constituent regional units, and recalculate Concept 2 inequality. The results are shown in figure 8.7. Before we discuss them, a methodological caveat is in order.

The data for the Indian states are given in 1993–94 constant prices, and their conversion into 1995 prices does not pose much of a problem. However, we are unable to adjust for the differences in regional price levels, and, in order to convert the data into 1995 international dollars, we simply apply the same 1995 PPP exchange rate to all states. An identical approach is followed in the case of China. In the Chinese case, however, there are more serious problems. The data are expressed in 1978 constant prices, and bringing them into the 1995 constant prices (using the all-China CPI) entails a much greater potential error. The same is true for the next step, an across-the-board conversion into the 1995 international dollars where, like in the Indian case, we use a single PPP exchange rate.[77] Since Chinese regional price levels are thought to be quite different (higher in richer provinces) using the same PPP exchange rate will boost income levels in rich provinces and depress them in poorer ones.[78] Finally, the all-China GDP obtained through a simple addition of provincial GDPs differs from the (official) all-China GDP that we have used before. The difference is minimal (about 1 to 2 percent) up to 1995, but then rapidly increases and reaches 15–17 percent in 1998–2000.[79] To make the calculations consistent, we have therefore adjusted by the same factor all regional GDPs so as to make the sum of regional GDPs equal to the all-China GDP used before. The same adjustment was done for the Indian data, although the discrepancy is much smaller there.

After making these adjustments, we calculate the Gini and Theil coefficients for the period 1980–2000 by substituting for China and India the observations for their provinces and states. Two things are clear: Concept 2 inequality is now higher, and the trend is unchanged until the mid-1990s when there is a slowdown or halt to a further decline in inequality. Interestingly, Gini and Theil indexes react differently to the introduction of provinces and states. Expressed in Gini terms, the overall weighted international inequality gets a level boost of about 6 to 7 Gini points, and there is no marked change in the overall trend of Concept 2 decline until almost the end of the period (figure 8.7 top panel). But in terms of the Theil entropy index, while the breakdown of China and India into provinces and states has at first almost no impact at all, at the end of the period it adds some 2 Theil points (figure 8.7, bottom panel). Moreover, since 1996, Concept 2 inequality approximated by the Theil index has ceased its decline which, as we have seen before, is one of the strong stylized facts of the past twenty years. Whence this difference between the Gini and Theil? The reason lies in the their definitions. Gini index is a mean-normalized and weighted sum of all bilateral income comparisons. Thus the relative position of each state vis-à-vis other states and countries will determine what happens to total inequality. The introduction of some forty new units with a range of incomes (mostly below the world mean) will add to the total sum of income differences. But for the Theil index, all units with incomes below the mean are inequality-reducing (if the country's income-to-overall-mean ratio is less than 1, then the logarithm will be negative) and the more so the poorer the country. In 1980, all Chinese provinces except Shanghai had per capita GDPs less than the world mean, and were inequality-reducing. This was especially the case for populous and poor provinces like Sichuan, Shandong and Henan (all with the populations in excess of 70 million in 1980). Using China as a single observation or broken-down by provinces did not make much difference. But the situation was different in 2000. There were five provinces with a combined population of 50 million with per capita incomes above the world mean.[80] They were contributing positively to Concept 2 inequality; at the same time, other Chinese and Indian regions' incomes were

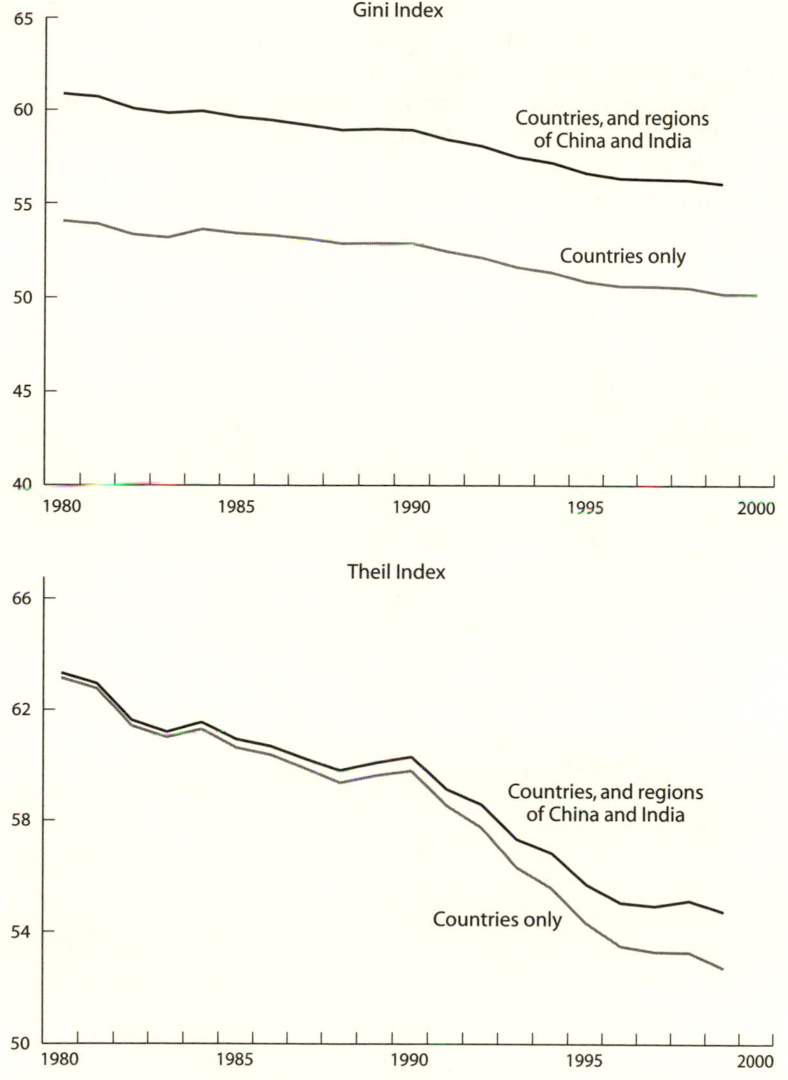


**Figure 8.7.** International population-weighted inequality: with China and India replaced by their provinces and states.

approaching the world mean from below and were "deducting" less from world inequality.

These results have two implications. First, the substitution of provinces and states for the two largest countries shows that the picture of Concept 2 inequality changes: growing interregional inequality in China and India has a discernable and positive effect on world inequality.[81] In particular, Concept 2 inequality measured by Theil coefficient is no longer decreasing. As more Chinese (and Indian) provinces become rich while others stay behind, world inequality will rise. Second, the calculations set a lower bound on global inequality—a concept to which we turn next. Global inequality, namely, inequality among individuals, at the turn of century must be greater than 56 in Gini terms, and 55 in Theil terms. This is because Concept 2 inequality ignores differences in income that exist within each country or state.

# 9

## High Global Inequality: No Trend?

> I say here, however, that I do not share in the apprehension held by many as to the danger of governments becoming weakened and destroyed by reason of their extension of territory. Commerce, education, and rapid transit of thought and matter by telegraph and steam have changed all this. Rather do I believe that our Great Maker is preparing the world, in His own good time, to become one nation, speaking one language.
>
> —ULYSSES S. GRANT, *Inaugural Speech*, 1873

WORLD or global inequality treats, in principle, all individuals in the world the same. It is concerned with their individual incomes and ranks them from the poorest to the richest regardless of the country where they live. Such world inequality can still, of course, be disaggregated into that part of inequality that is due to the differences in mean countries' incomes in the same way as overall inequality in a given country can be decomposed into a part of inequality due to differences in mean regional incomes.

The source of data for world income distribution are household surveys (HS). Since household survey data for several important countries or regions of the world have become available only comparatively recently (e.g., China since the early 1980s, USSR in the second half of the 1980s, and many African countries in the 1990s), we cannot calculate world distribution that would cover at least 80 to 90 percent of world population for any date prior to mid-1980s.[82] Recently there have been a number of attempts to calculate world inequality applying two different approximations.

The first consists in taking countries' GDPs per capita and a summary inequality statistic like the Gini coefficient or log standard deviation. Both GDP per capita and some summary inequality statistics have been available—even if very unevenly among the countries—for a much longer time. If we know the first two moments of the distribution (the mean and the variance) and/or the Gini coefficient, we can derive—on the assumption that incomes are lognormally distributed—the parameters of the distribution, and then in principle estimate level of income at each percentile. This was the approach adopted by Schultz (1998), Quah (1999), Chotikapanich, Valenzuela, and Rao (1997), and, more recently and with a few additions to the methodology, Sala-i-Martin (2002, 2002a). It is an ingenious approach because it is very powerful, given rather minimal information (one or two moments of distribution and one inequality statistic). However, the cost is that the assumptions, some of which are rather dubious, may drive the results. Since many assumptions are made simultaneously (e.g., that each country's distribution is lognormal; that GDP per capita gives the correct mean income; that income under- or overestimation compared to household surveys is constant, in percentage terms, across the income distribution), it is almost impossible to figure out what part of the results is due to the various assumptions and what to the actual, and very sparse, data. This is essentially the critique made in Milanovic (2003) with respect to Sala-i-Martin's calculations. This type of approximation faces two key problems. First, to the extent that empirical distributions diverge from the theoretical construct, the results are flawed; and indeed this is something that many authors have detected in applied empirical research (Bourguignon 2002; Cline 2004, pp. 35–6).[83] Second, the use of national accounts means (GDP per capita, or mean personal consumption) rather than household survey means assumes a proportional over- or (more commonly) underestimation by household surveys, which we know to be wrong. Namely, the rich tend to underestimate their consumption or income more than the poor, be it because of inadequate coverage of incomes from property or self-employment, top coding of incomes,[84] or simply underrepresentation in surveys due to noncompliance. On the latter point, Mistiaen and Ravallion (2003) find, using the U.S. Current Population Survey, that the underestimate of income of the top ventile is about 50 percent vs. the bottom decile's underestimate of 5 percent. Similarly, Banerjee and Piketty (2003) show that between a fifth and 40 percent of the gap between Indian household survey and national accounts growth rates can be explained by the lack of coverage of the income of the richest 1 percent. Thus, a simple upscaling of all incomes by a given parameter underestimates true inequality.[85]

The second approach, used by Bourguignon and Morrisson (1999) in a long-run study of world inequality, and by Berry and Serieux (2003), consists in taking the known distributions for a limited number of countries, and assuming that geographically and culturally similar countries have the same distributions. In the case of Bourguignon and Morrisson, since they tried to estimate global inequality going back more than 150 years, there was little choice but to assume that Russian income distribution stands also for the distributions in most of Eastern Europe; Argentina's approximates Latin America; India's distribution is used to represent Indonesia's, etc., until such time when distributions for other countries become available. The obvious problem with that approach is that the degree of approximation is huge: prerevolutionary Russia, with large land holdings, had very little in common with the distribution in the Balkans, where ownership of land was extremely fragmented. It is probably an acceptable approach for long-range historical sweeps when the divergence in mean country incomes (the "take-off" of Western Europe and its offshoots) was of such a magnitude that it dominated movements in within-country distributions; it is not an acceptable approximation for the recent period when, for the first time ever, we have access to income or expenditure surveys for most of the world. The first such study that relies solely on countries' household surveys to derive world income distribution for two benchmark years (1988 and 1993) was done by Milanovic (2002). This work is here extended to the third benchmark year, 1998.

### Explaining the Methodology

How were some of the methodological issues mentioned in chapter 2 dealt with here? First, as has become the accepted standard, the surveys have to be nationally representative; or in some cases when, in order to improve the precision of global estimates, large countries (China, India, Indonesia, and Bangladesh) have been divided into rural and urban areas, the surveys have to be representative for rural and urban areas as well. Second, the work combines income and expenditure surveys. This is less than ideal but was made inevitable by the tendency of countries to conduct either one or the other type of survey. Thus, surveys in Western and Eastern Europe and in Latin America tend to be income-based; surveys in Asian and African countries are predominantly expenditure-based with the exceptions of China, Japan, Korea, and a few smaller countries that rely on income surveys. Table 9.1 illustrates the regional "specialization" into either income- or expenditure-based surveys.[86]

There is, however, a tendency to move toward expenditure-based surveys in all regions. As table 9.1 shows, in the most recent benchmark year, all of Africa's surveys are expenditure-based; the proportion of expenditure- vs. income-based surveys in Asia is 2 to 1 in 1998 vs. about 1 to 1 in 1988; Eastern Europe/FSU, which used to be entirely income-based, is now half and half. It means that while out of a total of 102 surveys available in the benchmark year 1988, there were 80 income surveys, in 1998, out of 122 available surveys, only 59 were income-based. Table 9.2 shows that in terms of total population covered by income

**TABLE 9.1.**
Number of Income and Expenditure-Based Surveys by Region

| Region | 1988 Income | 1988 Expenditure | 1993 Income | 1993 Expenditure | 1998 Income | 1998 Expenditure |
|---|---|---|---|---|---|---|
| Africa | 3 | 11 | 3 | 27 | 0 | 24 |
| Asia | 9 | 10 | 8 | 18 | 8 | 20 |
| Latin America and the Caribbean | 18 | 1 | 16 | 4 | 20 | 2 |
| Eastern Europe and former USSR | 27 | 0 | 19 | 3 | 13 | 14 |
| WENAO | 23 | 0 | 23 | 0 | 18 | 3 |
| *Total* | *80* | *22* | *69* | *52* | *59* | *63* |

*Note:* "Expenditure" or "consumption" survey is used interchangeably.

compared to expenditure surveys, the percentage has moved from an almost 2 to 1 ratio in 1988 to only slightly above 1 to 1 in favor of income surveys in 1998. Of course, China accounts for most of this continuing preponderance of population covered by income surveys.

The surveys are "benchmarked" into three years, 1988, 1993, and 1998. The benchmark years were selected to be as close to the actual

**TABLE 9.2.**
Population Included in Income- and Expenditure-Based Surveys by Region (in millions)

| Region | 1988 Income | 1988 Expenditure | 1993 Income | 1993 Expenditure | 1998 Income | 1998 Expenditure |
|---|---|---|---|---|---|---|
| Africa | 20 | 273 | 5 | 510 | 0 | 482 |
| Asia | 1412 | 1322 | 1414 | 1646 | 1481 | 1776 |
| Latin America and the Caribbean | 368 | 6 | 406 | 19 | 454 | 10 |
| Eastern Europe and former USSR | 422 | 0 | 378 | 13 | 273 | 140 |
| WENAO | 652 | 0 | 715 | 0 | 640 | 118 |
| *Total* | *2874* | *1601* | *2918* | *2188* | *2848* | *2526* |
| *In percent* | *64* | *36* | *57* | *43* | *53* | *47* |

*Note:* "Expenditure" or "consumption" is used interchangeably.

years when direct international comparison of prices was conducted (since the domestic currency values, in order to be comparable, had to be converted into $PPP) as well as to maximize the number of available surveys.[87] If a country's survey were conducted in, say, 1989, its income or expenditure values would be deflated to year 1988 using the Consumer Price Index, and then the actual 1988 exchange rate, and the 1988 PPP exchange rate for personal consumption were applied to the converted data to obtain comparable amounts respectively in U.S. dollars and in international dollars of equal purchasing power parity.[88] The rule was, however, that the actual survey date should not be more than two years away from the benchmark year.[89] Thus, the "1993" surveys must have been conducted within the 1991–95 period. (Of course, if there were a choice among several surveys for a country and if they were of the same quality, the survey closest to the benchmark year would be chosen.) Nevertheless, this is an important approximation because in some cases the actual time span between the surveys in two benchmark years could be shorter or longer than five years.

A final issue concerns grouped vs. individual-level data. Ideally, if we had access to the individual-level data from all the surveys, we could calculate fairly detailed divisions, say, into centiles, for all countries and would thus be able to achieve a remarkably good degree of approximation of "true" inequality. Moreover, we would then be able to define more consistently both income and expenditure aggregates so that they are, as much as possible, the same across the countries. The first of these desiderata was increasingly satisfied as the share of the surveys where micro data were available gradually increased from 45 percent in 1988 to 66 percent in 1993 and then to 85 percent in 1998. For the two most populous countries (China and India), however, I had access to the grouped data only. The disadvantage of the grouped data is that some groups (data points) may be very large. At one extreme, there is a group a people, 180 million of them, in rural China who are all assigned the mean income of their group (695.6 yuan in 1993).[90] This, of course, imparts a downward bias to the Gini.[91] The drawback of having only grouped data was lessened by using grouped data for rural and urban areas—thus effectively doubling the number of data points—for the large countries where such data were available: China, India, Indonesia, and Bangladesh.[92] This enables not only a more precise estimation of total inequality, but more importantly, a meaningful decomposition of the contributors to world inequality since (as we shall see) rising differences in mean income between rural and urban China have become an important source of overall world inequality. Of particular importance in this respect are China and India because they account for almost 45 percent of the population in the sample. Alternatively, and preferably, if I had access to the provincial/state grouped income distribution data, I would have divided up China and India into provinces and states. That would have brought us even closer to true global inequality.

The overall average number of data points (fractiles) per survey is 10.8 in 1988, 11.4 in 1993, and 15.1 in 1998. This means that the data are denser than the decile data. Of course, the number of fractiles for all the countries for which I had access to microlevel data could have been increased almost without any limit (to several thousands), but that would not have made much sense, and I have therefore limited in all cases the maximum number of fractiles to twenty.

The second problem, namely, a consistent definition of income, expenditure, or consumption aggregates, is not solved: unless one has very detailed micro data, one depends on national definitions of income or expenditure aggregates. This has often been the case even when micro data were available because the aggregates would have already been defined. There are thus remaining problems of possible differences in definitions (e.g., valuation methods for home consumption, decision whether or not to include imputed rent, etc.), or recall periods. But—and it is important—in all cases the recipients are individuals (and quantiles are always quantiles of individuals, not households), and in all cases the welfare aggregate is household per capita expenditures or income.

For eighty-six countries,[93] there are household surveys for all three benchmark years. This is called "the common sample." The full sample is larger because there are countries included in one year, but not included in another. Thus the full sample for 1988 consists of 102 countries, and 121 and 122 countries in 1993 and 1998 respectively. The increase in the sample size is principally due to the much better coverage of Africa. For many of the African countries, the data on income distribution have become available for the early 1990s only. Table 9.3 shows the coverage of the common- and full-sample. The much greater (full-sample) coverage of Africa in 1993 and 1998 is apparent from the data.[94] The common-sample countries account for about 84 percent of the world population and about 91 percent of current-dollar GDP;[95] the full-sample countries cover 87 to 92 percent of world population and about 96 percent of world-dollar GDP.

## Global (Concept 3) Inequality, 1988–98

Table 9.4 shows the inequality measures calculated for the three benchmark years. Using either the Gini or Theil measure, or the full- or common-sample, or current dollars or $PPP, we see that inequality in-

**TABLE 9.3.**
How Much of the World Do the Surveys Cover? (in percentages)

| | *Poulation* | | | *GDP (in US$)* | | |
|---|---|---|---|---|---|---|
| *Full Sample* | *1988* | *1993* | *1998* | *1988* | *1993* | *1998* |
| Africa | 48.0 | 76.1 | 67.1 | 48.7 | 85.2 | 71.2 |
| Asia | 92.5 | 94.9 | 94.4 | 94.4 | 93.2 | 95.6 |
| E. Europe/FSU | 99.3 | 95.2 | 100 | 99.4 | 96.3 | 100 |
| LAC | 87.4 | 91.8 | 93.0 | 90.2 | 92.8 | 95.2 |
| WENAO | 92.4 | 94.8 | 96.6 | 99.3 | 96.2 | 96.3 |
| *World* | *87.3* | *92.4* | *91.6* | *96.5* | *95.4* | *96.0* |
| Common sample | | | | | | |
| Africa | 43.0 | 41.2 | 37.6 | 32.5 | 35.5 | 33.4 |
| Asia | 92.5 | 91.3 | 90.7 | 94.4 | 91.7 | 93.1 |
| E. Europe/FSU | 93.8 | 94.2 | 93.2 | 95.0 | 96.1 | 95.7 |
| LAC | 85.1 | 90.5 | 89.6 | 88.8 | 92.3 | 93.9 |
| WENAO | 83.5 | 83.5 | 82.1 | 92.9 | 91.7 | 90.5 |
| *World* | *84.8* | *84.3* | *83.1* | *91.8* | *90.9* | *90.6* |

creased in the first period and then declined in the second. Yet the 1998 level of world inequality was, again according to all measures of inequality, higher than in 1988. The most relevant measure of inequality, the Gini index for income[96] expressed in PPP dollars increased from about 62 in 1988 to a little over 65 in 1993, and then declined to a little over 64 five years later. There was thus first a 3-Gini point increase between 1988 and 1993, and then a 1-Gini point decrease. The changes in the Theil index magnify the Gini changes. The dollar-inequality that reaches the Gini level of 80 is probably among the highest, or perhaps the highest, inequality level ever recorded.

Figure 9.1 shows the Lorenz curves for the world population; figure 9.2 the distributions that underlie the Lorenz curves. The 1988 Lorenz curve dominates the two other curves, while the 1993 and 1998 curves intersect at the bottom (around the 15th percentile) and then again around the very top (at the 95th percentile). Note that three-quarters of the world population receives around one-quarter of the world $PPP income, or that the top 10 percent of the world population receives about one-half of the world income. Of course, if we look at actual dollar incomes, the numbers are even more dramatic: 90 percent of the world population (in 1998) receives a little less than one-third of the world income, or in other words, the top 10 percent receive two-thirds of world dollar income. In 1998, the decile ratio (average income of the top decile divided by the average income of the bottom decile) was 71

**TABLE 9.4.**
Global Inequality, 1988–98 (distribution of persons by $PPP and $ income per capita)

| | *Full Sample* | | | *Common Sample* | | |
|---|---|---|---|---|---|---|
| | *1988* | *1993* | *1998* | *1988* | *1993* | *1998* |
| *International dollars* | | | | | | |
| Gini index | 61.9 | 65.2 | 64.2 | 62.2 | 65.3 | 64.1 |
| | (1.8) | (1.8) | (1.9) | (1.8) | (1.6) | (1.9) |
| Theil index | 71.5 | 81.8 | 79.2 | 72.7 | 81.7 | 78.9 |
| | (5.8) | (6.1) | (6.3) | (5.6) | (5.5) | (6.6) |
| *US Dollars* | | | | | | |
| Gini index | 77.3 | 80.1 | 79.5 | 77.8 | 79.9 | 79.4 |
| | (1.3) | (1.2) | (1.4) | (1.4) | (1.6) | (1.5) |
| Theil index | 125.2 | 139.2 | 135.4 | 128.3 | 138.0 | 134.8 |
| | (7.1) | (7.5) | (8.3) | (8.1) | (9.3) | (8.7) |

*Note:* Gini and Theil standard errors given between brackets. The values for 1988 and 1993 are somewhat different from those reported in Milanovic (2002) due to the changes in the common-sample composition with the inclusion of the year 1998 (e.g., the surveys from Algeria, Switzerland, and Australia that were included in both 1988 and 1993 series were not available for 1998 and thus the size of the common sample was reduced). On the other hand, there were also some countries added to the common sample (Iran and Sri Lanka). The overall differences, however, are minimal.

to 1 if we use incomes converted in international dollars, and more than 320 to 1 if we use actual U.S. dollars.

The two five-year periods registered approximately the same real growth rate: 5.2 percent per capita over 1988–93, and 4.8 percent per capita between 1993 and 1998.[97] However, the growth incidence curves, shown in figure 9.3, look very different. During the first period, practically all growth rates up to the 85th percentile were negative. This was due to real income declines in Africa and in the world "middle class" located in Eastern Europe and Latin America.[98] But in the second period, the growth incidence curve reverses: along the broad spectrum of income distribution growth is above average (between 10 and 15 percent over the five-year period), and then it sharply decelerates after the 60th percentile, before shooting up for the very top ventile. Particularly striking is the fact that in both periods, it is the very poorest ventile that has registered the worst growth performance (–20 percent in the first period, –23 percent in the second).[99] While in the first period, growth was clearly anti-poor as all but the top 15 percent of the population registered growth rates below the mean, growth in the second period

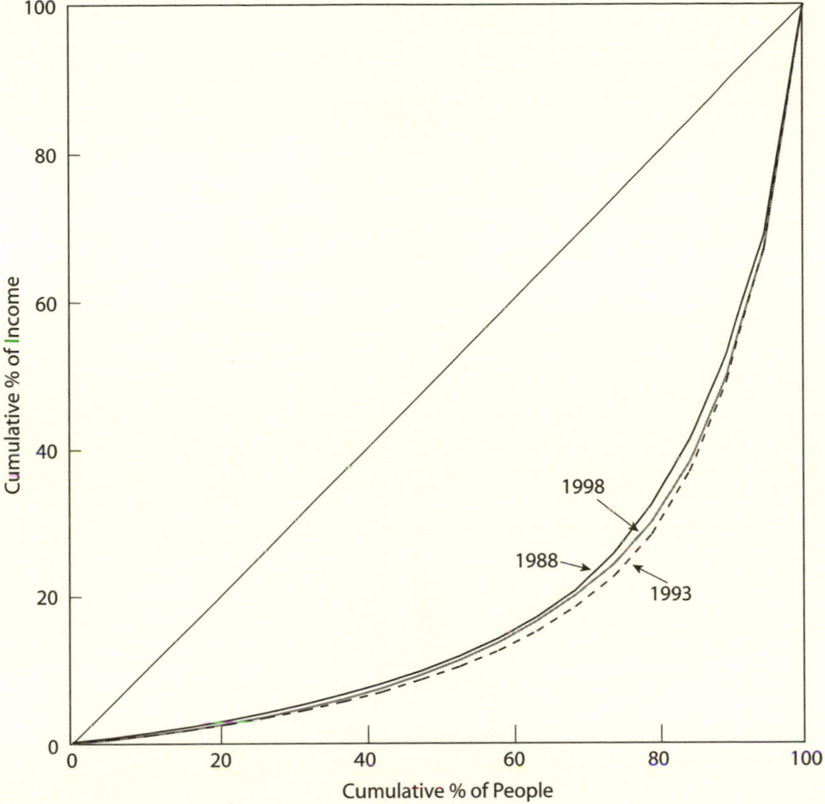


**Figure 9.1.** Global Lorenz curve (world individuals).

could be almost viewed as pro-poor were it not for the large decline in the income of the poorest.

## Gini Decomposition: Within- and Between-Country Inequality

If we decompose the Gini for the three benchmark years—using the standard decomposition explained in chapter 3—it turns out that between 71 and 83 percent of total inequality—depending on whether we use Gini or Theil index—is due to differences in mean incomes among the counties (table 9.5).[100] The shares are very stable. Of course, when we decompose the dollar Gini, the between-country share increases further as differences in mean incomes are magnified when we do not adjust for lower cost of living in poor countries. Now the between-

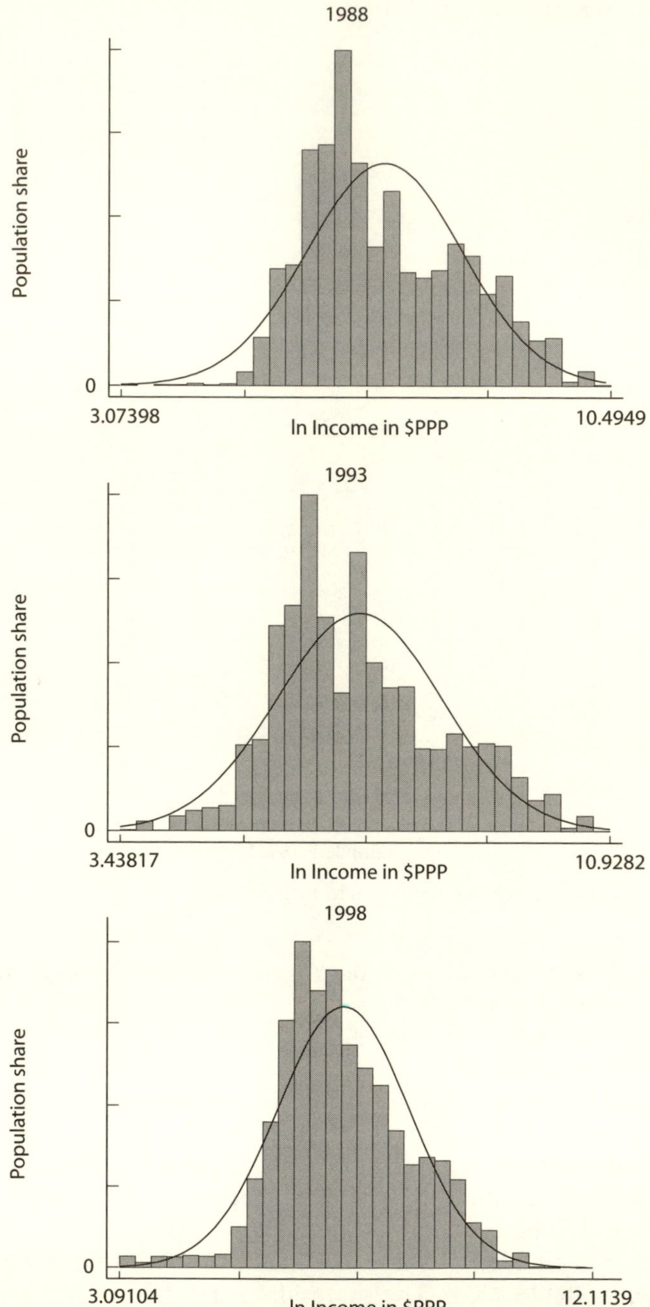


**Figure 9.2.** Global income distributions in 1988, 1993, and 1998. Horizontal axis: logarithm of income in PPP dollars. Vertical axis: population shares; normal distributions superimposed on the empirical distributions. Based on 1106 data points for 1988, 1392 for 1993, and 1796 for 1998.

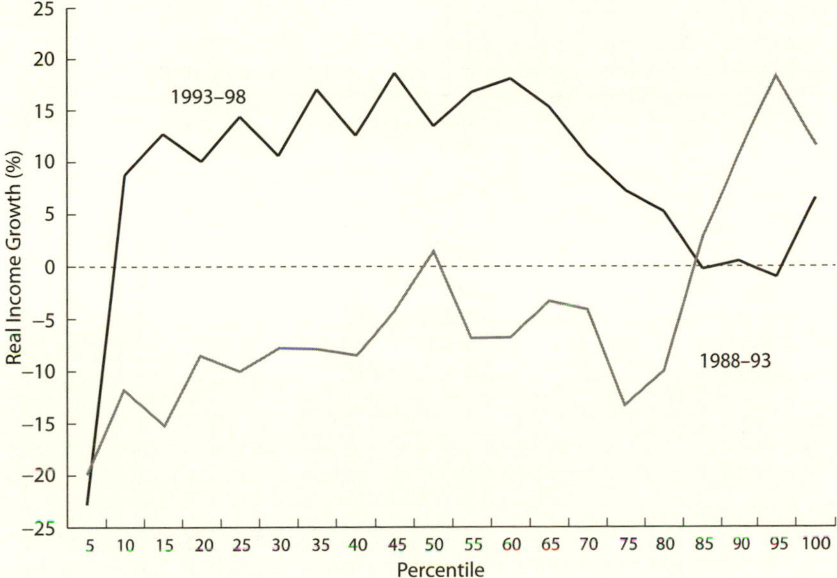


**Figure 9.3.** Growth incidence curves for the world, 1988–93 and 1993–98.

country differences account for between 85 and 90 percent of an overall, even greater inequality (that is, compared to the global Gini or Theil calculated from $PPP incomes).

Now, two natural questions arise: first, what explains the significant increase in world inequality between 1988 and 1993, and its more modest decline in the next five years; second, how would world inequality numbers change if instead of per capita income or expenditure calculated from household surveys we used per capita GDPs.

## What Explains the 1988–93 Increase in Inequality?

As we would expect from the previous analysis, the greatest contributors to the world Gini are large countries that are at the two poles of the income distribution spectrum: among the poor countries, China and India (each divided into rural and urban parts); and among the rich countries, the United States, Japan, Germany, France, and the United Kingdom. Table 9.6 shows that in 1993, 16.6 Gini points (that is, a quarter of total inequality) can be explained by the differences in mean incomes of the two poor and five rich countries.

But the largest contributors to the *level* of inequality need not be the largest contributors to the *change* in inequality between 1988 and 1993. Table 9.7 shows that the increasing income distance between, on the

**TABLE 9.5.**
Decomposition of Global Income Inequality, 1988–98 (common-sample countries; distribution of persons by income/expenditure per capita)

| | *Gini 1988* | *Gini 1993* | *Gini 1998* | *Theil 1988* | *Theil 1993* | *Theil 1998* |
|---|---|---|---|---|---|---|
| *International dollars* | | | | | | |
| Within-country inequality | 10.6 (17) | 11.1 (17) | 11.0 (17) | 20.3 (28) | 22.8 (28) | 23.2 (29) |
| Between-country inequality | 51.6 (83) | 54.2 (83) | 53.1 (83) | 52.4 (72) | 58.9 (72) | 55.7 (71) |
| Total world inequality | 62.2 (100) | 65.3 (100) | 64.1 (100) | 72.7 (100) | 81.7 (100) | 78.9 (100) |
| *US dollars* | | | | | | |
| Within-country inequality | 8.3 (11) | 8.2 (10) | 8.6 (11) | 18.3 (14) | 20.5 (15) | 22.3 (17) |
| Between-country inequality | 69.5 (89) | 71.7 (90) | 70.8 (89) | 110.0 (86) | 117.5 (85) | 112.5 (83) |
| Total world inequality | 77.8 (100) | 79.9 (100) | 79.4 (100) | 128.3 (100) | 138.0 (100) | 134.8 (100) |

*Notes:* Percentage contribution to total inequality between brackets. Within-country inequality in the case of the Gini coefficient includes both the "proper" within-country inequality and the overlap term. It is acceptable to ascribe the entire "overlap" term to the within-country component because the overlap term increases (as we saw at the end of chapter 3) when countries' income distributions become more unequal (and mean incomes do not change). The use of the Gini coefficient for decompositions has been criticized because it does not divide neatly into "within" and "between" components. However, some authors (Yitzhaki and Lerman 1991; Yitzhaki 1994; Lambert and Aranson 1993) have argued that the existence of the "overlap" component provides an important additional information about heterogeneity between the groups.

**TABLE 9.6.**
The Largest Between-Country Contributors to Inequality in 1993 (full-sample; in Gini points)

| *Poor* | *China (rural)* | *India (rural)* | *China (urban)* | *India (urban)* | *Total Gini Points* |
|---|---|---|---|---|---|
| *Rich* | | | | | |
| USA | 3.3 | 2.6 | 1.2 | 0.9 | 8.0 |
| Japan | 1.5 | 1.2 | 0.5 | 0.4 | 3.6 |
| Germany | 0.8 | 0.7 | 0.3 | 0.2 | 2.0 |
| France | 0.6 | 0.5 | 0.2 | 0.2 | 1.5 |
| UK | 0.6 | 0.5 | 0.2 | 0.2 | 1.5 |
| *Total* | *6.8* | *5.5* | *2.4* | *1.9* | *16.6* |

*Note:* Each cell represents the value of an individual intercountry term $\frac{1}{\mu}(y_j - y_i)p_i p_j$.

**TABLE 9.7.**
Key Changes in Intercountry Terms Between 1988 and 1993 (in Gini points)

| | (1) India (rural) | (2) China (rural) | (3) = (1) + (2) |
|---|---|---|---|
| Japan | +0.18 | +0.11 | |
| Germany | +0.15 | +0.12 | |
| France | +0.10 | +0.08 | |
| UK | +0.06 | +0.03 | |
| *Subtotal* | *+0.49* | *+0.34* | *+0.83* |
| China (urban) | +0.18 | +0.19 | |
| India (urban) | | +0.02 | |
| *Subtotal* | *+0.18* | *+0.21* | *+0.39* |

one hand, rural India and rural China, and, on the other, four rich countries added a little over 0.8 Gini point to world inequality. In addition, the rising difference in mean incomes between (i) urban China and (ii) rural India and rural China contributed an additional 0.4 Gini point. Finally, income declines in Eastern Europe/former Soviet Union were responsible for a 0.6 Gini point increase.[101]

We have thus identified the three main contributors to the rising Concept 3 inequality between 1988 and 1993. The first has to do with rising income differences between the top and the bottom: it is due to the slow growth of rural incomes in populous Asian countries compared to rich OECD countries. The second cause has to do with the pulling ahead of urban China vis-à-vis rural China and rural India. The urban-rural ratio increased by a half in China and it went up in India, too (table 9.8). The same phenomenon can be illustrated by calculating the mean income rank within world distribution of people in each country. The mean rank of population in urban China increased from the 53rd to the 62nd percentile while the mean ranks of populations in rural India and China stayed within 1 and 2 percentiles of where they were in 1988 (table 9.9). The third cause is the "hollowing out" of the world's middle class—a problem we have already identified with respect to Latin America and Eastern Europe since the early 1980s and early 1990s respectively. Here it is represented by the decline of incomes in Eastern Europe: for example, the mean income rank of the Russian population decreased from the 80th to the 73rd percentile.

### And Then What Happened between 1993 and 1998?

During the next five years, the developments were, in many respects, the reverse of what we had seen between 1988 and 1993. It was now the

**TABLE 9.8.**
China and India in Household Survey and National Account Data (in current $PPP)

| | *China* | | | *India* | | |
|---|---|---|---|---|---|---|
| | *1988* | *1993* | *1998* | *1988* | *1993* | *1998* |
| Rural income | 675 (74%) | 815 (72%) | 1306 (68%) | 431 (73%) | 451 (74%) | 633 (72%) |
| Urban income | 1114 (26%) | 1906 (28%) | 2992 (32%) | 678 (27%) | 727 (26%) | 1033 (28%) |
| Total income | 789 | 1120 | 1845 | 498 | 523 | 745 |
| GDP per capita | 1387 | 2333 | 3507 | 966 | 1264 | 2042 |
| Urban-rural ratio | 1.65 | 2.34 | 2.29 | 1.57 | 1.62 | 1.63 |
| HBS (all country) mean income to GDP per capita | 0.57 | 0.48 | 0.53 | 0.52 | 0.41 | 0.36 |

*Note:* Rural, urban and total income/expenditures are from household surveys. All amounts are in current $PPP. Income for China; expenditures for India. Percentage of total population given in brackets. HBS = household budget survey.

rural areas of China and India that were catching up with rich countries (table 9.9). While in the previous period their income distance from the rich world rose and added 0.8 Gini points to inequality, now the distance decreased and *subtracted* a full Gini point from overall inequality. This factor alone explains almost all of the change in inequality between 1993 and 1998 (minus 1.2 Gini points for common-sample countries). On the other hand, urban incomes in China continued to outpace income growth in rural India and rural China, adding again some 0.4

**TABLE 9.9.**
Mean World Income Ranks of Different Countries' Populations in 1988–98

| | *1988* | *1993* | *1998* | *Real Growth Between 1988 and 1993 (in %)* | *Real Growth Between 1993 and 1998 (in %)* |
|---|---|---|---|---|---|
| India (rural) | 20 | 18 | 20 | −14 | +24 |
| China (rural) | 33 | 34 | 41 | −1 | +42 |
| China (urban) | 53 | 62 | 66 | +40 | +39 |
| United States | 90 | 89 | 90 | +2 | +10 |
| Japan | 89 | 91 | 92 | +31 | +4 |
| Germany | 89 | 89 | 88 | +11 | 0 |
| Russia | 80 | 73 | 67 | −18 | −26 |

*Note:* Mean income rank is calculated as the average of income ranks of all deciles (individuals) in the country. This is not the same thing as the income rank of the person with mean country's income.

**TABLE 9.10.**
Key Changes in Intercountry Terms between 1993 and 1998 (in Gini points)

| | *(1) India (rural)* | *(2) China (rural)* | *(3) = (1) + (2)* |
|---|---|---|---|
| Japan | –0.07 | –0.19 | |
| Germany | –0.07 | –0.15 | |
| France | –0.08 | –0.14 | |
| USA | | –0.11 | |
| UK | –0.06 | –0.11 | |
| *Subtotal* | *–0.28* | *–0.71* | *–0.99* |
| China (urban) | +0.23 | +0.16 | |
| India (urban) | +0.02 | +0.04 | |
| *Subtotal* | *+0.25* | *+0.20* | *+0.45* |

points to inequality (see table 9.10).[102] Growth in urban India (vs. slower growth in rural areas) also contributed to inequality but much less. Finally, the third source of rising inequality in 1988–93 subsided as real incomes in Eastern Europe and former Soviet Union began to recover.[103]

In conclusion, the three factors that all worked toward increasing inequality between 1988 and 1993, behaved very differently over the next five-year period. One of them (rising income distance between rural and urban areas in China and India), continued almost unabated. Another—income distance between rural India and China and the West—reversed, contributing to inequality decrease. And the third, the crisis in transition countries, moderated, and basically no longer affected world inequality very much.

Abstracting from what seem to be the transitory phenomena, like the post-Communist and East Asian crises, we seem to be in the presence of an interesting situation where world inequality is driven by what happens to the relative incomes of the three large areas: (i) the rich countries of the West, (ii) urban incomes in China and India, and (iii) rural incomes in these two countries. The ratio between (ii) and (iii) has been rising and is unlikely to moderate. Moreover, while China and India are the most important examples of the trend, the urban-rural gap is rising in several other Asian countries (Bangladesh, Indonesia, Thailand). But as (ii) catches up to (i), world inequality is reduced. The crucial "swing" factor then becomes the ratio between (iii) and (i): what happens to rural incomes in China and India vs. incomes of the rich world. If the former catch up, world inequality goes down; if they do not, world inequality tends to rise. This is exactly what drove the increase in inequality between 1988 and 1993, and its reversal between 1993 and 1998.

Finally, one may wonder where in this story is Africa. Despite its dismal economic performance and rising population, it does not (yet) affect world inequality very much. Stagnation or decline in African incomes between 1993 and 1998 is responsible for about a 0.4 Gini point increase in world inequality. However, if Africa continues to fall behind and its population to rise, global inequality may be affected by relative income changes between the three areas mentioned earlier and Africa.

## Combining GDP per Capita and Household Survey Distributions

We have noted earlier (chapter 2) a systematic divergence between income or expenditure per capita calculated from household surveys and GDP per capita obtained from national accounts. This was raised as an issue in the calculation of world inequality (Castles 2001; Bhalla 2002). For example, while it is difficult in principle to argue that world inequality should *not* be calculated the same way as national inequality, that is from household surveys, one can raise the point that household surveys, since they deal with disposable income, leave out a large chunk of publicly provided services (free health and education), which are financed out of direct taxation and are "consumed" by households. Moreover their amounts vary from country to country quite significantly. To impute them to the specific households is, of course, very difficult and could be done only if we had very detailed and complete questionnaires and individual-level data for all surveys. Even for a single country it is a daunting task that entails a number of assumptions. It is all but impossible to do for several countries, let alone the whole world. Furthermore many income and expenditures surveys do not ask questions on school attendance or use of public health services.

Some of the discrepancy between mean income or expenditure from household surveys and GDP per capita is due to the non-inclusion in surveys of the items that are particularly significant in developed countries (publicly financed health and education; undisbursed corporate profits, depreciation, etc.) so that the mean survey income (expenditure)-to-GDP per capita ratio might be expected to go down as GDP per capita increases. On the other hand, there may be a systematic underreporting of income or expenditures in household surveys conducted in poor countries. For example, income from financial intermediation is not included in surveys. Implicit rent received from owner-occupied housing is often not included. Yet the share of both sources in GDP increases in the process of development (Deaton 2003). These points have been raised with respect to India, which has become something of a cause célèbre because of the widening discrepancy between the surging GDP per capita in the 1990s and the much more modestly increasing mean survey expenditures (Deaton and Drèze 2002, p. 3736).[104] The question is why, and which source is right. The problem has been extensively debated (Deaton 2000; Deaton and Drèze 2002; Ravallion 2000; National Committee for Statistics Task Force; Bhalla 2000), and the current view, after the latest "thick round" (large sample) of Indian survey, is that the discrepancy is less than it was thought, but the fact is that the discrepancy still remains. It is also reflected in table 9.8, where we saw that mean per capita expenditures calculated from the surveys have decreased as a share of GDP per capita from more than 50 percent in 1988 to 36 percent ten years later.

These problems have led some authors (most notably Bhalla 2002) to propose an alternative solution: simply to ignore mean per capita income (expenditures) obtained from household surveys and replace it with GDP per capita. There are obvious and severe problems with this approach. First, it assumes that while HSs provide a correct depiction of distribution, they do a poor job in estimating the level of income or expenditures—a hypothesis that we have no grounds to make and that is moreover explicitly questioned in the case of China, where the preponderance of the evidence is that national accounts, both in levels and growth rates, are upward biased and that household surveys do a much more realistic job in capturing the level of income (Rawski 2001).[105] Second, it also assumes that whatever is left out of survey income or expenditures (publicly provided services, capital income, or simply misreporting) is distributed in proportion to income recorded by household surveys. This is an even more debatable assumption because here we do have strong evidence that underreporting is increasing with income level. There are several reasons for this: capital income is known to be underreported mostly among top income-recipients (for the very simple reason that people on the bottom have hardly any such income); publicly provided services (e.g., tertiary education) are often skewed toward the rich, and survey noncompliance has been documented to be particularly high among the top deciles (Mistiaen and Ravallion 2003). Then, "upscaling" the survey-derived means to equal GDP per capita should be accompanied by pro-inequality correction in the underlying income distribution. None of the authors has done it, simply because there is no sufficient information to do so, in addition to the fact that proceeding to such corrections for a hundred countries at different points in time would be a Herculean task necessarily filled with dozens of arbitrary assumptions. Yet if one is willing to disregard all these objections, one can simply scale up all survey incomes by the ratio be-

**TABLE 9.11.**
World Income Inequality in 1988, 1993, and 1998 (common-sample countries; $PPP)

| | *1988* | *1993* | *1998* |
|---|---|---|---|
| *Gini* | | | |
| (1) Household-survey mean based | 62.3 | 65.3 | 64.1 |
| | (2.1) | (2.1) | (2.5) |
| (2) GDP per capita based | 64.1 | 65.5 | 63.5 |
| | (2.1) | (2.3) | (2.4) |
| Difference (1) – (2) | –1.9 | +0.2 | +0.6 |
| *Theil* | | | |
| (3) Household-survey mean based | 72.3 | 81.6 | 78.8 |
| | (6.2) | (6.5) | (8.1) |
| (4) GDP per capita based | 78.2 | 83.0 | 77.0 |
| | (6.8) | (7.2) | (8.1) |
| Difference (3) – (4) | –5.9 | –1.4 | +1.8 |

*Notes:* Standard errors given between brackets. The countries that were "broken" into urban and rural areas are shown here as "whole countries." This is why the household-survey based Ginis and Theils here differ from those in table 9.4. Note that we have to do this because GDPs per capita refer to whole countries, and to be comparable survey means need also to refer to whole countries.

tween GDP per capita and survey mean. If we do so for our countries, we obtain the results shown in table 9.11.[106]

Note first that the upscaling of survey incomes to GDP per capita still leaves the level of world inequality about the same as before. The difference in levels is negligible in 1993 and 1998: both the Ginis and the one-standard error ranges are almost the same. A difference exists for the 1988 results. There, forcing household-survey means to equal GDP per capita, produces higher indices of inequality: by almost 2 Gini points or 6 Theil points. Consequently, the increase in global inequality between 1988 and 1993 is moderated when we use GDP per capita instead of survey means. The increase becomes 1.4 Gini points against 3 Gini points, or less than 5 instead of almost 10 Theil points. Another implication of the higher level of inequality in 1988 (when "forcing" household-survey incomes to equal GDPs) is that the difference between global inequality in 1988 and 1998 is negative although very small and statistically not significant (see figure 9.4). Finally, note that the results depicted in figure 9.4 imply that for none of the years, and none of the concepts, can we establish that the calculated Ginis are statistically significantly greater (or smaller). We can, of course, be much

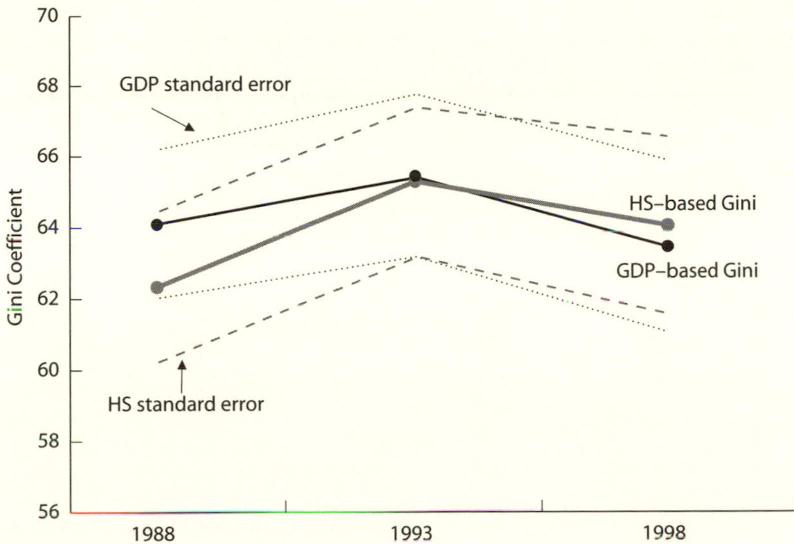


**Figure 9.4.** Global inequality with uncorrected survey means and when survey means are replaced by countries' GDPs per capita.

more certain about the absolute levels of inequality which in Gini terms range between 60 and 66.

Finally, we can do another check on the results by using the PPPs from one year only (1988). This entails deflating all incomes for 1993 and 1998 into local currency units expressed in the 1988 prices and then converting them by the use of 1988 PPPs. The advantage of this approach (which for the year 1988 obviously gives the same result) is that it controls for one source of variability, namely changing PPPs. The increase in inequality in 1993 is now much more modest (1.3 Gini points), and so is its subsequent decline in 1998 (see table 9.12). Using the Theil index, inequality keeps on increasing even in 1998. The use of single-year PPP reduces the level of inequality in all the cases and makes changes between the years less sharp. But it also implies that after inequality increased between 1988 and 1993, it did not go down, rather it might have continued on its upward trend.

## Comparing Different Studies of World Inequality across Individuals

The Concept 3 inequality has recently been studied by a number of authors. This is a new development made possible by the availability of (i) synthetic income inequality indicators like Gini coefficients, and in

**TABLE 9.12.**
Global Inequality Calculated Using 1988 PPPs and Incomes Expressed in 1988 Domestic Prices (full-sample countries)

| | *1988* | *1993* | *1998* |
|---|---|---|---|
| *Gini* | | | |
| (1) Current year PPPs | 61.9 | 65.2 | 64.2 |
| | (1.8) | (1.8) | (1.9) |
| (2) 1988 PPP only | 61.9 | 63.2 | 63.1 |
| | (1.8) | (1.9) | (2.0) |
| Difference (1) – (2) | 0 | +2.0 | +1.1 |
| *Theil* | | | |
| (3) Current year PPPs | 71.5 | 80.1 | 79.5 |
| | (5.8) | (1.2) | (1.4) |
| (4) 1988 PPP only | 71.5 | 75.7 | 76.7 |
| | (5.8) | (6.1) | (6.7) |
| Difference (3) – (4) | 0 | +4.4 | +2.8 |

*Notes:* Standard errors in parentheses.

some cases, quintiles, for a number of countries and years (most notably thanks to the Deininger-Squire and WIDER data bases),[107] as well as by (ii) the new data on GDP per capita in PPP terms available from the World Bank, the Penn World Tables (version 6.1), and Angus Maddison (2001) for most countries of the world and going back in time at least until 1960s. Basically, as we explained earlier, to proceed to a calculation of world income distribution, we need three building blocks: (i) national distributions available from household surveys, (ii) mean incomes again available from household surveys or from national accounts (GDP per capita), and (iii) PPP exchange rates. These building blocks, lacking in the past, have recently become available. There are, however, big problems with each of the building blocks. We shall review them one by one.

The biggest problems attend the estimation of the entire national distributions from very fragmentary data (that is, from only a few quantiles). As table 9.13 makes clear, the most common approach has been to calculate world distribution by using the Deininger-Squire or WIDER data base to get *approximations* of national distributions across individuals, and then to combine these approximations to get a world distribution. In addition, GDP per capita was used to get the absolute level of income of each percentile of income distribution. (Obviously, once a national distribution is approximated by a functional form, it is easy to generate income for as many fractiles as one wishes. Pushing it to the extreme, one author calculates incomes for each millesime of income distribution of all countries.[108]) The approximation can be done using quintiles, which are often provided by Deininger-Squire and WIDER databases (as was done by Sala-i-Martin 2002, 2002a), or by using Gini coefficients and mean income alone (see Quah 2002, Technical Appendix). In the latter case, for example, an a priori distribution is imposed (say, lognormal), and its parameters are derived from the knowledge of the mean and the Gini coefficient.[109] Nevertheless, the fact remains that once an approximation is done, and particularly if that approximation is based on only 5 data points per country/year, there is a large element of arbitrariness introduced. With only quintiles available, very large groups of people (e.g., in China, over 200 million people) are, at first, assigned the same income. The authors address this problem of "chunkiness" in distribution by smoothing it: either by imposing a theoretical distribution or by using nonparametric estimates. Of course, we do not know if the smoothing makes sense or not. Moreover, the error for large and rich income groups may substantially affect inequality results. For example, total incomes received by the top deciles in China and the United States—if calculated from the quintile shares published in the Deininger-Squire or WIDER databases—can vary by as much as 2 percent of *world* total income each and still be consistent with the published quintile shares (Milanovic 2003, p.13). For these two countries, therefore, we can have 4 percent of world income that, depending on the assumptions, we can "play with." Clearly, this is an amount that can easily affect our world inequality calculations.

Another problem with such approximations is that some authors use interchangeably distributions of individuals ranked by their per capita expenditures or income, and distributions of households ranked by household total income or expenditures.[110] Suppose, as is, for example, the case in Sala-i-Martin's two papers (2002, 2002a), that the calculation of national distributions across *individuals* is based on the Deininger-Squire quintiles where *households* are ranked by household total income. One then does not only have the approximation issue to deal with (guessing the entire distribution from five data points) but also a totally inappropriate instrument to do so: household distribution is used to approximate distribution of individuals. The entire problem is not even mentioned by either Sala-i-Martin or Bhalla (2002).

A final problem regarding distributions is specific to Sala-i-Martin and Bhalla, who both claim to have calculated *annual* Concept 3 inequality. Since we know that annual income distribution data for all countries in the world (which would have been needed for such a calculation) do not exist, the authors need somehow to "stretch" the exist-

**TABLE 9.13.**
Summary of Different Approaches to the Calculation of Concept 3 Inequality

| | *Income Distribution Source* | *Approximation of Individual Income Distributions* | *Approximation of Missing Country/Years (observations)* | *Mean Income From:* | *Type of PPP Used* |
|---|---|---|---|---|---|
| Milanovic (2002) | HS directly | No | No | HS directly | EKS |
| Bourguignon and Morrisson (1999/2002) | Various | No | Yes (big time) | GDP per capita (Maddison 1995 data) | Geary-Khamis |
| Sala-i-Martin (2002) | D-S, WDI | Yes (non-parametric) | Yes (big time: use of trends) | GDP per capita (PWT 6.1) | Geary-Khamis |
| Bhalla (2002) | D-S, WIDER, Milanovic | Yes (single-parameter Lorenz curve estimate) | Same distribution holds for all years (in most cases) | GDP per capita (WDI, PWT 5.6, etc). Personal consumption per capita from NA (the same sources as for income). If unavailable, regional share imputed. | Geary-Khamis |

| | | | | | |
|---|---|---|---|---|---|
| Dowrick and Akmal (2001) | D-S | Mostly no; in some cases single-parameter Lorenz curve estimate used | No | GDP per capita from ICP, plus extrapolation if country not part of ICP | Afriat |
| Dikhanov and Ward (2001) | WIDER | Yes ("quasi-exact" method) | No | Personal consumption per capita (World Bank data) | EKS |
| Sutcliffe (2003) | D-S, WDI | No | No | GDP data (Maddison, 2001) | Geary-Khamis |
| Chotikapanich et al. (1997) | D-S | Yes (lognormal distributions estimated from Gini and mean) | No | GDP per capita (PWT 5.6) | Geary-Khamis |
| Schultz (1998) | D-S | Yes (Lorenz curve estimated from quintiles) | Yes (big time) | GDP per capita (PWT 5.5) | Geary-Khamis |

*Note:* D-S = Deininger-Squire. EKS = Elteto, Koves, and Szulc. GDP = Gross domestic product (equivalent to GDI, gross domestic income, according to the recent change in national accounts terminologies). HS = Household survey. ICP = International Comparison Project. Milanovic = income distribution data for Eastern Europe available at http://www.worldbank.org/research/inequality/data.htm. PWT = Penn World Tables. WDI = World Development Indicators. WIDER = UN World Institute for Development Economics Research.

ing data to cover all the country/years. This is what I called the problem of "sparse data" (in time), a complement to the problem of fragmentary data (five quintiles that summarize entire distribution). Sala-i-Martin tries to estimate annual quintile shares from the data that are available for only a few years (on average 5.5) out of twenty-seven years covered in his studies. The already large degree of arbitrariness introduced by the fragmentary data is compounded by further assumptions that need to be made to "project" a given quintile share in year $t$ to derive the same quintile's share in a year that could be as far back as $t-20$ or as far in the future as $t+20$. The assumption of linear change in time between these two dates (as used by Sala-i-Martin) is of course entirely arbitrary: it would be, for example, a grave mistake to assume a linear relationship between the share of the U.S. bottom quintile in 1960 and in 1990. During that period, the bottom quintile share first increased and then went down. The end points tell us very little about the intervening change.[111]

Bhalla's (2002) approach is, if anything, even more questionable. He too presents annual Concept 3 Ginis for the period 1950–2000. These values, however, are calculated from individual country distributions for only three benchmark years (1960, 1980, and 2000).[112] It seems, although Bhalla does not say it explicitly, that for all the intervening years the distributions are assumed to stay the same and only mean incomes, that is GDPs per capita, change. To make matters worse, an inspection of the three benchmark distributions quickly reveals that most often even these are not independent distributions from different years, but that one available distribution, say in, year 1987 for a country X, is first assumed to hold for that country for all the three benchmark years, and then for all the years between 1950 and 2000 as well! In consequence, Bhalla and Sala-i-Martin keep countries' income distributions essentially fixed (or changing minimally and smoothly) during the fifty- and twenty-seven-year periods that they study and therefore calculate—despite their claims to the contrary—Concept 2 rather than Concept 3 inequality.[113]

Moving to the second building block—the mean income—we notice in table 9.13 that all authors who use approximations for national income distributions do not also seem to trust national household surveys for the means (or they do not have access to the means) and apply GDP per capita, or in one case, personal consumption per capita, to the distributional shares in order to obtain the absolute amounts of income by quantile. This introduces another inconsistency: the use of distribution data from surveys, but with the mean from national accounts, a practice that we have criticized before. But the problem is not only that national accounts and household survey data do not always agree.

Much less noticed is the disagreement among the various sources of national accounts data. We have seen before, at the end of chapter 8, how the use of Maddison's data rather than the Chinese official or World Bank data for China's GDP affects the calculations of Concept 2 inequality. The differences are not limited to China as Sutcliffe (2003, p. 12) shows. For the year 1998, only between 35 and 49 percent of country GDP per capita observations from the three sources (PWT 6.1, Maddison 2001, and World Bank) are within 10 percent of each other. The greatest differences are between Maddison and the World Bank data. Then, not surprisingly, when Concept 3 inequality is calculated by applying GDP per capita data to country distributions, it will also matter *which* GDP per capita series we use. Sutcliffe's (2003) calculations show a stable global inequality between 1980 and 2000 when GDP data are taken from Maddison (2001), and a decreasing global inequality when using World Bank data.

The third building block has problems too. As has been pointed out (most recently by Dowrick and Akmal 2001, and Reddy and Pogge 2002), the use of GDP per capita values from the Penn World Tables or Maddison's (2001) calculations underestimates international and world inequality because the Geary-Khamis PPPs underlying these GDP values impart an upward bias to poor countries' incomes. The main reason is that quantities of services and goods consumed in poor countries are estimated at "international" prices that are much closer to prices that prevail in rich countries (since rich countries' weight in "world" price determination is greater). There is thus the Gerschenkron effect—a country's income will always appear greater if assessed at other country's prices. The high cost of services in (say) the United States, inflates GDP in India, where such services are relatively cheap and consumed in large quantities. Instead of the Geary-Khamis approach to PPP determination used in the Penn World Tables and by Maddison, Dowrick and Akmal (2001) suggest the use of the Afriat index. The Elteto-Koves-Szulc (EKS) approach to PPP determination (used in this work) is supposed to yield the results close to those obtained by the Afriat index (see Dikhanov and Ward 2001). Whether one uses the Geary-Khamis or Afriat or EKS approach to PPPs does make a difference for the inequality results. It is not only that with the Afriat PPPs the level of inequality is higher (as we would expect) but also that the trend reverses (see table 9.14 reproduced from Dowrick and Akmal 2001). Thus, as Dowrick and Akmal argue, the use of the most common PPP (Geary-Khamis) will tend to bias the level of world inequality down, and in addition may bias the trend.

We thus see that there are nonnegligible problems with each of the three building blocks: lack of individual-level distributions for most of

**TABLE 9.14.**
Gini Coefficients of Global Inequality Calculated with Different PPPs

| | *Penn World Tables (Geary-Khamis PPP)* | *Afriat PPP* |
|---|---|---|
| 1980 | 65.9 | 69.8 |
| 1993 | 63.6 | 71.1 |
| Change | –2.3 | +1.3 |

*Source:* Dowrick and Akmal (2001, table 5, p.32).

the countries in the world, questionable mixing of household surveys and national accounts data, intertemporal projections of quintile shares, and overestimates of poor countries' income implied by the Geary-Khamis PPPs. Milanovic's (2002, and here) approach is the only one based on the direct use of household surveys. However, it is not free of the problems—even if we disregard the issue of household survey reliability, which, of course, affects all the approaches equally. We lack individual-level data from Chinese and Indians surveys (which decisively influence world income distribution); and income and expenditure measures are combined.

Figure 9.5 depicts the global Gini coefficients obtained by the various authors.[114] We note first that the values are within a relatively narrow range between 62 and 68. One can be, in effect, pretty confident that world inequality (across individuals) has been in the middle-60s of Gini points over the past twenty or even thirty years. What the authors do not agree on is the direction of change. Dikhanov and Ward (2001), Bourguignon and Morrisson (1999/2002), and Dowrick and Akmal (2001) all find a slight increase in inequality between the 1970s and the 1990s. Milanovic (2002, and here) finds a sharp increase between 1988 and 1993 followed by a decline in the next five-year period. Sutcliffe (2003) calculates a stable inequality (using Maddison's data) and a declining one (when using the World Bank data). Chotikapanich, Valenzuela, and Rao (1997) find a decline in the 1970s followed by an increase in the 1980s. Sala-i-Martin (2002, 2002a) and Bhalla (2002) find a consistent decline in inequality during almost the entire period of the past thirty years. As detailed comparisons of the various approaches (here and in appendix 5) make clear, this is due to a host of very strong assumptions made by both authors.[115] Such assumptions were necessary to overcome the paucity of data both in terms of number of data points for each distribution, and even more so in terms of country/years for which even such fragmentary data were available. But most of these as-

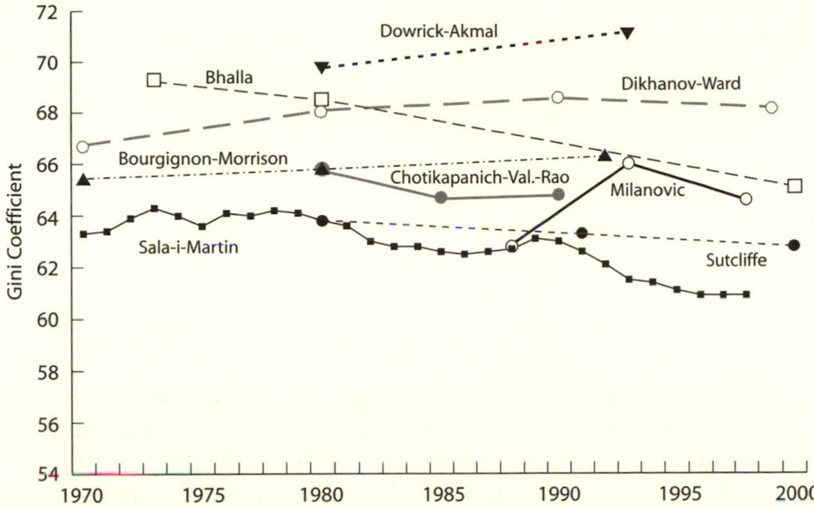


**Figure 9.5.** Gini coefficients of Concept 3 inequality, 1970–2000 (various authors). Bhalla (2002) shows, in a graphic form, values for all years. The numeric values from Bhalla, reproduced here, are given for only a few years. All sources are given in table 9.13.

sumptions (e.g., the use of the same distribution for all years as in Bhalla, or artificial smoothing of quintile share changes as in Sala-i-Martin) are not neutral: they bias the calculated results down, affect the trend, and come very close to presenting what is a thinly disguised Concept 2 inequality as global inequality.

# 10

## A World without a Middle Class

WHAT is the world's middle class? Does the question make sense? No: if we believe that the concept has a meaning only if there is a community with similar customs, language, and history, and with a government ruling over a precisely delimited territory. Yes: if treat the world as a single entity as we have done throughout. We shall now turn to this question, which in the context of a single country is, since Aristotle, linked with the question of social stability. One could argue that—even in the world context—it may be reasonable to ask whether a small middle class may not be conducive to global instability. We shall leave this speculative question for later.

Consider first the distribution of world population by 2000 GDP per capita (in PPP terms) of the country where they live. This distribution is shown in figure 10.1.[116] The most striking fact, even at a first glance, is the emptiness in the middle. First, note that 70 percent of world population lives in countries whose GDP per capita is less than $PPP 5,000. For example, more than 200 million people live in the poorest countries whose annual GDP per capita is less than $PPP 1,000. Between $PPP 1,000 and $PPP 2,000, we find populous countries such as India, Bangladesh, Nigeria, and Vietnam. Between $PPP 2,000 and $PPP 4,000, there are Indonesia, Pakistan, the Philippines, and the Ukraine. Between $PPP 4,000 and $PPP 5,000, we find China and Russia. Next, about 12 percent of people live in countries with GDP per capita levels between $PPP 5,000 and $PPP 8,000. And then within the broad middle income range, which encompasses incomes from $PPP 8,000 to $PPP 20,000, there is only 4 percent of the world population. The remaining 14 percent of world population live in the rich world, that is in the countries whose GDP per capita is above $PPP 20,000.

This distribution (figure 10.1) is related to the Concept 2 inequality. We can go further than this by looking at the Concept 3 distribution, which, of course, reflects the actual incomes of people in different countries. Then, using household survey data, we obtain the distribution of world population for the year 1998, as shown in figure 10.2. We notice the crowding around the left end of the graph, or in other words, we see that the distribution is heavily skewed to the right. A little over 40 percent of the world population lives on an income/expenditure less than

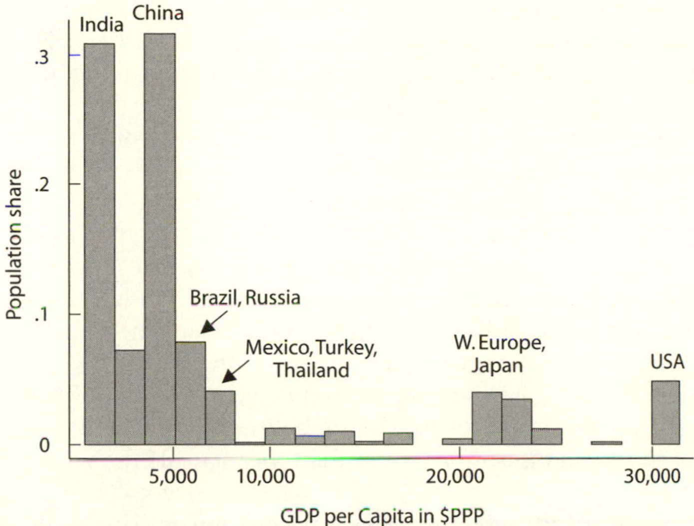


**Figure 10.1.** Distribution of people in the world according to GDP per capita in international dollars of the country where they live (year 2000). Luxembourg (GDP PPP = 47,515) is omitted. GDP shown in 1995 international dollars.

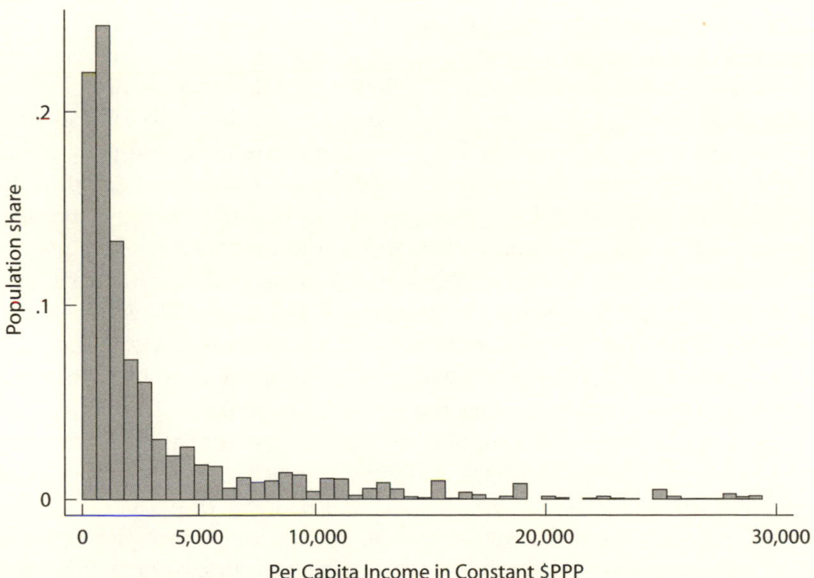


**Figure 10.2.** World income distribution (based on household survey data; year 1998). Horizontal axis is truncated at income level of $PPP 30,000. Amounts shown in 1998 international dollars.

$PPP 1,000 per capita annually;[117] 75 percent of world population lives with an income less than the world mean income of $PPP 3,526; the top 10 percent of world distribution includes all those with incomes above $PPP 9,600 per capita per annum.

If we then define the middle class (as was done by Birdsall, Graham, and Pettinato 2000) to include all those whose incomes fall within 75 percent and 125 percent of the median,[118] we find that only 17.4 percent of world population can be called the "middle class." Compare this with the similarly defined middle class in the countries most devoid of it, like Brazil (20.7 percent of the population), or Chile (21.5 percent). OECD countries' middle-class share, in contrast, ranges between 35 and 40 percent of the population. In effect, in the Birdsall, Graham, and Pettinato (2000) dataset, which covers thirty countries, only one country (Panama) has a middle class share below 20 percent (19.4 percent), and this is still significantly greater than the share of the world middle class.

This world middle class receives only 6.5 percent of world 1998 income: its per capita income is therefore a little over 37 percent of the world mean (6.5 divided by 17.4). Again, if we compare this with the results in Birdsall, Graham, and Pettinato (2000), where the middle-class income in Western economies is estimated at about 85 percent of country mean, in transition countries at about 80 percent of the mean, and in Latin America at about 60 percent of the mean, we see that the world middle class is not only much smaller than in any individual country but also is relatively much poorer.[119] A rule of thumb for within-country inequality studies is that the share of the bottom decile in total income is between 3 and 3.5 percent; its average income is accordingly about 30–35 percent of the overall mean. At the world level, we see that the middle class has a relative income that is in the same range as relative income of the bottom decile within an individual country.

Yet another way to look at this issue is presented in Milanovic and Yitzhaki (2001). They define the world middle class as consisting of all people whose income falls between the average income (calculated from household surveys) of Brazil and average income of Italy, the lowest-income country among the G7. We can replace the latter with the average income of Portugal to make it consistent with our earlier analysis in chapter 7. This includes everyone with 1998 incomes ranging between $PPP 3,987 (Brazil) and $PPP 6,060 (Portugal). Conveniently, it turns out that Brazil's average per capita income of just under $PPP 4,000 is quite close to the per capita poverty line, which entails eligibility for welfare benefits in developed Western nations. We find that 77.3 percent of the world population lives below the rich countries' poverty line. The size of the middle class (that is, individuals with in-

**TABLE 10.1.**
Poor, Middle Class and Rich in the World, according to Three Inequality Concepts

| | (1) *Concept 1* *Percent (number) of Countries* | (2) *Concept 2* *Percent of World Population Living in Countries with Average Per Capita Income Being...* | (3) *Concept 3* *Percentage of World Population with Per Capita Income Being...* |
|---|---|---|---|
| Poor (below mean income of Brazil) | 58 (79) | 70.1 | 77.4 |
| Middle class | 21 (28) | 13.9 | 6.7 |
| Rich (above mean income of Portugal) | 21 (29) | 16.0 | 15.9 |
| Out of which WENAO | 15 (21) | 13.0 | 10.0 |
| *Total* | *100(136)* | *100* | *100* |

*Note:* Columns (1) and (2) based on GDP per capita. Column (3) based on the data from household surveys (full sample; 122 countries in 1998). Brazil and Portugal always included in the higher group (respectively middle income and rich).

comes between $PPP 3,987 and $PPP 6,060 per year) is only 6.7 percent. The percentage of the rich is about 16 percent.[120]

Table 10.1 summarizes the poor, the middle class and the rich according to the three concepts of inequality. If we look only at the number of countries that are poor (using the same criterion: that is, having GDP per capita less than Brazil), there are seventy-nine such countries. If we consider the percentage of the population who live in poor countries, it is 70.1 percent. Finally, if we are interested in the actual percentage of people who have per capita income/expenditures below the level of mean income of Brazil, they are 77.4 percent of the people in the world. The interpretation of other cells is the same. For us, the most interesting fact is the scarcity of the middle class. Slightly less than 14 percent of world population lives in middle-income countries, and 6.7 percent of individuals in the world have incomes that place them among the world middle class.

The last row confirms the already-noticed dominance of WENAO countries among the rich world. That prevalence, however, is less in terms of truly rich individuals (only two-thirds of whom live in WENAO countries) than in terms of total population living in rich countries (more than 80 percent).[121] The implication is, of course, that there are quite a few rich people outside the WENAO region, whether the countries themselves may be poor or in the middle. It is worth noting, for example, that the richest ventile in South Africa belongs to the top percentile in the world;[122] Brazil's situation is the same. The composition of the world's top income percentile illustrates this fact. There we find the richest income groups from the following countries: Brazil, Greece, France, Canada, South Africa, Hong Kong, Italy, Ireland, Luxembourg, Barbados, United States, and Chile. Now, South Africa, according to its GDP per capita, belongs to the poor countries, while Brazil is on the dividing line between the poor and middle-class countries, and Chile's GDP per capita puts it in the middle group. Yet a significant number of people from these countries belong to the richest 1 percent of the world population.

Table 10.2 focuses on the issue of correspondence between country's mean income and actual income of the people who live there. If we look at the second column, we see that in 1998 there were 4160 million people (77.4 percent of total world population included in our household survey data) who had an income smaller than the mean income of Brazil. Almost 3.9 billion of thus-defined poor people lived in poor countries, that is, in countries whose survey-based mean income was less than that of Brazil. In other words, 93 percent of poor people live in poor countries, about 5 percent live in middle-income countries, and 2 percent of the world poor live in rich countries. But when we move to the rich people and rich countries, the very strong correspondence between one's location and income weakens.[123] Although about 83 percent of rich people do live in rich countries (707 million out of the total of 855 million), more than 11 percent of the world rich live in poor countries, and more than 6 percent of the world rich live in middle-income countries.

A different way to look at Table 10.2 is to look at its rows. We note

**TABLE 10.2.**
Correspondence between Poor Countries and Poor People in the World (in million people; 1998 household survey data)

| | *Persons* | | | |
|---|---|---|---|---|
| *Countries* | *Poor* | *Middle Income* | *Rich* | *Total Population* |
| Poor | 3879 | 210 | 96 | 4185 |
| Middle income | 189 | 35 | 52 | 277 |
| Rich | 92 | 115 | 707 | 913 |
| Total population | 4160 | 360 | 855 | 5375 |

*Note:* Full sample countries (122 countries). Definition of the poor, middle class, and rich as in table 10.1.

that out of all people who live in rich countries (913 million), 77 percent (707 million) are rich too. Yet 92 million, or 10 percent of people living in rich countries are poor. Or differently, from all the people living in poor countries (almost 4.2 billion), 93 percent or almost 3.9 billion are poor too. There are nevertheless 5 and 2 percent of people in these countries who belong respectively to the world middle class or to the rich. It is somewhat of a curiosity that about the same number of people (92 and 96 million) are either poor people living in rich countries or rich people living in poor countries.

## Transfers to Reduce World Poverty

Let us now suppose that, in such an uneven world where not all the poor live in poor countries and not all the rich live in rich countries, we want to make transfers that would reduce world poverty. Such transfers are (still) mostly made on a bilateral basis: from a rich country to a poor country. We may also want to avoid the likelihood of a regressive transfer, that is, the possibility that the transfer is generated by taxing somebody in a rich country who may turn out to be poorer than the recipient in a poor country. If the two countries' distribution do not overlap at all, that is if even the poorest residents of a rich country are better off than the richest citizens of the poor country, the likelihood of a regressive transfer is zero. This is approximately the situation that obtains among Group A countries listed in table 10.3.[124] This group combines countries where transfers from a rich to poor country would be extremely unlikely to be regressive. In the rich countries, ranging from Japan to France, the average income of the people in the bottom decile is so high as to place them at between the 72nd and 83rd percentile of world income distribution. These are rich countries with relatively equal income distributions (in contrast to the United States). Now, consider the mean income of the people belonging to the *top* decile or ventile, in countries ranging from rural India to Cameroon. Their income puts them between the 51th and 69th percentile of world distribution. Therefore, these two distributions, for example, Japan's and rural India's, practically do not overlap. Or, to give another example, a Frenchman on welfare or unemployment benefits (who would presumably belong to the bottom decile of income distribution in France) would still be better off than a top decile person in Madagascar. Obviously, we cannot guarantee that absolutely *no one* will overlap: it is virtually certain that there would be a few rich people in Madagascar who would be better off than some poor persons in France. However, statistical importance of such an overlap is minimal. At most, and depending both on

**TABLE 10.3.**
Percentile Rankings in the World Distribution of the Bottom Decile in Rich Countries and the Top Decile in Poor Countries (1998 household survey data)

| *Rich Countries* | *Bottom Decile or Ventile* | *Poor Countries* | *Top Decile or Ventile* |
|---|---|---|---|
| Group A countries (almost no overlap of distributions = low likelihood of regressive transfers | | | |
| Japan | 83 | Rural India | 51 |
| Norway | 81 | Madagascar | 54 |
| Finland | 76 | Rural Indonesia | 55 |
| Canada | 76 | Ethiopia | 59 |
| Taiwan | 75 | Niger | 64 |
| Sweden | 74 | Cameroon | 69 |
| Germany | 73 | | |
| France | 72 | | |
| Group B countries some overlap of distributions = some likelihood of regressive transfers) | | | |
| Portugal | 47 | Bangladesh | 76 |
| Spain | 65 | Egypt | 80 |
| United States | 69 | Kyrghyzstan | 84 |
| | | Kazakhstan | 87 |
| | | Morocco | 89 |
| Group C countries (greater overlap = greater likelihood of regressive transfers) | | | |
| All rich countries | | Peru | 90 |
| | | Philippines | 91 |
| | | Colombia | 98 |
| | | Brazil | 100 |
| | | South Africa | 100 |

*Note:* Ranking is the rank of the person with a mean income of the bottom (or top) decile or ventile. All incomes are in $PPP.

the skewness of the upper tail of the poor countries' distributions, or (a very unlikely) skewness of the left-end tail of the rich countries' distributions, there could be about 3 to 4 percent of people of the two countries combined whose incomes might overlap. It is therefore highly unlikely that a transfer from a rich to a poor country, both belonging to Group A, would be regressive. Actually, even if the transfer were purely random, the chance of it ending up in the pockets of a richer person would be very small (3 to 4 percent).

The situation is different, however, for Group B countries consisting, on the one hand, of a few advanced countries that are either not so rich (Portugal) as to make even their poorest citizens wealthy by world standards, or that have very skewed income distributions (the United States) and, on the other hand, a number of poor countries where the top decile is fairly well-off (around the 80th world percentile). For this group the likelihood of a regressive transfer cannot be entirely dismissed. And even less so for Group C countries (Philippines, Colombia, Brazil, South Africa), whose top decile is very rich by world standards. Group C countries' distributions overlap in a nontrivial way, that is, it is not only the proverbial Mobutu and his family who are richer than some people in rich countries.

# Part IV

CONCLUDING COMMENTS

# 11

# The Three Concepts of Inequality in Historical Perspective

> We may conclude . . . that per capita relative income disparity between the populations of Europe, North America and Oceania, and the populations of Asia and Africa has probably widened over the last fifty years, and this widening disparity is even more likely to be true if we cover the last century.
>
> —SIMON KUZNETS, *Regional Economic Trends*, 1954

## From the Industrial Revolution to Today

Thanks to recent historical research in countries' income levels (Maddison 2001) and inequality (among others by Morrisson 2000), we are able to make reasonably informed estimates of concepts 1, 2, and 3 inequality going all the way back to 1820, that is, to the beginning of the modern times. In principle, calculations of concepts 1 and 2 should be easier and more reliable because for them we need only two pieces of information: GDP per capita and population (both provided by Maddison). However, the problem—even if this information were fully correct—is that for large parts of the world we do not have GDP per capita for the early nineteenth century. There are no data for Africa, most of (what used to be called) Indo-China, the Philippines, Korea, Turkey and the Middle East, the Balkans, and all of Latin America and the Caribbean with the exception of Brazil. Thus our coverage of the world is less than complete, albeit increasing, until the mid-twentieth century. Fortunately, Maddison's data do include China and India, which keeps the population coverage around 80 percent even in the nineteenth century. We see in table 11.1 that both the number of countries and the population coverage in the calculations steadily rise from twenty-six countries and 79 percent of the world population in 1820 to 127 countries and 92 percent of the world population in 1960.

For Concept 3, we use Bourguignon and Morrisson (1999/2002) data up to the most recent period, where we use the results from this book. The Bourguinon and Morrisson data, by construction, cover all the world but achieve this through the "assignment" of the available income distribution data to "similar" countries that lack them. Thus the precision of the estimates is far less than for the most recent period.

Consider first the issue of convergence or divergence among countries' incomes. The results shown in figure 11.1 (top panel) illustrate the process of the "Great Divergence" that began with the modern industrial development and growth in the West. During the first globalization century, that is, between 1820 and 1913, the Concept 1 inequality doubled if measured by the Gini and more than tripled if measured by the Theil index. The number of countries included in the sample increased over the same period from twenty-six in 1820 to forty-six in 1913, and so a part of the increase in inequality may be spurious. However, when we keep the 1820 sample of countries fixed, and run the same inequality statistics across them, the results are practically unchanged: the 1913 Gini and Theil are 32.6 and 17.3 vs. respectively 19.6 and 5.9 more than a century before. Thus the great divergence in between-country incomes seems to hold even on a rather restricted sample of twenty-six countries whose GDP data are available throughout the entire period.[125]

In the interwar period, Concept 1 inequality (calculated across 45 or 46 countries) slightly declined, only to rise dramatically as the consequence of uneven outcomes during World War II. Although Concept 1 inequality in 1952 is calculated across 71 countries and is not directly comparable to that calculated across 45 countries in 1938, keeping the sample constant between the two years shows again that the increase was not a spurious one: for the same sample of countries, Gini increased from about 35 to slightly over 43, and Theil from 19 to more than 30.[126] Finally, over the most recent half century, intercountry inequality, as we have seen in chapters 4 and 5, continued to rise. In conclusion, it seems undeniable that mean incomes of countries over the past two centuries have been getting more and more dissimilar, the only exception to this trend being the interwar period. As in a kind of Big Bang, to which the industrial revolution can be likened, parts of the world that used to be similar in income levels have steadily diverged, and continue to do so.

The population-weighted international inequality charts the same evolution as Concept 1 inequality up to World War I (see figure 11.1 bottom panel).[127] The Gini and Theil coefficients of both concepts are almost the same up to that point, even if the increase in the Concept 2 inequality is sharper (because the initial inequality in 1820 was less). After World War I, and most dramatically during World War II, how-

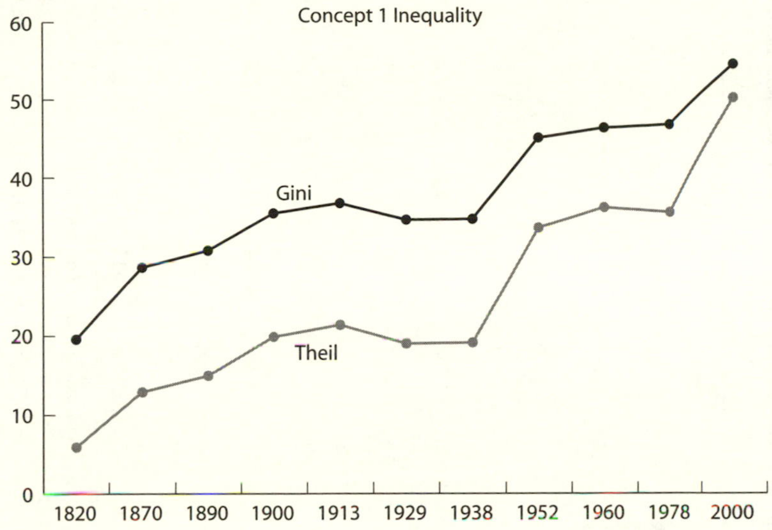


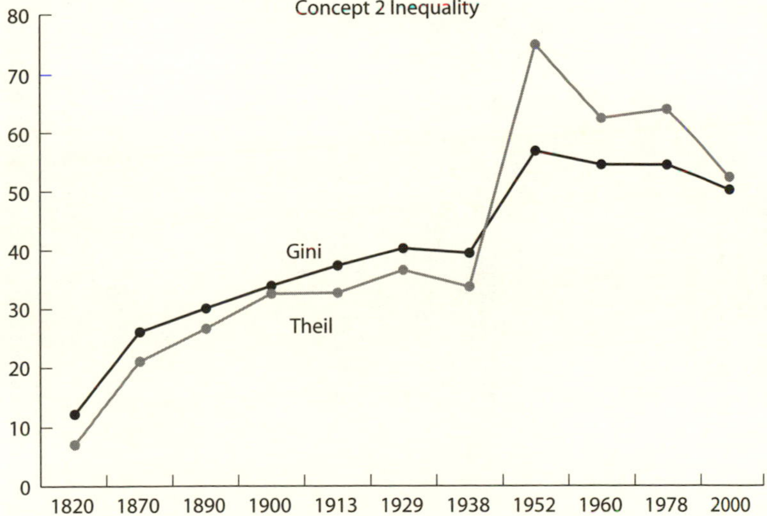


**Figure 11.1.** Inequality concepts 1 and 2 in historical perspective, 1820–2000.

ever, Concept 2 inequality shoots up as poor and populous China continues on its economic decline, and the richest (and relatively populous) United States pulls ahead of the rest of the world.[128] Thus the sharper increase of Concept 2 compared to Concept 1 inequality is due

**TABLE 11.1.**
World Inequality in Historical Perspective (Gini coefficients)

| | *1820* | *1870* | *1890* | *1900* | *1913* | *1929* | *1938* | *1952* | *1960* | *1978* | *1988* | *1993* | *2000* |
|---|---|---|---|---|---|---|---|---|---|---|---|---|---|
| International inequality (Concept 1) | 19.6 | 28.7 | 30.8 | 35.5 | 36.8 | 34.7 | 34.8 | 45.1 | 46.3 | 46.7 | 49.8 | 52.9 | 54.3 |
| Number of countries | 26 | 30 | 28 | 41 | 48 | 45 | 45 | 71 | 127 | 130 | 137 | 138 | 136 |
| Weighted international inequality (Concept 2) | 12.0 | 26.1 | 30.1 | 34.0 | 37.4 | 40.3 | 39.5 | 56.9 | 54.5 | 54.4 | 52.9 | 51.6 | 50.2 |
| Population included (in m) | 836 | 972 | 1,108 | 1,150 | 1,509 | 1,729 | 1,878 | 1,981 | 2,794 | 3,985 | 4,813 | 5,237 | 5,781 |
| Population coverage (in %) | 79 | 77 | 76 | | 88 | 85 | | 79 | 92 | 90 | 98 | 99 | 99 |
| Global income inequality (Concept 3) | 50.0 | 56.0 | 58.8 | | 61.0 | 61.6 | | 64.0 | 63.5 | 65.7 | 62.2 | 65.3 | 64.1 |
| Population included (in m) | 1,057 | 1,266 | 1,450 | | 1,719 | 2,042 | | 2,511 | 3,025 | 4,414 | 4,475 | 5,107 | 5,383 |
| Population coverage (in %) | 100 | 100 | 100 | | 100 | 100 | | 100 | 100 | 100 | 91 | 96 | 92 |
| Estimated world population (in million) | 1,057 | 1,266 | 1,450 | | 1,719 | 2,042 | | 2,511 | 3,025 | 4,414 | 4,900 | 5,300 | 5,845 |

*Note:* Concept 1: For years 1820–1938 calculated from Maddison (2001); period 1952–2000: as in previous chapters. Concept 2: For years 1820–1938 calculated from Maddison (2001); period 1952–2000: as in previous chapters. Concept 3. Period 1820–1978, from Bourguignon and Morrisson (2002, table 1); period 1988–2000: as in chapter 9. Concept 3 actual data are for 1910 (instead of 1913), 1950 (instead of 1952), and 1998 (instead of 2000). Estimated world population: for 1920 to 1978 from Bourguignon and Morrisson (2002, table 1), for 1988 to 2000 as in the previous chapters. The Bourguignon Morrisson Concept 3 calculations include, by construction, the entire population of the world.

to slower growth/decline of poor and *populous* countries. By 1952 Concept 2 inequality is at its peak. Afterward, as discussed in previous chapters, the two concepts have moved differently: Concept 1 inequality continued to rise while Concept 2 inequality was brought down as poor and populous countries, rather than falling behind, were now catching up.

The drastic changes during the period of World War II and, more recently, since the late 1970s, suggest that developments in China and the United States (the two thirds of our "triangle") were crucial for what we observe. This is indeed true, but it is not sufficient to explain the changes. If we calculate Concept 2 inequality without China, there is still a dramatic increase between 1938 and 1952, even if it some 4 Gini points less (see figure 11.2). Only during the past several decades it is China alone that explains the decline in the Concept 2 inequality. Similarly, if we take out the United States, the wartime increase in Concept 2 inequality is less (by some 8 Gini points) but is nonetheless substantial (13 Gini points). Therefore, the dramatic worsening of Concept 2 inequality during the last war was not solely due to the decline of China and the progress of the United States.

Inequality among world citizens starts at an already very high level (Gini of 52 in 1820), much above those of concepts 1 and 2. It then increases to reach the level of about 61 around the time of World War I and 65 in the early 1950s.[129] Since then, with the exception of a dip in

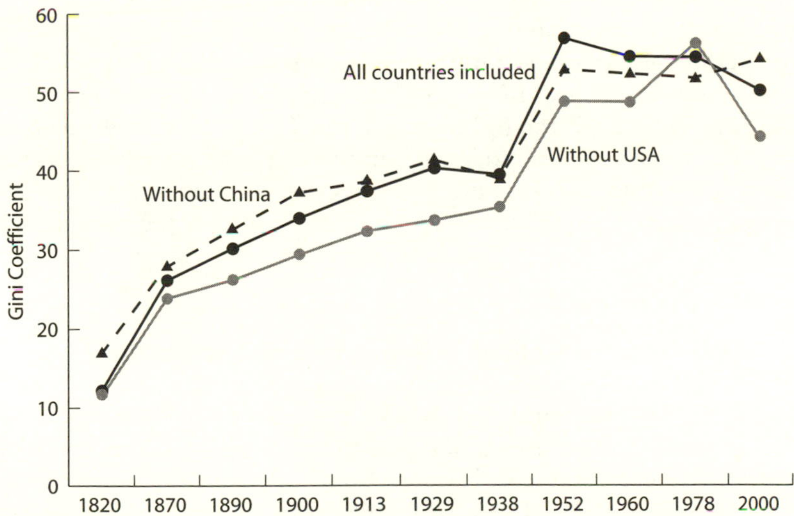


**Figure 11.2.** Concept 2 (Gini) inequality without China and without the United States, 1820–2000.

1988, it has remained at that level.[130] The difference in levels between Concept 3 and Concept 2 inequality provides us with information regarding the relative importance of within- vs. between-country inequality. In 1820, Concept 3 inequality was vastly higher than Concept 2 inequality: Gini of 50 vs. Gini of 12. Thus, the bulk (almost 80 percent according to the Gini, and 85 percent according to the Theil) of inequality among individuals was due to inequality within nations. By 1952, however, this has totally changed: the difference between the two concepts has declined from 38 Gini points to less than 7. It was a tremendous change that reflects three key historical developments between 1820 and 1950. First, rising differences among countries' mean incomes; second, relative decline of poor and populous countries; and third, diminishing within-country inequalities. While in the past, one's income depended much more on the class he belonged to than on the place (country) where he lived, by mid-twentieth century, it was the country much more than the social class that mattered. In the second half of the 20th century however, the situation reversed again: the importance of within-country inequality rose (see figure 11.3).

In a big historical sweep, these developments allow us to distinguish the pre-1950 and post-1950 periods. The first was characterized by (i) strong divergence among countries, (ii) relative decline of populous countries, (iii) increasing inequality among world citizens, and (iv) decreasing within-country inequality. In the second period, after 1950, (i) the divergence among countries continued although at a slower pace, (ii) populous and poor countries started to catch up with the rich world, (iii) inequality among world citizens moved slightly up, and (iv) the overlap, and perhaps within-country inequalities, increased again. In other words, the features (i) and (iii) continued, but at a slower pace, while the features (ii) and (iv) reversed. In effect, it is the reversal of feature (ii)—namely, the end to India's and China's falling behind the rich world—that causes the increase in the overlap component, as some part of poor countries' populations now "mingle" with people from the rich countries.

## Are There "Laws of Motion" of World Income Distribution?

The overview of historical evolution of income inequality among countries or world citizens immediately suggests to the reader the possibility of drawing broader conclusions about the forces that explain such developments and about their probable future evolution. This is based on an implicit view that, in the evolution of inequality, be it among the states or individuals, there are some regularities that we can, in princi-

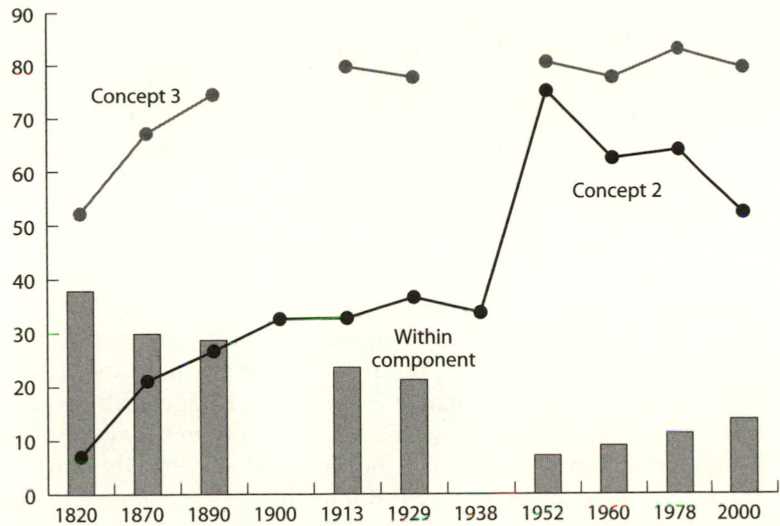


**Figure 11.3.** Decomposition of Concept 3 Theil inequality, 1820–2000.

ple, uncover. Thus Firebaugh (2003) in his recent book emphasizes the changing ratio between Concept 2 and Concept 3 inequality, that is the reversal in the trend of the population-weighted international inequality, which, as we have seen, had occurred some twenty years ago. He believes that this is an epochal change and that we are now entering the stage of "inequality transition," where the forces originally harnessed by industrial and technological revolutions will spread to other countries, and as they do so, enable the poor countries to grow faster than the rich. International and global inequality will begin its downward move, charting a gigantic inverted U shape: exploding after the industrial revolution, continuing its rise almost to the present, and then going on the decline. In other words, the worst of global inequality is behind us. Lucas (2002) has a similar view. Again as the technology spreads faster and more easily (due to lower costs of telecommunications and transport) and as institutions become more similar, the outcomes will too. In Lucas's view, we are bound to return to the global level of inequality that obtained prior to the industrial revolution—a level much lower than what is the case today. Finally, similar exercises, although in the context of the convergence analysis, are undertaken by Quah (1993a) and Jones (1997). They try, using the transition matrices of countries' rankings in international income distribution, to calculate the long-run equilibrium distribution of countries' GDPs per capita. The assumption motivating their analysis is of course that there is such a thing as a long-run distribution of countries' incomes.

Do these grand theories about the future evolution of inequality make sense? After all, similar theories have a long pedigree in economics. Almost no significant economist has failed to predict where the trends he (more rarely, she) has detected will lead humankind. Thus, Ricardo famously predicted (unless the Corn Laws were repealed) a growing share of the national income to accrue to landlords. Malthus predicted a world where population would always tend to run ahead of the means of sustenance, thus expecting no increase in real per capita income. Hobson and Lenin held that only the expansion of the external markets, and imperialism, could keep capitalism alive. Marx expected the profit rate to decline. Schumpeter argued that large, monopoly producers would outsell their competitors and their eventual socialization would be simply a technical matter. Even Simon Kuznets, an apostle of careful and detailed empirical work, is better known today for his inverted-U curve hypothesis, which he formulated carefully and most tentatively, than for his other work. But as this short review of the predictions of some of the most famous economists reveals, they were all (with the possible exception of Kuznets) wrong. Regularities that they were convinced to have discovered were just not there. This should at least give us pause when we consider the temptation to extrapolate the past developments into the future.

Consider first the view that there will be an "inequality transition." This is based, as said before, on the break in the trend of Concept 2 inequality. That break in trend is entirely due to China's spectacular growth over the past twenty years. To argue that the new, downward trend will continue is to argue not only that China will continue on its growth path (for if it does, it will soon become rich enough to push Concept 2 inequality back up), but also that the poor, populous countries like Nigeria, Bangladesh, or Pakistan are also going to be launched on a high-growth trajectory. Can we be sure of that? As soon as the grand statement is, as it were, peeled down to what it really means, we conclude that there is no inevitability that the developments which it implies will indeed happen. There is no inevitability that China and India will continue to grow, and even less that the currently poor and populous countries will catch up. Lucas's view that the spread of technology should help them is in essence a static one. It is based either on the view that there are discrete technological advances that then spread to the rest of the world, or that there is a continuous technological progress but that its spread, because of faster communication, also accelerates, allowing poor countries to catch up. But it is equally plausible to argue that the speed of technological progress can outpace the speed of the information dissemination, so that by the time invention A reaches a poor country, the rich country has already moved to a production process, not of the B (higher) generation, but an even higher (D) generation. Then, relative gaps must rise.

Similar is the criticism that can be leveled at Quah's (1993a) and Jones's (1997) attempt to find an "equilibrium" distribution of countries' incomes. One may fail to see the usefulness of their exercise. First, because factors that produce a given distribution are highly idiosyncratic and do not obey any regularity (e.g., were oil prices to jump, the transition matrix would look very different from the one based on very low oil prices); second, there is not any theoretical or common-sensical long-run distribution of countries' incomes. It suffices that one country, like the USSR, splinters into fifteen countries (a political event par excellence) to change totally the income distribution of countries. Finally, there is no reason why all countries in the world may not come to within a whisker of the richest country in the world, or why the distribution of countries' GDPs per capita would be lognormal or of any other shape.

So what can we do? We can, I think, pretty confidently chart and explain the past evolution in various international and global inequality measures, but we cannot project these trends into the future. We cannot do so because there are fundamentally no "laws of motion" of world-income distribution. The outcome depends not only on whether poor countries, like China, use technology well enough to catch up, but also on whether political and institutional developments in these countries are consistent with what is needed to grow fast or not. How will China handle its democratizaton? Will it happen, when and how? Will China break up? China's long-term and recent past is full of sudden shifts—to mention only a momentous decision to stop all maritime explorations in the sixteenth century, the Cultural Revolution, or the Deng Xiaoping ascendancy. None of these events were inevitable and yet each of them had a tremendous impact on Chinese economic development. And, of course, this is true not only for China. History has produced so many zigzags that what seems an inevitable development today is shown tomorrow to have been a chimera. The political and social developments that crucially determine what happens to the economy are not easily, or at all, predictable. Other factors that determine world income distribution are similarly impossible to gauge: will mobility of labor among countries increase or not? Will population growth rates in sub-Saharan Africa decline? What will be the impact of AIDS on growth rates in these countries as well as in India? Will the political conflict between Islamic fundamentalism and the West escalate and condemn the countries of the Middle East to be a permanent "arc of instability" with low economic growth or not? We cannot answer any of these questions with certainty. And yet they are key to predicting what happens to economic growth in different parts of the world, and thus to world-income distribution.

Thus I think that our conclusion should be that we can indeed explain past trends, because the history that underlies them (e.g., the Chinese Civil War, the Bolshevik revolution, colonialism, or the industrial revolution) is known to us, and the link between them and the observed outcomes can reasonably be made. But we cannot make sensible projections because we do not know the future political and social, and hence economic, history of the world. It is not because history is random, but because it is created through the interaction between an "objective reality" (institutions, preferences, the past) and actions of people endowed by free will. History is, as Vico wrote, what people make of it. Deterministic theories are incomplete because they cannot take into account that second element, human freedom of action (*le libre arbitre*). Moreover, under the false air of inevitability, they sap all effort to effect social change. The best critique of the deterministic theories was, I think, made by Tocqueville (1978) in his *Souvenirs*, written in 1850, and it is worth quoting in full (my translation):

> I hate . . . these absolute systems that make all the events in history depend on primary causes, linking one to another by an inevitable chain, and that, so to speak, take out people from the general history of humankind. I find them narrow in their pretended grandeur, and false under their guise of mathematical truths. I believe, whatever the view of the writers who have invented these sublime theories to nourish their own vanity and to facilitate their work, that many of the important historical facts cannot be explained but by accidental circumstances, and that many others remain inexplicable. And that finally, chance, or rather that mixing of the secondary causes, which we thus call, since we do not know how to tell them apart, explain a lot of what we see on the world stage. But I strongly believe that chance does not do anything that is not prepared in advance. The existing reality, nature of the institutions, state of mind of people, customs, are the raw materials with which chance constructs the facts that surprise and awe us.

# 12

## Why Does Global Inequality Matter and What to Do about It?

> The central economic issue related to globalization is that of inequality.
>
> —AMARTYA SEN, *"Globalization and Poverty,"* from a lecture given at Santa Clara University, October 29, 2002.

### The Current Situation: Plutocracy at a Global Level . . .

The arguments against global inequality and in favor of some redistribution or help for the world's poorest are inextricably linked with the argument about the need for democratization at the global level. This is a carbon copy of the argument, made in the nineteenth century at the national level, linking the spread of franchise and the empowerment of the poor. Note however, that, at the global level we cannot even speak of "democracy," but in an almost Soviet-speak, the best we can do is to argue for "democratization," that is, for the introduction of some elements of democratic (one person, one vote) decision-making in the international arena. This is because a move to "democracy" would require a world government and a huge redistribution of political power that is, under current conditions, impossible to envisage. The best one can hope for is some redress of the current imbalance of power: most of the power is currently held by the rich countries, and to the extent that in these countries themselves, it is the rich people that are politically the most active and powerful, global power too is held by a relatively small number of very rich people.

At the global level, and in sharp contrast to what is increasingly the trend at the national level, it is plutocracy rather than democracy that we live in—even if plutocracy's codification (not always in name but certainly in spirit) in charters of different international organizations and treaties does represent an advancement in comparison to the old days of colonialism when the rich ruled untrammeled by any global strictures. It has become almost commonplace to point out that the rules of the game in all important international organizations are disproportionately influenced by the rich world, and among them by specific interest groups. The point was forcefully illustrated by Stiglitz (2002) regarding the role of the U.S. Treasury and financial interests in influencing the policies of the World Bank and the IMF. The World Trade Organization, despite an appearance of democracy in the sense that decisions are made unanimously, is also—as argued, for example, by Nayyar (1997 and 2003), Khor (2001), Jomo (2002), and Bardhan (2000)—controlled by rich countries. The "green room" negotiations where the really important issues are decided in small circles have come in for much criticism. So have many WTO decisions relating to the protection of intellectual property rights and unwillingness to allow the provision of cheaper generic drugs in poor countries,[131] the exemption of agriculture and, until recently, textiles from tariff liberalizations, the emphasis on the liberalization of financial services where the rich countries enjoy comparative advantage, the prohibitively high costs of dispute resolution, and so forth. Global bodies tend to be either irrelevant if representative, or if relevant, to be dominated by the rich.

A stark example of the latter situation is provided by the quota and voting rights enjoyed by member countries of the IMF. There, as well as in the World Bank, votes do not follow either what may be deemed a truly global one person = one vote formula, or the international formula of one country = one vote (as, for example, in the United Nations General Assembly). The voting rights match rather closely the one dollar = one vote rule. Figure 12.1 shows the Lorenz curves of IMF voting rights and world distribution of (PPP) income. The horizontal axis gives the cumulative percentage of all people in the world ranked according to their country's GDP per capita in international dollars (from the poorest country, Sierra Leone, to the richest, Luxembourg). On the vertical axis, we have the cumulative percentage of voting rights (or IMF quota) and the cumulative percentage of world total income. As can be seen, the voting rights are even more concentrated than the distribution of world income: the former's Gini is 61 vs. the income's Gini of 54.[132] The poorest 40 percent of the world population has less than 10 percent of the vote in the IMF and accounts for exactly 10 percent of world income. On the other hand, the 10 percent of the world population living in the richest countries has 43 percent of the IMF vote and controls 40 percent of world income. Incidentally, as the figure shows (see the portion between A and B), the biggest loser seems to be China which, with 22 percent of the world population and 14 percent of world income, has only 3 percent of IMF voting rights. In other words, each Chinese counts as one-twenty-seventh of each American.[133] Moreover, as Leech (1998) shows, using different power indexes, the actual concentration of political power in the IMF is greater than implied by the

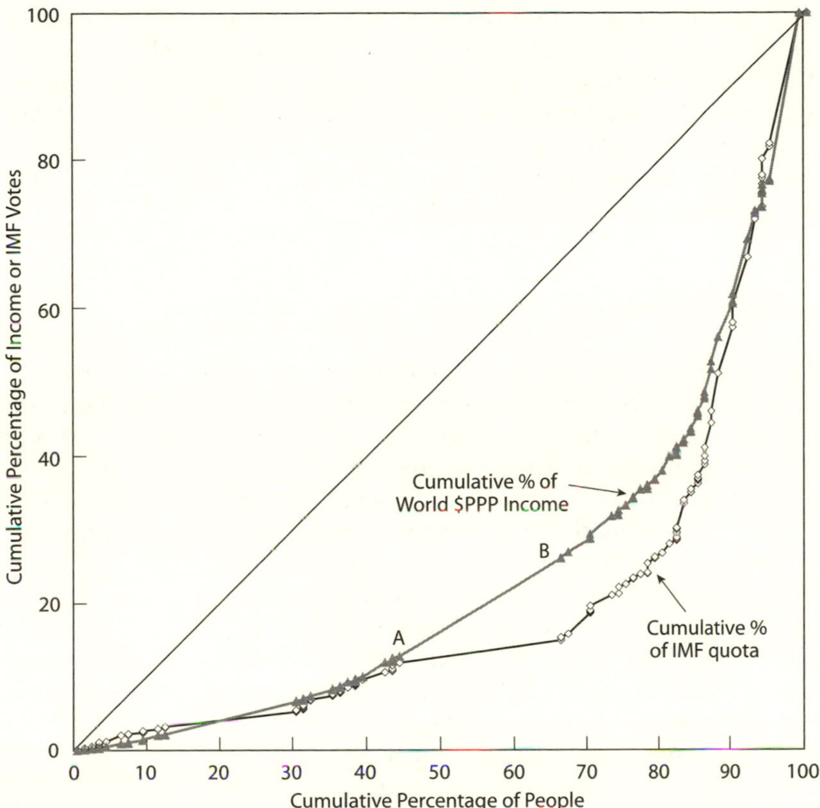


**Figure 12.1.** Distribution of voting rights at the IMF and world income. People are ranked by the mean income of their country. Income is GDP per capita in $PPP terms.

voting rights; for example, U.S. actual power share is around 23 percent even if its share of the votes is 17.7 percent (Leech 2002, p. 389).

The even more pro-rich bias of the IMF votes than implied by the distribution of world income is not surprising if we reflect that the IMF formula that is used to calculate each country's votes is based on total GDP as expressed at market exchange rates (which reduces the share of the poor countries whose exchange rates are low) and the country's trade. But it illustrates well that the current arrangements in global institutions that do matter are very far from the rules that prevail within nations-states, where voting rights, if not necessarily real political power, are not proportional to one's wealth or income. In the global arena, however, we seem to be much more comfortable with plutocratic than even partly democratic decision-making. As long as the current rules are in effect it is probably vain to expect a major move toward redistribution at the world scale: democratization of decision-making is the prerequisite for it. More to the point, in the short- to medium-run, redistribution of income toward the world poor will continue to take place through its existing two channels: concessional elements in loans granted by international financial organizations, and official bilateral aid. We shall consider briefly the latter.

### . . . and a Bilateral Aid That Is Not Focused on the Poor

Both poverty and inequality in the recipient countries are only incidental objectives in rich countries' decisions on bilateral aid. That is, the objective of bilateral aid, in deed not in words, is not to achieve maximum poverty reduction in the world. As it has often been argued (Diven 2001; Omoruyi 2001; Ali, Malvanda, and Suliman 1999), international aid responds more to political and economic objectives in donor countries than to the pure global welfare considerations. Table 12.1 shows the concentration coefficients of bilateral aid by rich countries. The total amount of official aid included here is $22 billion, and it includes all Development Assistance Committee (DAC) countries with the exception of New Zealand and Portugal. The more negative the concentration coefficient, the more the aid is directed toward countries with low GDP per capita (in PPP terms). With the concentration coefficient of zero, aid is practically randomly distributed, while a positive concentration coefficient implies that aid is pro-rich in the absolute sense: richer countries receive more of it in per capita terms than poor countries. (Note, however, that even such aid would reduce Concept 2 inequality because it is likely to be less pro-rich than the actual distribution of world income.)

The results show that important countries with strong geopolitical interests are less efficient in the allocation of aid. This is true for the United States, the European Union, Japan, France, and Germany. Great Britain is an exception. But even smaller countries are more mindful of their political interests than of poverty alleviation in general. Thus Greece helps mostly Balkan and Eastern Mediterranean countries, Portugal its former colonies, Spain, Latin American countries. Overall, rich countries' aid concentration coefficient is mildly pro-poor with the value of –11.1.

An often overlooked advantage of more targeted bilateral aid is that it buys a lot of "bang for the buck" because poorer countries' domestic price levels are lower than those of rich countries. Therefore one dollar of bilateral aid goes further in a poor country than at home. The $22 billion

**TABLE 12.1.**
Official Bilateral Aid and Its Targeting (year 2001)

| | *Percentage Share in Total Bilateral Aid* | *Concentration Coefficient* | *The "Boost" Factor* |
|---|---|---|---|
| Belgium | 0.7 | –75.5 | 3.9 |
| Ireland | 0.5 | –74.1 | 4.8 |
| Norway | 1.3 | –69.6 | 4.4 |
| Great Britain | 5.5 | –69.5 | 4.4 |
| Switzerland | 0.8 | –67.8 | 4.7 |
| Denmark | 1.9 | –63.6 | 4.7 |
| Luxembourg | 0.2 | –62.6 | 4.3 |
| Netherlands | 3.4 | –48.4 | 4.7 |
| Sweden | 1.6 | –47.3 | 3.7 |
| Finland | 0.4 | –40.4 | 3.6 |
| Austria | 2.1 | –34.6 | 2.7 |
| Spain | 2.4 | –24.8 | 3.1 |
| Japan | 28.1 | –21.5 | 4.2 |
| Greece | 0.4 | –21.1 | 3.6 |
| Italy | 1.4 | –2.6 | 4.4 |
| France | 9.4 | –1.9 | 2.7 |
| Germany | 5.2 | –1.2 | 3.8 |
| Canada | 1.4 | 0.6 | 3.9 |
| Australia | 1.6 | 14.6 | 3.2 |
| USA | 16.8 | 20.2 | 3.3 |
| European Union | 13.7 | 28.7 | 2.9 |
| *Total* | *98.8* | *–11.1* | *3.7* |

*Note:* The shares do not add up to 100 because Portugal and New Zealand are not included. This is due to the lack of data on GDP per capita in international dollars for many of their recipient countries (e.g., São Tome and Principe, Cape Verde, Vanuatu, Solomon Islands etc), thus precluding the calculation of a meaningful concentration coefficient. The "boost" factor is calculated as the ratio between the value of international aid at international prices and at current exchange rates. PPP value of aid for each recipient is calculated by dividing the dollar amount received by the recipient country's relative price level (world price level = 1). Countries are ranked by their level of aid targeting.

*Source:* http://www.oecd.org/countrylist/0,2578,en_2825_34447_1783495_1_1_1_1,00.html. The concentration coefficients are calculated for the 2001 official bilateral aid disbursed to ten largest recipients for each donor. European Union has an aid program separate from the individual aid programs of its country-members.

of aid included in our calculations is equivalent to some $73 billion if evaluated at international prices. Poor countries' gains from bilateral aid are thus 3.7 times greater than the cost of this aid to the rich countries.

Are the countries that are more "generous" domestically, that is, that have greater domestic welfare programs, also more likely to be generous globally? This seems to be the case (figure 12.2) as there is a posi-

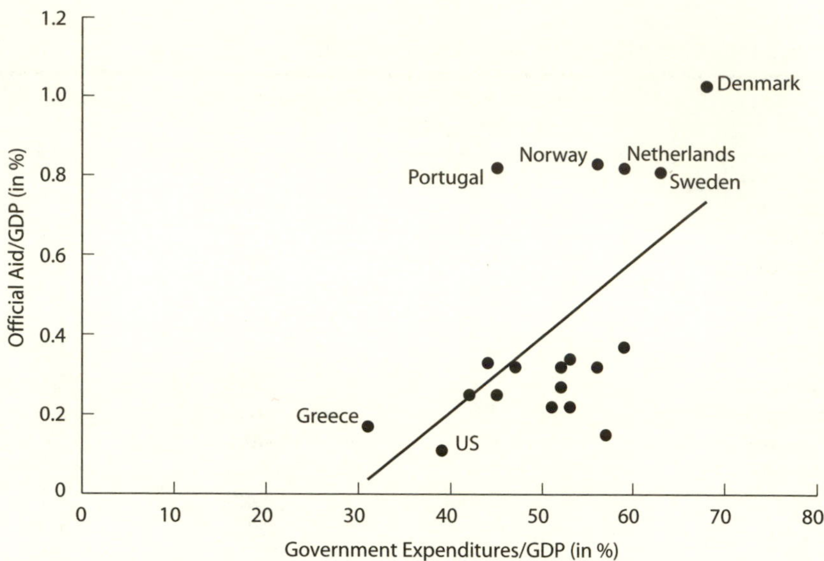


**Figure 12.2.** Relationship between domestic government spending and official foreign aid (both in percent of GDP). *Source:* Official aid: see note to table 12.1. Government expenditures: World Development Indicators and World Bank SIMA database (year 1998).

tive, even if weak, relationship between the extent of domestic spending (measured by government expenditures/GDP ratio) and official bilateral aid (as a share of GDP). Both may be "explained" by a certain redistributionist philosophy. What is important for us to realize is that such a philosophy, even if incomparably more generous domestically, does not seem to end at one's borders—which is indeed good news for the case of global redistribution. It is thus not surprising that the largest donors (in terms of their GDP) are the same North European countries that also exhibit a very high share of government spending in GDP.

## But Does Global Inequality Matter?

Why would world inequality matter? This is a legitimate question. Even at a national level, there are those (e.g., Feldstein 2002; Krueger, 2002) who would argue that inequality does not matter, so long as poverty (assuming that it could be defined only in an absolute sense) is low. Despite these views, there is an increasing consensus that inequality at the national level matters, either because it may slow down growth (see Perotti 1996, 1993; Alesina and Perotti 1994) or because it leads to political instability or to market failures that in turn also slow down growth (Keefer and Knack 2002; Hoff 1996), or because people are simply inequality-averse (see Fong, Bowles, and Gintis 2003). And there is, of course, a long-standing view going back to Plato and Aristotle that high inequality is indeed a social pathology, for (according to Plato) an unequal society is not truly one, but two, societies.

However, these views of inequality are all at the national level. Inequality may matter when people perceive each other as equals, when they jointly elect a parliament and a government that represents them. They may then hold that wide inequality in economic outcomes is unacceptable. But at the international level, the similarities—cultural, religious, ethnic, linguistic—are much weaker, cleavages are deeper, and there is no single institution that people of the world, as citizens, elect. Thus no one can be said to be "in charge" of world inequality.

This view may be in the process of changing. As the world becomes more integrated, at least two developments will tend to increase the relevance of inequality on the world scale.

The first is the awareness of differences in incomes. As people interact more with each other or can see on their TV screens vastly different levels of wealth enjoyed by the people in different countries, the awareness of inequality increases. Globalization thus by itself contributes to the sharpening of the perception of inequality regardless of whether inequality is in fact increasing or not. It does so by heightening people's awareness of, on the one hand, differences in income and wealth, and, on the other, showing a fundamental human similarity between them. As was, in a similar context, noted by *Al Ahram*'s political commentator Mohamed Sid-Ahmed (2002),

> Foremost among [new developments] was the accelerated pace of globalisation, especially in the field of communications and the information revolution. As the planet shrank, it brought into sharper focus the discrepancies between societies and between people within the same society. What came to be called the global village syndrome also invested once distant events, towards which people were more or less neutral, with a new intensity, forcing them to adopt stands that often brought them into conflict with one another. Perceptions changed as distances from and between events seemed to vanish.

This is a process not much different from the one that occurred a century or two ago in Europe when increased within-national interaction simultaneously created nations out of localized ethnic groups and heightened the awareness of income differences. So long as peasants stayed put in their villages, and defined their nationality as being "from here-abouts" (Hroch 1993, p. 11), there was no likelihood that anything like national consciousness would emerge. Once the obstacles to mobility were removed, as when the industrial revolution was set in motion, and nationalities were created out of hitherto stateless peasants, the issues of national inequality and poverty became much more present in people's minds.[134]

If one holds that people's utility functions include not only their absolute level of income but their relative position in income distribution too, then globalization must, by changing the reference point upward, make people in poor countries feel more deprived. This means that globalization alone—even if there is no change in the overall world income distribution or absolute income levels—will foster among the people in poor countries the feeling of being left out. It is the same effect that we would expect greater inequality to produce within a single country. The effect was foreseen much before the current wave of globalization by Simon Kuznets, who in 1954 wrote that even if there is an all-around increase in absolute income, "the political misery of the poor, the tension created by the observation of the much greater wealth of other communities . . . may . . . only increase" (Kuznets 1965, p. 174).

This process of increased mutual awareness is not confined to the poor world. It extends—and perhaps even more because of greater access to modern technology—to the rich world too. As Gunnar Myrdal observed more than thirty years ago, the very idea that rich countries should help the poor countries is both novel—since it dates from the end of World War II—and implies the conception of "world welfare." For "abolishing the policies in developed countries that are averse to underdeveloped countries and, still more, that would help them positively, assume[s] that people in the former countries would accept to one degree or another, the conception of a *welfare world*" (1970, p. 208; emphasis in the text).

The second development is the ease of migration (and reduced cost of travel). Although migration today is less than a century ago, the forces that impel people to migrate are as strong. It is simply that the recipient countries today are much more closed to immigration than they were then. However, as inequalities in incomes increase or, even if constant, are perceived to be great, and as the cost of travel goes down, the pressure to migrate will continue unabated. It is unrealistic to hold that large income differences between the Northern and Southern shore of the Mediterranean, or between Mexico and the United States, or between Indonesia and Malaysia, can continue without adding further pressure to migrate. The governments of the rich countries, despite their fortress mentality, are fighting a losing battle because the economic incentives on the side of the out-migrants and those who can employ them in the rich countries are working against them. To see how this incentive to migrate is related to global inequality, observe the fact that the Gini coefficient can be interpreted also as one-half of the mean-normalized expected gain (or loss) from having another (random) person's income.[135] A world Gini of 65 thus means, to a very poor person, that his expected income might increase by 1.3 times the mean, that is, by about $PPP 4,600 if he became somebody else—a thing that he can do by migrating to a rich country.

### What to Do?

But even if we have a descriptive analysis of world inequality, what are the concrete steps that, based on such an analysis, one could suggest to remedy the problem? There are several.

First, there are, I think, reasons for redistribution on a world scale. One case for such a redistribution is moral; another is more utilitarian and pragmatic, and would involve redistribution among the countries whose income distributions do not overlap so to minimize the likelihood of a regressive income transfer (along the lines of our analysis in chapter 10).

Let us consider first the moral arguments against a too great world inequality. They are based on the proposition that excessive inequality is morally abhorrent, as argued, for example, by Singer (2002); or on the past and present responsibility of the rich world for the plight of the poor (Pogge 2002). The latter point is not quite as fanciful as some people hold. For example, Leszek Balcerowicz, the head of the National Bank of Poland, in a discussion on world poverty argued, in opposition to Joe Stiglitz, that rich countries have no responsibility toward the poor. This is because poor countries are poor because of the civil wars, unfavorable geographic positions, or wrong economic policies (IWM Newsletter 2003). But can one seriously believe that colonization, or, more recently, the Cold War had nothing to do with furthering civil wars and adding to the misery of the poor countries? Didn't the Congo's leaders just copy the plundering mode of governance that they observed during Belgian rule? Was not Mobutu installed and kept in power precisely to deny the Congo to the Communists and the Soviet bloc? Aren't the lack of viability of many African states and their chronic ethnic conflicts related to the way in which these states were created—with no reference at all to local conditions and affinities (see a beautiful description of colonization of Africa in Wesseling 1996)? Or to invert the question: would not Europe be in a state of permanent war today if its borders were drawn as arbitrarily by foreign powers as the African borders were? If, for example, Germans could always outvote

Czech and Poles, and French would rule northern Spain? After all, when the domestic political conditions are unsettled the economy always takes a second place. In effect, the issue of past responsibility has been brought to the fore by the recent reparations paid to the Jewish survivors by the Swiss banks, and by the German firms that employed slave labor during World War II, and finally by the similar claims voiced by African-Americans in the United States. While formal reparations for past misdeeds are both unlikely and difficult to justify and implement, a recognition of some responsibility toward poor countries is certainly in order.

It may be important to underline, however, that the moral argument in favor of world redistribution is not shared by Rawls (1999), who believes that, at most, there is responsibility of the rich to help the poor nations that are "prevented by poverty from organizing [themselves] as a liberal or decent society" (cited in Pogge 2002, p. 2). Rawls is similarly opposed to any world-level redistribution other than that due to "unjustified distributive effects" of international cooperative agreements. In his view, within a community of "decent nations" there is no reason why there should be intercountry transfers: if Denmark cares about its citizens, and the United States does too, there is no reason to endorse any transfer of income between Denmark and the United States. Any difference in income between these two societies is the result of different choices: one society might value leisure or immediate consumption more than another, which may value hard work and savings (see Kapstein 2002, p.8).

The problem with Rawls's approach is that it answers the question by assuming away the problem. Indeed there is no case for redistribution among societies that are very similar in terms of their ideology and income. But that is not an interesting question, for no one would disagree with Rawls's statement. The interesting question is whether there are moral grounds for redistribution between *different* (rich and poor) societies. There, Rawls might at most accept that with regard to the societies that are striving to become "decent," the rich nations may have some responsibility to help them achieve this goal. But nothing more; and surely, it would seem, no responsibility toward those societies that are not "decent." Thus, for example, most of Africa, and large chunks of Asia and the Middle East, would be exempt from any sympathy or help because their governments (and by implication, their societies) are neither liberal and decent nor apparently striving to be so. It is a very harsh logic indeed that assimilates societies to governments: for if a government is a tyranny, it does not mean that the people do not strive to have a decent society. They just have no way to demonstrate that wish.

Kapstein (2002) identifies four approaches to the issue of international economic justice: that of people concerned with winners and losers within national borders; those concerned with widening international gaps (as between the "North" and the "South"); cosmopolitans concerned with increasing gaps among individuals in the world, and proceduralists who are not interested in outcomes (the growing gap) but in whether the rules are fair and are being observed. The second and the third approaches are more sympathetic to a redistribution at the world scale even if their starting points are different (countries vs. individuals). The first, which is basically Rawls's approach, ignores the problem of global inequality, while the proceduralists or libertarians are unconcerned with it. Thus, according to the proceduralists, the whole concept of "social justice" is devoid of a meaning. As Hayek writes in *Law, Legislation and Liberty* (1976, 2:69–75), the only issue is whether or not the rules have been accepted and followed. There is no justice in the outcome of a game of chess. We only ask whether the rules have been observed or not; a "better" player might lose because he made a silly mistake.[136] But let us use the game of soccer rather than chess as the metaphor for economic life. Hayek's contention immediately crumbles since it becomes apparent that whether a rule was observed or not is often very fuzzy and a matter of dispute: "did the ball pass the goal line?" "Was the player off-side?" "Did the ball touch the player's hand?" While a rule, in the abstract, is precise (we know what the rule of off-side is and that players are not allowed to touch ball by hand), whether that rule has been obeyed or not is a matter of judgment. Thus in a real life, even if the rules are accepted by all the players (a situation that is far from obvious in economic life), their observance is a matter of dispute. Perhaps if real life were more like chess than soccer, proceduralists might have a stronger point. But it is not, and, since procedures (rules) themselves are neither unanimously accepted, nor can they always be thought fair (because they reflect the power of those who create them), proceduralists' case boils down to a plea to preserve the status quo: the existing distribution of power and money.

To the proceduralists, the very concept of inequality is suspect. Let is suppose that three people have each an income of $100. After one year, due to the differences in work effort and luck, they find themselves with incomes of $120, $150, and $200. Inequality is much greater now. But why should it matter at all, they ask, given that everyone is better off? It is a Pareto improvement, and if the person with $120 complains of inequality, it is because she must be envious. Or is it so? Could what the rich person calls "envy" be something that a poor person would simply deem lack of fairness? Do not proceduralists assume the issue away when they implicitly claim that (i) the original distribution of endowments is fair, and (ii) that the entire difference in outcomes is explained by the differences in work effort and luck? In real world, the initial endowments of $100 might be due, in one case, to inheritance, in another to theft, and in the third to savings. Let then the person who inherited his $100 double it in the next period, and the one who stole his first $100 end up with $150. Wouldn't the person who worked hard and ended up with $120 complain of such an outcome? Would we consider it fair? If I steal $100, put it on the right number in the casino, and make $1000, what should I be expected to pay back: the initially stolen amount or all of it? As soon as these questions are asked, that is, when the fairness of initial endowments is questioned, distribution issues arise even if—and it is a big "if"—the rules of the game are observed.

But going back to the issue of what defines a "community" and arguing that with globalization its size is likely to expand, thus leading, sooner or later, to the acceptance of redistributive transfers, we face practical issues as how to best implement such a system. That some systemic redistribution, in contrast to the current system of bilateral and voluntary contributions from rich countries, will eventually take place is a view that is now being shared by the World Bank. Its chief economist François Bourguignon noted that there was convergence with the alter-globalists on certain topics including the creation of international taxes—whether it be a Tobin tax on financial flows, or a tax on plane tickets, on $CO_2$ emission, or on weapon exports.[137] This convergence, if indeed real, represents a major step forward.

If a global system of redistribution is implemented, it must observe in its functioning the same rules that "regulate" transfers within nation-states: the requirement that transfers be globally progressive, that is, flow from richer households to poorer. This is important not only because of welfare considerations, but for political economy reasons as well. Rich countries and their voters are often loath to increase international aid if they cannot be reasonably sure that the money paid by their taxpayers will not end up lining up the pockets of rich people living in poor countries. Obviously, one way of ensuring that this does not happen is to improve pro-poor targeting of the projects undertaken with aid money and to improve accountability and governance in the recipient countries. But the distribution effects of the projects are difficult to estimate, and take a long time to be known. Deciding behind the "veil of ignorance" regarding the likely effect of the projects, the case can be made that international aid should favor countries that are poor and where income distribution is relatively equal. The reason is that in such countries, as we have seen in the examples given in chapter 10, transfers are less likely to be globally regressive: income distributions of the donor and the recipient country do not overlap at all, or almost at all, and regardless of the quality of the project, globally regressive transfers are unlikely.

Translated in terms of the eligibility requirement that the poor countries have to satisfy to qualify for soft loans (as, e.g., those given by the World Bank affiliate, the International Development Agency, IDA), this means that countries will, in addition to being poor, also need to be relatively egalitarian. Thus, instead of the GDP per capita (or in addition to GDP per capita) one could use the ranking of the country's top decile in world income distribution. Another possibility would be to "correct" GDP per capita by the ratio between the mean and median income. This ratio is normally greater than 1, and it is the greater the more unequal the distribution. Take the examples of Nigeria and Bangladesh. The two countries have approximately the same average income, but Nigeria's income distribution is much more unequal. The mean-to-median ratio in Nigeria is 1.7 vs. 1.2 in Bangladesh. Multiplying GDP per capita with this ratio will therefore "blow up" Nigeria's income, making it more difficult to be eligible for IDA loans. This would penalize countries with very rich top-income groups and help those where even the rich are poor by world standards. The argument to help the latter is that the likelihood of a globally regressive transfer is minimal. The argument against helping the first group of countries is that their own rich should be willing to share some of their gains with the poor before expecting the rest of the world to contribute.[138]

We shall end with one statistical, but very important, point. The current analysis and the pitfalls and issues we had to face in assembling disparate household survey data also highlight the need to undertake a worldwide household income or expenditure survey. This seems a small point compared to ideological issues whether some redistribution at all should take place, or to the practical issues of what to tax and whether a global taxing authority is acceptable. Indeed, one can envisage a worldwide household survey without any of the accompanying redistributive measures. And such a survey would be worth undertaking for the reasons of better knowledge of the socioeconomic situation of the world even if no policy changes would follow from it. But I believe that this is unlikely: once a general survey of living conditions is undertaken, and vast disparities in income and wealth become more apparent, the pressure to redress some of them will be unstoppable. Thus what may seem at first a purely technical or statistical exercise will have clear policy repercussions.

Technical obstacles to conducting such a survey are minimal. The sampling, the design, the enumerators—all these problems are solvable. The obstacles are, of course, the cost of such a survey (and the agency that would conduct it) and, more importantly, the political problems. These problems range from probable unwillingness of some governments to allow an international organization, and hence foreign-controlled enumerators and analysts, to get a first-hand insight into the welfare and conditions of the life of their people. Powerful players may be arrayed against such a survey. They may cover a large part of the political spectrum: from the oppressive governments that are unwilling to share the results of their own surveys, to the governments of the rich countries that may view a worldwide survey as a step toward eventual international policy in favor of redistribution of income, to the liberals who would be opposed to it because of confidentiality reasons. One can add to it the nationalist right-wing forces who would regard it as a further encroachment of national sovereignty by international organizations. Yet, I believe, that once the idea of such a survey takes hold, and it can be shown that the technical problems are not insuperable, there would be relentless pressure to conduct it—eventually.[139]

And ditto for the redistribution on the global scale. We are bound to move toward global community and global democracy, and once we do, many of the functions of today's national governments—including dealing with extreme cases of inequality and poverty—will be taken over by new global institutions. The road to that goal will be long and arduous. One need simply glance at the "democratic deficit" experienced by the European Union. How much more difficult it would be to create such institutions on the global level! Yet, if we consider the path that has been traversed in the past two centuries—from a consortium of powers ruling the world without bothering to consult anyone else and bent on the sheer exploitation of the weak, to today's host of international institutions and the willingness, however begrudgingly, to share wealth—and if we project these developments into the future, there is, I think, little doubt that further inclusion of all peoples and globalization of decision-making awaits us there. At that point, issues like global inequality will acquire almost the same importance that national inequality nowadays has in national political discussions. It will be indeed an issue whose time has come.

# Appendix 1

List of Countries and Years for Which GDP Per Capita (in international dollars of equal purchasing power parity) Is Available

| | *Code* | *Country* | *Period* | | *Code* | *Country* | *Period* |
|---|---|---|---|---|---|---|---|
| 1 | AGO | Angola | 1960–2000 | 41 | FJI | Fiji | 1960–2000 |
| 2 | ALB | Albania | 1980–2000 | 42 | FRA | France | 1950–2000 |
| 3 | ARG | Argentina | 1950–2000 | 43 | GAB | Gabon | 1960–2000 |
| 4 | ARM | Armenia | 1958–2000 | 44 | GBR | United Kingdom | 1950–2000 |
| 5 | AUS | Australia | 1950–2000 | 45 | GHA | Ghana | 1955–2000 |
| 6 | AUT | Austria | 1950–2000 | 46 | GIN | Guinea | 1959–2000 |
| 7 | BEL | Belgium | 1950–2000 | 47 | GMB | Gambia, The | 1960–2000 |
| 8 | BEN | Benin | 1960–2000 | 48 | GNB | Guinea-Bissau | 1960–2000 |
| 9 | BFA | Burkina Faso | 1960–2000 | 49 | GRC | Greece | 1950–2000 |
| 10 | BGD | Bangladesh | 1960–2000 | 50 | GTM | Guatemala | 1950–2000 |
| 11 | BGR | Bulgaria | 1950–2000 | 51 | GUY | Guyana | 1950–2000 |
| 12 | BHS | Bahamas, The | 1960–2000 | 52 | HKG | Hong Kong, China | 1960–2000 |
| 13 | BLR | Belarus | 1958–2000 | 53 | HND | Honduras | 1950–2000 |
| 14 | BOL | Bolivia | 1950–2000 | 54 | HRV | Croatia | 1952–2000 |
| 15 | BRA | Brazil | 1950–2000 | 55 | HTI | Haiti | 1960–2000 |
| 16 | BRB | Barbados | 1960–2000 | 56 | HUN | Hungary | 1950–2000 |
| 17 | BWA | Botswana | 1960–2000 | 57 | IDN | Indonesia | 1954–2000 |
| 18 | CAF | Central African Rep. | 1960–2000 | 58 | IND | India | 1950–2000 |
| 19 | CAN | Canada | 1950–2000 | 59 | IRL | Ireland | 1950–2000 |
| 20 | CHE | Switzerland | 1950–2000 | 60 | IRN | Iran, Islamic Rep. | 1955–97 |
| 21 | CHL | Chile | 1950–2000 | 61 | ISR | Israel | 1950–2000 |
| 22 | CHN | China | 1952–2000 | 62 | ITA | Italy | 1950–2000 |
| 23 | CIV | Cote d'Ivoire | 1960–2000 | 63 | JAM | Jamaica | 1953–2000 |
| 24 | CMR | Cameroon | 1960–2000 | 64 | JOR | Jordan | 1954–2000 |
| 25 | COG | Congo, Rep. | 1960–2000 | 65 | JPN | Japan | 1950–2000 |
| 26 | COL | Colombia | 1950–2000 | 66 | KAZ | Kazakhstan | 1958–2000 |
| 27 | CRI | Costa Rica | 1950–2000 | 67 | KEN | Kenya | 1950–2000 |
| 28 | CSK | Czechoslovakia | 1960–92 | 68 | KGZ | Kyrgyz Rep. | 1958–2000 |
| 29 | CZE | Czech Republic | 1984–2000 | 69 | KHM | Cambodia | 1987–2000 |
| 30 | DEU | Germany[a] | 1950–2000 | 70 | KOR | Korea, Rep. | 1953–2000 |
| 31 | DJI | Djibouti | 1971–2000 | 71 | KWT | Kuwait | 1962–96 |
| 32 | DNK | Denmark | 1950–2000 | 72 | LAO | Lao PDR | 1984–2000 |
| 33 | DOM | Dominican Rep. | 1950–2000 | 73 | LKA | Sri Lanka | 1950–2000 |
| 34 | DZA | Algeria | 1960–2000 | 74 | LSO | Lesotho | 1960–2000 |
| 35 | ECU | Ecuador | 1950–2000 | 75 | LTU | Lithuania | 1958–2000 |
| 36 | EGY | Egypt, Arab Rep. | 1950–2000 | 76 | LUX | Luxembourg | 1950–2000 |
| 37 | ESP | Spain | 1950–2000 | 77 | LVA | Latvia | 1958–2000 |
| 38 | EST | Estonia | 1958–2000 | 78 | MAR | Morocco | 1951–2000 |
| 39 | ETH | Ethiopia | 1950–2000 | 79 | MDA | Moldova | 1960–2000 |
| 40 | FIN | Finland | 1950–2000 | 80 | MDG | Madagascar | 1960–2000 |

**APPENDIX 1.** (*cont.*)

| | Code | Country | Period | | Code | Country | Period |
|---|---|---|---|---|---|---|---|
| 81 | MEX | Mexico | 1950–2000 | 112 | SLE | Sierra Leone | 1960–2000 |
| 82 | MLI | Mali | 1960–2000 | 113 | SLV | El Salvador | 1950–2000 |
| 83 | MNG | Mongolia | 1981–2000 | 114 | SUN | USSR | 1950–90 |
| 84 | MOZ | Mozambique | 1960–2000 | 115 | SVK | Slovak Republic | 1984–2000 |
| 85 | MRT | Mauritania | 1960–2000 | 116 | SVN | Slovenia | 1952–2000 |
| 86 | MUS | Mauritius | 1950–2000 | 117 | SWE | Sweden | 1950–2000 |
| 87 | MWI | Malawi | 1950–2000 | 118 | SYC | Seychelles | 1960–2000 |
| 88 | MYS | Malaysia | 1954–2000 | 119 | TCD | Chad | 1960–2000 |
| 89 | NER | Niger | 1960–2000 | 120 | TGO | Togo | 1960–2000 |
| 90 | NGA | Nigeria | 1951–2000 | 121 | THA | Thailand | 1950–2000 |
| 91 | NIC | Nicaragua | 1950–2000 | 122 | TKM | Turkmenistan | 1958–2000 |
| 92 | NLD | Netherlands | 1950–2000 | 123 | TTO | Trinidad & Tobago | 1951–2000 |
| 93 | NOR | Norway | 1950–2000 | 124 | TUN | Tunisia | 1961–2000 |
| 94 | NPL | Nepal | 1958–2000 | 125 | TUR | Turkey | 1950–2000 |
| 95 | NZL | New Zealand | 1950–2000 | 126 | TWN | Taiwan, China | 1951–2000 |
| 96 | PAK | Pakistan | 1950–2000 | 127 | TZA | Tanzania | 1960–2000 |
| 97 | PAN | Panama | 1951–2000 | 128 | UGA | Uganda | 1950–2000 |
| 98 | PER | Peru | 1950–2000 | 129 | UKR | Ukraine | 1958–2000 |
| 99 | PHL | Philippines | 1950–2000 | 130 | URY | Uruguay | 1950–2000 |
| 100 | PNG | Papua New Guinea | 1960–2000 | 131 | USA | United States | 1950–2000 |
| 101 | POL | Poland | 1950–2000 | 132 | UZB | Uzbekistan | 1965–2000 |
| 102 | PRI | Puerto Rico | 1950–98 | 133 | VEN | Venezuela, Rep. | 1950–2000 |
| 103 | PRT | Portugal | 1952–2000 | 134 | VNM | Vietnam | 1984–2000 |
| 104 | PRY | Paraguay | 1950–2000 | 135 | YEM | Yemen, Rep. | 1990–2000 |
| 105 | ROM | Romania | 1950–2000 | 136 | YUF | Yugoslavia | 1952–90 |
| 106 | RUS | Russian Federation | 1958–2000 | 137 | YUG | Serbia/Montenegro | 1952–98 |
| 107 | RWA | Rwanda | 1951–2000 | 138 | ZAF | South Africa | 1950–2000 |
| 108 | SAU | Saudi Arabia | 1960–2000 | 139 | ZAR | Congo, Dem. Rep. | 1950–98 |
| 109 | SDN | Sudan | 1956–2000 | 140 | ZMB | Zambia | 1951–2000 |
| 110 | SEN | Senegal | 1960–2000 | 141 | ZWE | Zimbabwe | 1950–2000 |
| 111 | SGP | Singapore | 1960–2000 | | | | |

[a]Until 1991 only West Germany. From then on, unified Germany.

*Note:* For the former Soviet republics, data for 1959, 1961, 1962, and 1963 are not available.

# Appendix 2

## The Effect on the Gini of "Stacking Up" Regions

We need to clarify how in general the addition of a country (or several countries) affects the Concept 1 Gini. Let us suppose that we add a new country, $l$. (I use the subscript $l$ to indicate that its income may lie somewhere in the middle of income distribution.) Let the Gini before a new country was added be

$$G = \frac{1}{\mu_1}\frac{1}{n^2}\sum_{i}^{n}\sum_{j>i}^{n}(y_j - y_i). \tag{A1}$$

where $i, j \neq l$.

The new Gini G* becomes

$$G^* \frac{1}{\mu_1{}^*}\frac{1}{(n+1)^2}\sum_{i}^{n}\sum_{j>i}^{n}(y_j - y_i) + \frac{1}{\mu_1{}^*}\frac{1}{(n+1)^2}\sum_{i \neq l}^{n}|\, y_i - y_l \,| \tag{A2}$$

The second term on the right-hand side of equation (A2) must be positive. However, $G^*$ is not necessarily greater than $G$ because the larger sample size $(n + 1)$ reduces the first term on the RHS, and so might a possible increase in mean income. Since the new and the old mean are related as

$$\mu_1{}^* = \frac{1}{n+1}\left(\sum_{i \neq l} y_i + y_l\right) = \frac{n}{n+1}\mu_1 + \frac{1}{n+1}y_l = \frac{n\mu_1 + y_l}{n+1},$$

we can rewrite equation (A2):

$$\begin{aligned} G^* &= \frac{1}{(n\mu_1 + y_l)(n+1)}\sum_{i}^{n}\sum_{j>i}^{n}(y_j - y_i) + \frac{1}{(n\mu_1 + y_l)(n+1)}\sum_{i \neq l}|\, y_i - y_l \,| = \\ &= \frac{1}{n^2\mu_1 + y_l(n+1) + n\mu_1}\sum_{i}^{n}\sum_{j>i}^{n}(y_j - y_i) \\ &+ \frac{1}{n^2\mu_1 + y_l(n+1) + n\mu_1}\sum_{i \neq l}|\, y_i - y_l \,| . \end{aligned} \tag{A3}$$

The first term in (A3) will always be smaller than $G$ because $y_1 (n + 1) + n\mu > 0$.[140] Depending on how much smaller than the initial G, and how great the second term, the new Gini $G^*$ may go either up or down. Therefore, the addition of a new country or region may move the Gini in either direction.

# Appendix 3

GDP Per Capita in 2000 vs. the Highest GDP Per Capita Achieved by the Country (period 1950–2000)

| | *At the Peak in 2000* | *Less Than 10% Below the Peak* | *Between 10% and 30% Below the Peak* | *More Than 30% Below the Peak* |
|---|---|---|---|---|
| Africa | Botswana | Burkina Faso (1999) | Algeria (1985) | Cameroon (1986) |
| | Egypt | Ethiopia (1980) | Central African Rep. (1977) | Cote d'Ivoire (1978) |
| | Mauritius | Gambia (1984) | Ghana (1971) | Djibouti (1971) |
| | Sudan | Guinea (1999) | Guinea-Bissau (1997) | Gabon (1976) |
| | Tunisia | Kenya (1990) | Mali (1979) | Madagascar (1971) |
| | | Lesotho (1997) | Nigeria (1977) | Niger (1963) |
| | | Malawi (1979) | Senegal (1961) | Sierra Leone (1980) |
| | | Mauritania (1970) | Rwanda (1983) | Zambia (1955) |
| | | Morocco (1998) | Zimbabwe (1991) | |
| | | South Africa (1981) | | |
| | | Tanzania (1976) | | |
| | | Uganda (1969) | | |
| Number of countries | 5 | 12 | 9 | 8 |
| Percentage of countries | 15 | 35 | 26 | 24 |
| Average level | 1 | 0.952 | 0.821 | 0.523 |
| Overall average level | 0.823 | | | |
| Asia | Bangladesh | Japan (1997) | Indonesia (1997) | |
| | China | Malaysia (1997) | Jordan (1986) | |
| | Hong Kong | Philippines (1982) | Papua New Guinea (1994) | |
| | India | Yemen (1990) | Fiji (1996) | |
| | Lao PDR | Thailand (1996) | | |

**APPENDIX 3.** *(cont.)*
GDP Per Capita in 2000 vs. the Highest GDP Per Capita Achieved by the Country (period 1950–2000)

| | *At the Peak in 2000* | *Less Than 10% Below the Peak* | *Between 10% and 30% Below the Peak* | *More Than 30% Below the Peak* |
|---|---|---|---|---|
| | Nepal<br>Pakistan<br>Sri Lanka<br>Singapore<br>S. Korea<br>Taiwan<br>Vietnam | | | |
| Number of countries | 12 | 5 | 4 | 0 |
| Percentage of countries | 57 | 24 | 19 | |
| Average level | 1 | 0.969 | 0.857 | |
| Overall average level | 0.965 | | | |
| Latin America and the Caribbean | Barbados<br>Brazil<br>Chile<br>Dominican R.<br>Mexico<br>Panama | Argentina (1998)<br>Bolivia (1978)<br>Colombia (1997)<br>Costa Rica (1999)<br>Ecuador (1997)<br>Guatemala (1980)<br>Guyana (1976)<br>Honduras (1979)<br>Peru (1981)<br>Trinidad & Tob. (1982) | El Salvador (1978)<br>Jamaica (1972)<br>Paraguay (1981)<br>Venezuela (1977) | Nicaragua (1977) |

| | | | | |
|---|---|---|---|---|
| Number of countries | 6 | 10 | 4 | 1 |
| Percentage of countries | 29 | 47 | 19 | 5 |
| Average level | 1 | 0.945 | 0.798 | 0.448 |
| Overall average level | 0.909 | | | |
| Eastern Europe/FSU | Poland | Czech (1989) | Belarus (1989) | Armenia (1985) |
| | Hungary | Estonia (1990) | Bulgaria (1988) | Kyrgyz Rep. (1989) |
| | Slovak Rep. | | Kazakhstan (1988) | Latvia (1989) |
| | Slovenia | | Mongolia (1989) | Lithuania (1988) |
| | | | | Moldova (1989) |
| | | | | Romania (1986) |
| | | | | Russia (1989) |
| | | | | Turkmenistan (1975) |
| | | | | Ukraine (1989) |
| | | | | Uzbekistan (1983) |
| | | | | Serbia/MN (1981) |
| Number of countries | 4 | 2 | 4 | 11 |
| Percentage of countries | 19 | 10 | 19 | 52 |
| Average level | 1 | 0.917 | 0.790 | 0.534 |
| Overall average level | 0.708 | | | |
| WENAO | Australia | Turkey (1998) | | |
| | Austria | | | |
| | Belgium | | | |
| | Canada | | | |
| | Denmark | | | |
| | Finland | | | |
| | France | | | |

**APPENDIX 3.** *(cont.)*

GDP Per Capita in 2000 vs. the Highest GDP Per Capita Achieved by the Country (period 1950–2000)

| | *At the Peak in 2000* | *Less Than 10% Below the Peak* | *Between 10% and 30% Below the Peak* | *More than 30% Below the Peak* |
|---|---|---|---|---|
| | Germany | | | |
| | Greece | | | |
| | Ireland | | | |
| | Israel | | | |
| | Italy | | | |
| | Luxembourg | | | |
| | Netherlands | | | |
| | New Zealand | | | |
| | Norway | | | |
| | Portugal | | | |
| | Spain | | | |
| | Sweden | | | |
| | Switzerland | | | |
| | UK | | | |
| | US | | | |
| Number of countries | 22 | 1 | 0 | 0 |
| Percentage of countries | 96 | 4 | | |
| Average level | 1 | 0.986 | — | — |
| Overall average level | 0.9993 | | | |

*Note:* The year of the peak is given in the brackets. Average level calculated with respect is the peak (=1). The average level of 0.9 means that the unweighted average GDP per capita of the countries in the year 2000 is 10% below the highest ever achieved GDP per capita.

# Appendix 4

The Year When the Country Has for the First Time Achieved Its 2000 Level of GDP Per Capita

| *Region* | *At the Peak in 2000* | *Less than 20 Years before 2000* | *Between 20 and 40 years before 2000* | *Before 1960 (or the first year when data are available)* |
|---|---|---|---|---|
| Africa | Botswana<br>Egypt<br>Mauritius<br>Sudan<br>Tunisia | Burkina Faso (1999)<br>Guinea (1999)<br>Morocco (1998)<br>Lesotho (1996)<br>South Africa (1980) | Djibouti (1971)<br>Guinea-Bissau (1964)<br>Kenya (1979)<br>Ethiopia (1979)<br>Nigeria (1970)<br>Tanzania (1971)<br>Cote d'Ivoire (1968)<br>Mauritania (1970)<br>Algeria (1977)<br>Cameroon (1978)<br>Gabon (1974)<br>Zimbabwe (1971)<br>Gambia (1978)<br>Malawi (1978) | Mali (1960)<br>Central African Republic (1960)<br>Madagascar (1960)<br>Niger (1960)<br>Senegal (1960)<br>Sierra Leone (1960)<br>Zambia (1960)<br>Ghana (1957)<br>Rwanda (1951)<br>Uganda (1951) |
| Asia | Bangladesh<br>China<br>India<br>Lao PDR<br>Sri Lanka<br>Taiwan<br>Vietnam<br>Nepal<br>Singapore<br>Pakistan<br>Hong Kong<br>South Korea | Yemen (1990)<br>Japan (1997)<br>Malaysia (1997)<br>Indonesia (1997)<br>Thailand (1996) | Papua New Guinea (1972)<br>Fiji (1979)<br>Jordan (1979)<br>Philippines (1979) | |
| Latin America and the Caribbean | Barbados<br>Chile<br>Dominican R.<br>Panama<br>Brazil<br>Mexico | Argentina (1998)<br>Costa Rica (1999)<br>Colombia (1994)<br>Trinidad & Tobago (1982) | Ecuador (1977)<br>Paraguay (1979)<br>Bolivia (1974)<br>Guatemala (1979)<br>Guyana (1975)<br>Honduras (1978)<br>El Salvador (1974)<br>Jamaica (1968)<br>Peru (1973) | Nicaragua (1950)<br>Venezuela (1955) |

**APPENDIX 4.** (*cont.*)

| *Region* | *At the Peak in 2000* | *Less than 20 Years before 2000* | *Between 20 and 40 years before 2000* | *Before 1960 (or the first year when data are available)* |
|---|---|---|---|---|
| Eastern Europe/ FSU | Poland<br>Hungary<br>Slovakia<br>Slovenia | Belarus (1985)<br>Bulgaria (1984)<br>Czech (1986)<br>Estonia (1988)<br>Mongolia (1981) | Armenia (1968)<br>Kazakhstan (1970)<br>Kyrgyz (1967)<br>Latvia (1976)<br>Lithuania (1972)<br>Romania (1976)<br>Russia (1973)<br>Uzbekistan (1971)<br>Serbia/MN (1968) | Moldova (1964)<br>Turkmenistan (1958)<br>Ukraine (1968) |
| WENAO | Australia<br>Austria<br>Belgium<br>Canada<br>Denmark<br>Finland<br>France<br>Greece<br>Ireland<br>Israel<br>Italy<br>Luxembourg<br>Netherlands<br>Norway<br>Portugal<br>Spain<br>Sweden<br>UK<br>USA<br>Germany<br>New Zealand<br>Switzerland | Turkey (1998) | | |

# Appendix 5

Comparison of Different Studies of Global (Concept 3) Income Inequality
General Approach and Results

| | *Period* | *Years* | *Results* | *Gini Values* | *Source of Distribution Data* | *Mean Income* | *PPPs Used* | *Number of Countries* | *Main Problems* |
|---|---|---|---|---|---|---|---|---|---|
| Milanovic (this volume) | 1988–98 | 1988<br>1993<br>1998 | Inequality increases then declines | 63 ('88)<br>66 ('93)<br>65 ('98) | HS data | HS mean | EKS (World Bank) | 86 (common sample) to 122 total (full sample) | Mixes X and Y. |
| Bourguignon-Morrison (1999) | 1820–1990 | 1950<br>1960<br>1970<br>1980<br>1992 | Inequality increases | 64 ('50)<br>64 ('50)<br>65 ('70)<br>66 ('80)<br>66 ('92) | Various sources: Morrisson, HS etc. | NA (GDP per capita from Maddison 1995) | Geary-Khamis (Maddison) | 33 country groups | Combines HS data and NA.<br>Mixes X and Y.<br>"Representative" countries used<br>Very few data points. |
| Sala-i-Martin (2002) | 1970–98 | All | Inequality slightly increases then declines | 63 ('70)<br>64 ('80)<br>63 ('90)<br>61 ('98) | Quintiles from HSs (D-S, WDI) | NA (GDP per capita from PWT 6.1) | Geary-Khamis (PWT) | (A) 68 countries with more than 1 income share observation; (B) 29 countries with only 1 observation; (C) 28 countries with no data. Former USSR not included. | Very few data points (quintiles).<br>Extrapolates for country/years for which data are unavailable (86% of country/years).<br>Group C countries: all population assigned the same income.<br>Mixes HS data and NA.<br>Mixes Y and X data. |

**APPENDIX 5.** (*cont.*)

Comparison of Different Studies of Global (Concept 3) Income Inequality

General Approach and Results

| | *Period* | *Years* | *Results* | *Gini Values* | *Source of Distribution Data* | *Mean Income* | *PPPs Used* | *Number of Countries* | *Main Problems* |
|---|---|---|---|---|---|---|---|---|---|
| | | | | | | | | | Unclear how HH and per capita data from D-S are treated (mixed?). |
| Bhalla (2002) | 1950–2000 | All | Inequality increases then declines | 66 ('60) 69 ('80) 65 ('00) | Quintiles from HSs (D-S, WIDER and Milanovic) | NA (GDP per capita and personal consumption per capita from WDI and PWT 5.6) | Geary-Khamis | 136 (42 with three distributions, 66 with two, 28 with one distribution only) | Very few data points. Income distributions for three benchmark years only (1960, 1980 and 2000). For all other years (96% of country/years) assumes distribution to be unchanged. For countries with one distribution only, distribution is supposed to be the same for all fifty years. Mixes HS data and NA. |

| | | | | | | | | | |
|---|---|---|---|---|---|---|---|---|---|
| Dikhanov and Ward (2001) | 1970–99 | 1970 1980 1990 1999 | Inequality slightly increases | 67 (1970) 68 (1999) | Quintiles and Ginis from WIDER | NA (personal consumption expenditures per capita from World Bank) | EKS (World Bank) | 45 countries (but they are not always the same) | Combines HS data and NA. Mixes Y and X. |
| Dowrick and Akmal (2001) | 1980–93 | 1980 1993 | Inequality slightly increases | 70 ('80) 71 ('93) | Quintiles and Ginis from D-S | NA (GDP per capita) | Afriat (own calculations) | 47 countries with quintile data; unclear how many more are included | Combines HS data and NA. Unclear how Y and X are treated (mixed?). Unclear how HH and per capita data are treated (mixed?). |
| Sutcliffe (2003) | 1980–2000 | 1980 1990 2000 | Stable | 64 ('80) 63 ('90) 63 ('00) | Quintiles from HSs (D-S, WDI) | NA (GDP per capita from Maddison 2001 and WDI) | Geary-Khamis (Maddison and WDI) | 163 | Combines HS data and NA. Unclear how Y and X are treated (mixed?). |
| Chotikapanich et al. (1997) | 1980–90 | 1980 1985 1990 | Stable | 66 ('80) 65 ('85) 65 ('90) | D-S | NA (GDP per capita from PWT 5.6) | Geary-Khamis (PWT) | 36 | Combines HS data and NA. Unclear how HH and per capita data are treated (mixed?). |

**APPENDIX 5.** (*cont.*)
Comparison of Different Studies of Global (Concept 3) Income Inequality
General Approach and Results

| | *Period* | *Years* | *Results* | *Gini Values* | *Source of Distribution Data* | *Mean Income* | *PPPs Used* | *Number of Countries* | *Main Problems* |
|---|---|---|---|---|---|---|---|---|---|
| Schultz (1998) | 1960–89 | 1960 1970 1980 1989 | Increases then declines | [variance of logs] | D-S | NA (GDP per capita from PWT 5.5) | Geary-Khamis (PWT) | 56 from D-S. For other 64 countries inequality measures estimated. | Combines HS data and NA. Mixes Y and X. Unclear how HH and per capita data are treated (mixed?). Double approximation: variance of logs estimated from D-S quintiles; for countries without data, approximation based on regression |

*Notes:* DS = Deininger-Squire database. HH = households. HS = household survey. Milanovic: World income distribution available on http://www.worldbank.org/research/inequality/data.htm. NA = national accounts. PWT = Penn World Tables (different versions). WDI = World Development Indicators (from the World Bank). WIDER = WIDER database. X = expenditures or consumption. Y = income.

**APPENDIX 5.** *(cont.)*
Approximations to National Distributions

| | *Approximation of Individual Country Distributions* | *How Approximation is Done* | *Approximation of Missing Country/Years* | *If no Distribution Data at All* | *Combines HS and NA* |
|---|---|---|---|---|---|
| Milanovic (2002) | No | No approximation; each point is one observation | Take the closest year | Country not included | No |
| Bourguignon and Morrisson (1999/2002) | No | No approximation; each point is one observation | Take the closest year and country grouping | Take the closest country | Yes (applies GDP per capita to distributions) |
| Sala-i-Martin (2002) | Yes, using D-S database (quintiles) | Kernel estimates (smoothing) for each country/year | Linear trend | Mean income used (inequality = 0) | Yes (applies GDP per capita to distributions) |
| Bhalla (2002) | Yes, using D-S, WIDER and Milanovic database | Single parameter Lorenz curve estimate | Same distribution holds for all years | Country not included | Yes (applies GDP or personal consumption per capita to distributions) |

**APPENDIX 5.** (*cont.*)
Approximations to National Distributions

| | *Approximation of Individual Country Distributions* | *How Approximation is Done* | *Approximation of Missing Country/Years* | *If no Distribution Data at All* | *Combines HS and NA* |
|---|---|---|---|---|---|
| Dowrick and Akmal (2001) | Yes, using D-S data base (quintiles and Ginis) | No approximation if quintiles available; If Gini only available Chotikapanich approximation of the Lorenz curve used | Take the closest year | Country not included | Yes (applies GDP per capita to distributions) |
| Dikhanov and Ward (2001) | Yes, using WIDER data (Ginis) | Using "quasi-exact distribution rendering" | Take the closest year and country | Country not included | Yes (applies personal consumption per capita to distributions) |
| Sutcliffe (2003) | No | No approximation; each point is one observation | Distribution the same as in previous years | Mean income used (inequality = 0) | Yes (applies GDP per capita to distributions) |
| Schultz (1998) | Yes, using D-S data base (quintiles) | Variance of log estimated from D-S quintiles | Regression | Use regressions to estimate log variance | Yes (applies GDP per capita to distributions) |
| Chotikapanich et al. (1997) | Yes, using D-S data base (Ginis) | Lognormal distribution estimated based on mean income and Gini | Take the closest year | Country not Included | Yes (applies GDP per capita to distributions) |

# Appendix 6

Various Measures of International Inequality, 1950–2000

| *Relative Mean Deviation* | | | *Coefficient of Variation* | | |
|---|---|---|---|---|---|
| *Year* | *World Weighted* | *World Unweighted* | *Year* | *World Weighted* | *World Unweighted* |
| 1950 | 0.446 | 0.340 | 1950 | 1.116 | 0.840 |
| 1951 | 0.446 | 0.350 | 1951 | 1.130 | 0.882 |
| 1952 | 0.523 | 0.350 | 1952 | 1.419 | 0.900 |
| 1953 | 0.515 | 0.348 | 1953 | 1.399 | 0.896 |
| 1954 | 0.510 | 0.351 | 1954 | 1.377 | 0.894 |
| 1955 | 0.508 | 0.347 | 1955 | 1.374 | 0.891 |
| 1956 | 0.507 | 0.352 | 1956 | 1.362 | 0.906 |
| 1957 | 0.505 | 0.346 | 1957 | 1.346 | 0.890 |
| 1958 | 0.496 | 0.344 | 1958 | 1.316 | 0.884 |
| 1959 | 0.498 | 0.344 | 1959 | 1.315 | 0.888 |
| 1960 | 0.478 | 0.350 | 1960 | 1.281 | 0.956 |
| 1961 | 0.507 | 0.359 | 1961 | 1.307 | 0.957 |
| 1962 | 0.511 | 0.361 | 1962 | 1.330 | 0.959 |
| 1963 | 0.511 | 0.361 | 1963 | 1.324 | 0.956 |
| 1964 | 0.514 | 0.365 | 1964 | 1.322 | 0.965 |
| 1965 | 0.488 | 0.354 | 1965 | 1.294 | 0.949 |
| 1966 | 0.488 | 0.353 | 1966 | 1.299 | 0.947 |
| 1967 | 0.490 | 0.351 | 1967 | 1.300 | 0.940 |
| 1968 | 0.494 | 0.352 | 1968 | 1.305 | 0.939 |
| 1969 | 0.493 | 0.356 | 1969 | 1.293 | 0.945 |
| 1970 | 0.487 | 0.355 | 1970 | 1.266 | 0.932 |
| 1971 | 0.486 | 0.352 | 1971 | 1.264 | 0.923 |
| 1972 | 0.490 | 0.352 | 1972 | 1.275 | 0.923 |
| 1973 | 0.490 | 0.355 | 1973 | 1.274 | 0.928 |
| 1974 | 0.488 | 0.351 | 1974 | 1.259 | 0.914 |
| 1975 | 0.483 | 0.349 | 1975 | 1.243 | 0.899 |
| 1976 | 0.486 | 0.352 | 1976 | 1.256 | 0.898 |
| 1977 | 0.484 | 0.351 | 1977 | 1.256 | 0.896 |
| 1978 | 0.482 | 0.350 | 1978 | 1.258 | 0.894 |
| 1979 | 0.484 | 0.354 | 1979 | 1.263 | 0.902 |
| 1980 | 0.480 | 0.356 | 1980 | 1.248 | 0.907 |
| 1981 | 0.479 | 0.356 | 1981 | 1.248 | 0.906 |
| 1982 | 0.474 | 0.355 | 1982 | 1.234 | 0.903 |
| 1983 | 0.473 | 0.358 | 1983 | 1.236 | 0.913 |
| 1984 | 0.473 | 0.362 | 1984 | 1.248 | 0.925 |

**APPENDIX 6.** (*cont.*)

| Year | Relative Mean Deviation: World Weighted | Relative Mean Deviation: World Unweighted | Year | Coefficient of Variation: World Weighted | Coefficient of Variation: World Unweighted |
|---|---|---|---|---|---|
| 1985 | 0.469 | 0.365 | 1985 | 1.246 | 0.935 |
| 1986 | 0.467 | 0.368 | 1986 | 1.247 | 0.942 |
| 1987 | 0.464 | 0.374 | 1987 | 1.245 | 0.954 |
| 1988 | 0.463 | 0.378 | 1988 | 1.245 | 0.966 |
| 1989 | 0.464 | 0.381 | 1989 | 1.252 | 0.978 |
| 1990 | 0.464 | 0.386 | 1990 | 1.259 | 0.995 |
| 1991 | 0.459 | 0.392 | 1991 | 1.245 | 1.007 |
| 1992 | 0.455 | 0.405 | 1992 | 1.243 | 1.034 |
| 1993 | 0.449 | 0.412 | 1993 | 1.229 | 1.051 |
| 1994 | 0.447 | 0.418 | 1994 | 1.223 | 1.062 |
| 1995 | 0.440 | 0.419 | 1995 | 1.209 | 1.063 |
| 1996 | 0.436 | 0.419 | 1996 | 1.200 | 1.060 |
| 1997 | 0.433 | 0.421 | 1997 | 1.199 | 1.063 |
| 1998 | 0.432 | 0.422 | 1998 | 1.204 | 1.070 |
| 1999 | 0.430 | 0.425 | 1999 | 1.199 | 1.083 |
| 2000 | 0.426 | 0.428 | 2000 | 1.193 | 1.097 |

| Year | Standard Deviation of Logs: World Weighted | Standard Deviation of Logs: World Unweighted | Year | Gini Coefficient: World Weighted | Gini Coefficient: World Unweighted |
|---|---|---|---|---|---|
| 1950 | 1.099 | 0.882 | 1950 | 0.524 | 0.439 |
| 1951 | 1.095 | 0.869 | 1951 | 0.530 | 0.449 |
| 1952 | 1.311 | 0.877 | 1952 | 0.569 | 0.451 |
| 1953 | 1.257 | 0.858 | 1953 | 0.562 | 0.448 |
| 1954 | 1.231 | 0.860 | 1954 | 0.561 | 0.450 |
| 1955 | 1.235 | 0.855 | 1955 | 0.563 | 0.446 |
| 1956 | 1.208 | 0.861 | 1956 | 0.559 | 0.452 |
| 1957 | 1.213 | 0.863 | 1957 | 0.557 | 0.448 |
| 1958 | 1.156 | 0.859 | 1958 | 0.546 | 0.447 |
| 1959 | 1.154 | 0.861 | 1959 | 0.546 | 0.449 |
| 1960 | 1.114 | 0.858 | 1960 | 0.545 | 0.463 |
| 1961 | 1.237 | 0.911 | 1961 | 0.561 | 0.475 |
| 1962 | 1.269 | 0.918 | 1962 | 0.567 | 0.477 |
| 1963 | 1.257 | 0.928 | 1963 | 0.565 | 0.478 |
| 1964 | 1.241 | 0.939 | 1964 | 0.564 | 0.483 |
| 1965 | 1.189 | 0.896 | 1965 | 0.557 | 0.469 |
| 1966 | 1.178 | 0.901 | 1966 | 0.557 | 0.469 |
| 1967 | 1.207 | 0.907 | 1967 | 0.559 | 0.469 |
| 1968 | 1.245 | 0.916 | 1968 | 0.563 | 0.470 |

APPENDIX 6. *(cont.)*

| *Standard Deviation of Logs* | | | *Gini Coefficient* | | |
|---|---|---|---|---|---|
| *Year* | *World Weighted* | *World Unweighted* | *Year* | *World Weighted* | *World Unweighted* |
| 1969 | 1.221 | 0.923 | 1969 | 0.558 | 0.474 |
| 1970 | 1.185 | 0.928 | 1970 | 0.548 | 0.472 |
| 1971 | 1.187 | 0.927 | 1971 | 0.547 | 0.468 |
| 1972 | 1.209 | 0.942 | 1972 | 0.551 | 0.471 |
| 1973 | 1.214 | 0.956 | 1973 | 0.551 | 0.474 |
| 1974 | 1.218 | 0.954 | 1974 | 0.548 | 0.470 |
| 1975 | 1.194 | 0.951 | 1975 | 0.542 | 0.466 |
| 1976 | 1.224 | 0.960 | 1976 | 0.547 | 0.468 |
| 1977 | 1.213 | 0.963 | 1977 | 0.546 | 0.467 |
| 1978 | 1.193 | 0.967 | 1978 | 0.544 | 0.467 |
| 1979 | 1.198 | 0.982 | 1979 | 0.545 | 0.472 |
| 1980 | 1.180 | 0.989 | 1980 | 0.541 | 0.474 |
| 1981 | 1.166 | 0.987 | 1981 | 0.539 | 0.474 |
| 1982 | 1.145 | 0.986 | 1982 | 0.534 | 0.473 |
| 1983 | 1.126 | 0.998 | 1983 | 0.532 | 0.477 |
| 1984 | 1.117 | 1.028 | 1984 | 0.536 | 0.484 |
| 1985 | 1.102 | 1.032 | 1985 | 0.534 | 0.487 |
| 1986 | 1.092 | 1.044 | 1986 | 0.533 | 0.490 |
| 1987 | 1.080 | 1.054 | 1987 | 0.532 | 0.495 |
| 1988 | 1.064 | 1.058 | 1988 | 0.529 | 0.499 |
| 1989 | 1.060 | 1.064 | 1989 | 0.529 | 0.503 |
| 1990 | 1.051 | 1.069 | 1990 | 0.529 | 0.509 |
| 1991 | 1.040 | 1.070 | 1991 | 0.525 | 0.513 |
| 1992 | 1.026 | 1.080 | 1992 | 0.521 | 0.523 |
| 1993 | 1.009 | 1.089 | 1993 | 0.516 | 0.528 |
| 1994 | 1.001 | 1.108 | 1994 | 0.514 | 0.534 |
| 1995 | 0.989 | 1.107 | 1995 | 0.509 | 0.534 |
| 1996 | 0.984 | 1.112 | 1996 | 0.506 | 0.534 |
| 1997 | 0.985 | 1.123 | 1997 | 0.506 | 0.536 |
| 1998 | 0.979 | 1.129 | 1998 | 0.505 | 0.538 |
| 1999 | 0.970 | 1.133 | 1999 | 0.502 | 0.541 |
| 2000 | 0.973 | 1.137 | 2000 | 0.502 | 0.545 |

| *Mehran Measure* | | | *Piesch Measure* | | |
|---|---|---|---|---|---|
| *Year* | *World Weighted* | *World Unweighted* | *Year* | *World Weighted* | *World Unweighted* |
| 1950 | 0.563 | 0.590 | 1950 | 0.505 | 0.363 |
| 1951 | 0.573 | 0.594 | 1951 | 0.508 | 0.376 |
| 1952 | 0.571 | 0.593 | 1952 | 0.567 | 0.379 |

**APPENDIX 6.** (*cont.*)

| | *Mehran Measure* | | | *Piesch Measure* | |
|---|---|---|---|---|---|
| *Year* | *World Weighted* | *World Unweighted* | *Year* | *World Weighted* | *World Unweighted* |
| 1953 | 0.567 | 0.588 | 1953 | 0.560 | 0.377 |
| 1954 | 0.574 | 0.591 | 1954 | 0.555 | 0.379 |
| 1955 | 0.580 | 0.586 | 1955 | 0.554 | 0.376 |
| 1956 | 0.578 | 0.593 | 1956 | 0.550 | 0.382 |
| 1957 | 0.578 | 0.591 | 1957 | 0.546 | 0.377 |
| 1958 | 0.567 | 0.591 | 1958 | 0.535 | 0.376 |
| 1959 | 0.568 | 0.592 | 1959 | 0.535 | 0.377 |
| 1960 | 0.588 | 0.601 | 1960 | 0.523 | 0.394 |
| 1961 | 0.602 | 0.622 | 1961 | 0.541 | 0.402 |
| 1962 | 0.607 | 0.625 | 1962 | 0.547 | 0.403 |
| 1963 | 0.606 | 0.628 | 1963 | 0.544 | 0.404 |
| 1964 | 0.604 | 0.633 | 1964 | 0.544 | 0.408 |
| 1965 | 0.607 | 0.613 | 1965 | 0.532 | 0.397 |
| 1966 | 0.605 | 0.615 | 1966 | 0.533 | 0.397 |
| 1967 | 0.609 | 0.616 | 1967 | 0.534 | 0.395 |
| 1968 | 0.614 | 0.618 | 1968 | 0.537 | 0.396 |
| 1969 | 0.609 | 0.623 | 1969 | 0.533 | 0.400 |
| 1970 | 0.599 | 0.623 | 1970 | 0.523 | 0.396 |
| 1971 | 0.598 | 0.620 | 1971 | 0.522 | 0.393 |
| 1972 | 0.602 | 0.624 | 1972 | 0.526 | 0.394 |
| 1973 | 0.602 | 0.629 | 1973 | 0.526 | 0.397 |
| 1974 | 0.600 | 0.626 | 1974 | 0.522 | 0.392 |
| 1975 | 0.594 | 0.623 | 1975 | 0.515 | 0.388 |
| 1976 | 0.600 | 0.626 | 1976 | 0.521 | 0.389 |
| 1977 | 0.599 | 0.626 | 1977 | 0.519 | 0.388 |
| 1978 | 0.597 | 0.626 | 1978 | 0.518 | 0.387 |
| 1979 | 0.605 | 0.633 | 1979 | 0.516 | 0.391 |
| 1980 | 0.602 | 0.635 | 1980 | 0.510 | 0.393 |
| 1981 | 0.600 | 0.635 | 1981 | 0.509 | 0.393 |
| 1982 | 0.595 | 0.634 | 1982 | 0.503 | 0.392 |
| 1983 | 0.594 | 0.639 | 1983 | 0.501 | 0.396 |
| 1984 | 0.606 | 0.649 | 1984 | 0.501 | 0.401 |
| 1985 | 0.594 | 0.623 | 1985 | 0.499 | 0.404 |
| 1986 | 0.604 | 0.655 | 1986 | 0.498 | 0.408 |
| 1987 | 0.603 | 0.661 | 1987 | 0.496 | 0.413 |
| 1988 | 0.599 | 0.664 | 1988 | 0.494 | 0.417 |
| 1989 | 0.599 | 0.669 | 1989 | 0.494 | 0.421 |
| 1990 | 0.599 | 0.674 | 1990 | 0.494 | 0.427 |
| 1991 | 0.596 | 0.677 | 1991 | 0.489 | 0.431 |
| 1992 | 0.593 | 0.685 | 1992 | 0.485 | 0.441 |

**APPENDIX 6.** (*cont.*)

| Mehran Measure | | | Piesch Measure | | |
|---|---|---|---|---|---|
| *Year* | *World Weighted* | *World Unweighted* | *Year* | *World Weighted* | *World Unweighted* |
| 1993 | 0.591 | 0.691 | 1993 | 0.479 | 0.447 |
| 1994 | 0.592 | 0.698 | 1994 | 0.474 | 0.452 |
| 1995 | 0.590 | 0.699 | 1995 | 0.468 | 0.452 |
| 1996 | 0.589 | 0.700 | 1996 | 0.465 | 0.452 |
| 1997 | 0.590 | 0.702 | 1997 | 0.464 | 0.453 |
| 1998 | 0.591 | 0.704 | 1998 | 0.463 | 0.455 |
| 1999 | 0.586 | 0.707 | 1999 | 0.460 | 0.458 |
| 2000 | 0.588 | 0.710 | 2000 | 0.459 | 0.462 |

| Kakwani Measure | | | Theil Entropy Measure | | |
|---|---|---|---|---|---|
| *Year* | *World Weighted* | *World Unweighted* | *Year* | *World Weighted* | *World Unweighted* |
| 1950 | 0.270 | 0.168 | 1950 | — | 0.313 |
| 1951 | 0.270 | 0.175 | 1951 | — | 0.331 |
| 1952 | 0.355 | 0.175 | 1952 | 0.750 | 0.337 |
| 1953 | 0.346 | 0.173 | 1953 | 0.728 | 0.332 |
| 1954 | 0.340 | 0.175 | 1954 | 0.710 | 0.334 |
| 1955 | 0.339 | 0.173 | 1955 | 0.708 | 0.331 |
| 1956 | 0.336 | 0.177 | 1956 | 0.698 | 0.340 |
| 1957 | 0.334 | 0.174 | 1957 | 0.691 | 0.332 |
| 1958 | 0.323 | 0.173 | 1958 | 0.662 | 0.329 |
| 1959 | 0.323 | 0.174 | 1959 | 0.663 | 0.332 |
| 1960 | 0.304 | 0.184 | 1960 | 0.624 | 0.362 |
| 1961 | 0.333 | 0.193 | 1961 | 0.678 | 0.375 |
| 1962 | 0.338 | 0.194 | 1962 | 0.692 | 0.378 |
| 1963 | 0.337 | 0.195 | 1963 | 0.688 | 0.378 |
| 1964 | 0.338 | 0.199 | 1964 | 0.688 | 0.386 |
| 1965 | 0.318 | 0.188 | 1965 | 0.650 | 0.367 |
| 1966 | 0.319 | 0.188 | 1966 | 0.652 | 0.367 |
| 1967 | 0.323 | 0.188 | 1967 | 0.660 | 0.365 |
| 1968 | 0.329 | 0.189 | 1968 | 0.671 | 0.367 |
| 1969 | 0.326 | 0.192 | 1969 | 0.662 | 0.372 |
| 1970 | 0.318 | 0.191 | 1970 | 0.642 | 0.367 |
| 1971 | 0.318 | 0.188 | 1971 | 0.641 | 0.362 |
| 1972 | 0.324 | 0.190 | 1972 | 0.654 | 0.365 |
| 1973 | 0.325 | 0.193 | 1973 | 0.655 | 0.370 |
| 1974 | 0.322 | 0.189 | 1974 | 0.647 | 0.362 |
| 1975 | 0.316 | 0.187 | 1975 | 0.632 | 0.355 |
| 1976 | 0.322 | 0.188 | 1976 | 0.646 | 0.357 |

**APPENDIX 6.** (*cont.*)

| Kakwani Measure | | | Theil Entropy Measure | | |
|---|---|---|---|---|---|
| *Year* | *World Weighted* | *World Unweighted* | *Year* | *World Weighted* | *World Unweighted* |
| 1977 | 0.320 | 0.188 | 1977 | 0.643 | 0.356 |
| 1978 | 0.318 | 0.188 | 1978 | 0.639 | 0.356 |
| 1979 | 0.320 | 0.192 | 1979 | 0.644 | 0.364 |
| 1980 | 0.314 | 0.194 | 1980 | 0.631 | 0.367 |
| 1981 | 0.312 | 0.193 | 1981 | 0.627 | 0.366 |
| 1982 | 0.306 | 0.193 | 1982 | 0.614 | 0.365 |
| 1983 | 0.304 | 0.196 | 1983 | 0.610 | 0.373 |
| 1984 | 0.303 | 0.202 | 1984 | 0.613 | 0.384 |
| 1985 | 0.299 | 0.204 | 1985 | 0.606 | 0.389 |
| 1986 | 0.297 | 0.207 | 1986 | 0.604 | 0.395 |
| 1987 | 0.294 | 0.211 | 1987 | 0.599 | 0.404 |
| 1988 | 0.291 | 0.214 | 1988 | 0.594 | 0.411 |
| 1989 | 0.291 | 0.218 | 1989 | 0.596 | 0.418 |
| 1990 | 0.291 | 0.222 | 1990 | 0.598 | 0.430 |
| 1991 | 0.285 | 0.226 | 1991 | 0.585 | 0.437 |
| 1992 | 0.280 | 0.234 | 1992 | 0.577 | 0.455 |
| 1993 | 0.273 | 0.239 | 1993 | 0.563 | 0.466 |
| 1994 | 0.269 | 0.244 | 1994 | 0.556 | 0.477 |
| 1995 | 0.263 | 0.245 | 1995 | 0.543 | 0.478 |
| 1996 | 0.259 | 0.245 | 1996 | 0.535 | 0.478 |
| 1997 | 0.258 | 0.247 | 1997 | 0.533 | 0.481 |
| 1998 | 0.256 | 0.249 | 1998 | 0.533 | 0.486 |
| 1999 | 0.254 | 0.252 | 1999 | 0.527 | 0.494 |
| 2000 | 0.252 | 0.255 | 2000 | 0.523 | 0.502 |

| Theil Mean Log Deviation Measure | | | | | |
|---|---|---|---|---|---|
| *Year* | *World Weighted* | *World Unweighted* | *Year* | *World Weighted* | *World Unweighted* |
| 1950 | 0.603 | 0.354 | 1965 | 0.735 | 0.391 |
| 1951 | 0.602 | 0.359 | 1966 | 0.731 | 0.394 |
| 1952 | 0.878 | 0.364 | 1967 | 0.754 | 0.395 |
| 1953 | 0.828 | 0.354 | 1968 | 0.786 | 0.400 |
| 1954 | 0.799 | 0.357 | 1969 | 0.766 | 0.408 |
| 1955 | 0.801 | 0.352 | 1970 | 0.732 | 0.407 |
| 1956 | 0.778 | 0.360 | 1971 | 0.733 | 0.403 |
| 1957 | 0.778 | 0.357 | 1972 | 0.755 | 0.411 |
| 1958 | 0.725 | 0.354 | 1973 | 0.760 | 0.421 |
| 1959 | 0.726 | 0.357 | 1974 | 0.757 | 0.415 |
| 1960 | 0.672 | 0.372 | 1975 | 0.733 | 0.410 |

**APPENDIX 6.** *(cont.)*

| *Theil Mean Log Deviation Measure* | | | | | |
|---|---|---|---|---|---|
| *Year* | *World Weighted* | *World Unweighted* | *Year* | *World Weighted* | *World Unweighted* |
| 1961 | 0.787 | 0.404 | 1976 | 0.761 | 0.415 |
| 1962 | 0.816 | 0.408 | 1977 | 0.751 | 0.416 |
| 1963 | 0.806 | 0.413 | 1978 | 0.736 | 0.417 |
| 1964 | 0.798 | 0.423 | 1979 | 0.743 | 0.429 |
| 1980 | 0.723 | 0.434 | 1991 | 0.602 | 0.517 |
| 1981 | 0.711 | 0.433 | 1992 | 0.588 | 0.534 |
| 1982 | 0.690 | 0.432 | 1993 | 0.569 | 0.547 |
| 1983 | 0.675 | 0.442 | 1994 | 0.559 | 0.564 |
| 1984 | 0.670 | 0.463 | 1995 | 0.544 | 0.565 |
| 1985 | 0.656 | 0.468 | 1996 | 0.536 | 0.567 |
| 1986 | 0.648 | 0.477 | 1997 | 0.535 | 0.575 |
| 1987 | 0.637 | 0.488 | 1998 | 0.531 | 0.581 |
| 1988 | 0.623 | 0.494 | 1999 | 0.523 | 0.588 |
| 1989 | 0.622 | 0.503 | 2000 | 0.521 | 0.594 |
| 1990 | 0.617 | 0.512 | | | |

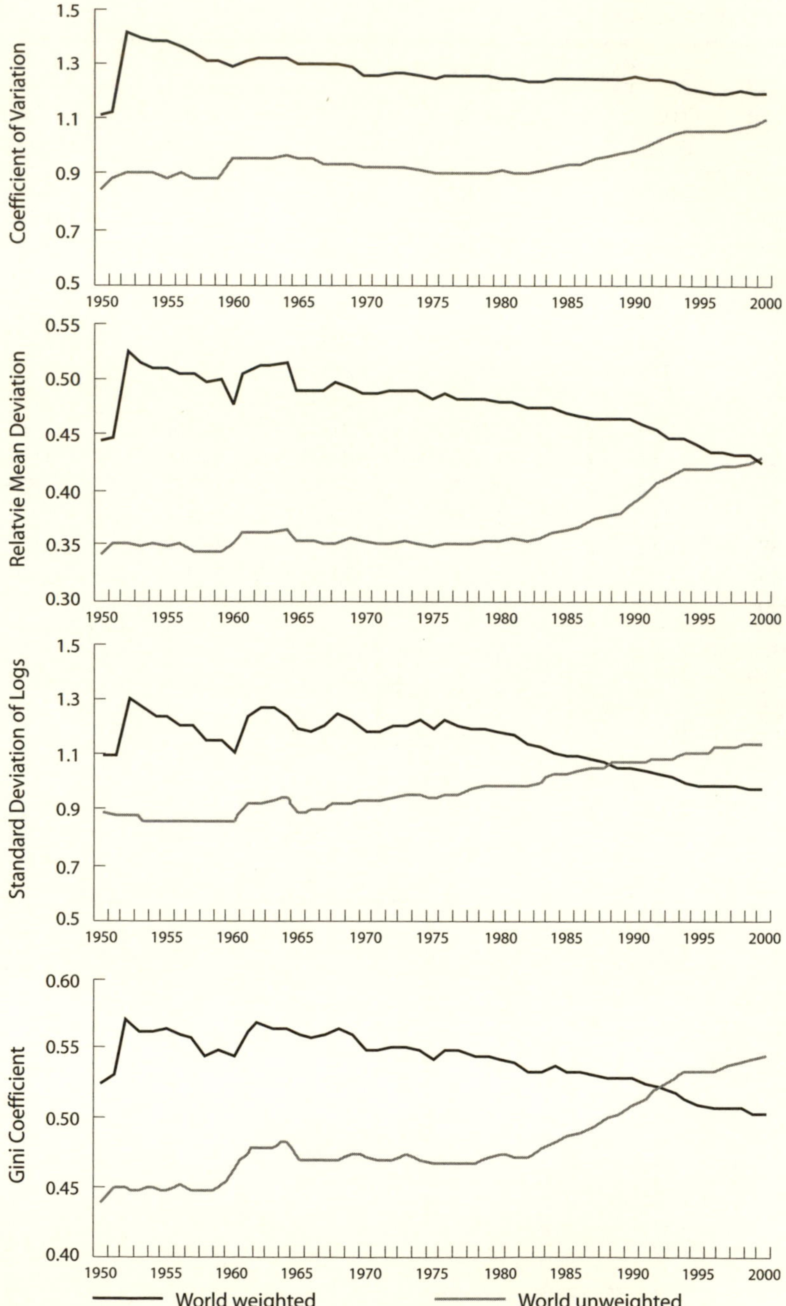


**Figure A6.1.** Inequality measures 1950–2000.

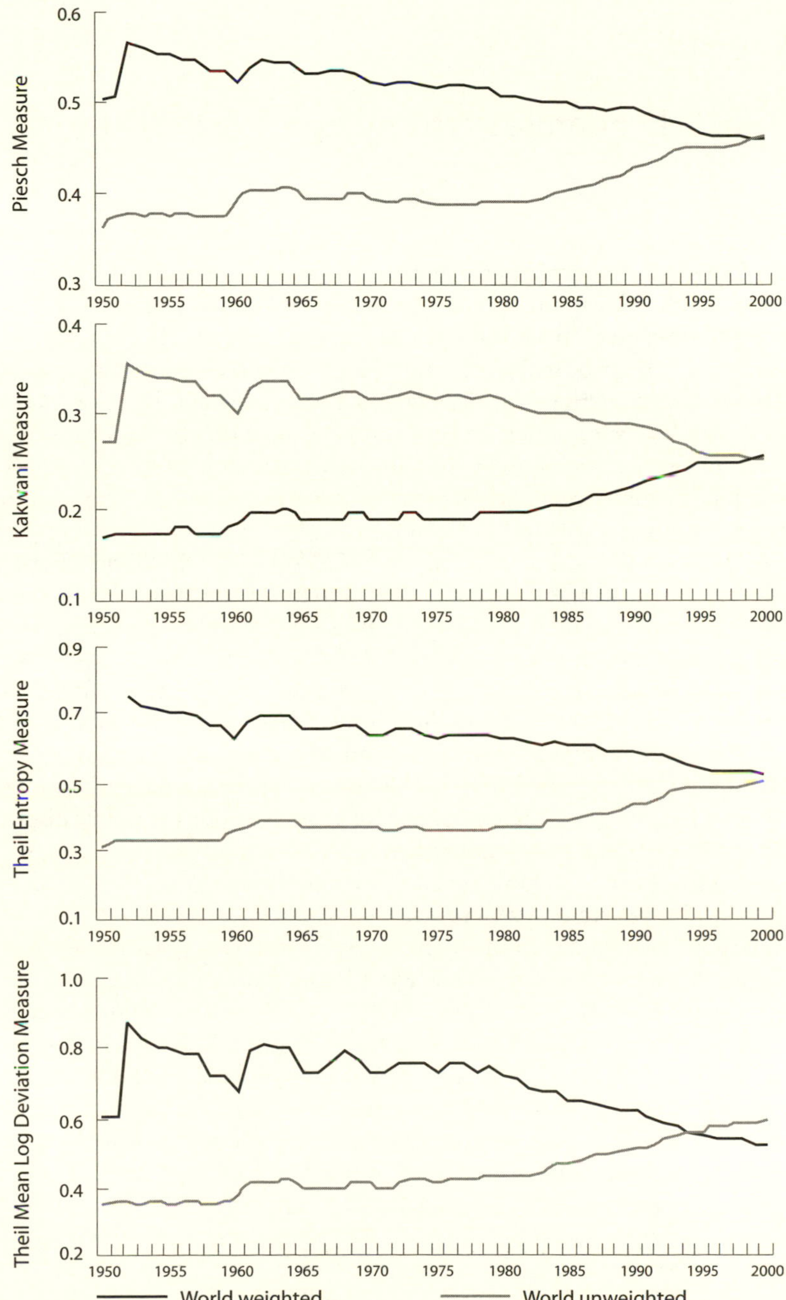


**Figure A6.2.** Inequality measures 1950–2000.

# Appendix 7

## China's Economic Performance, 1950–2000

The Chinese economic performance has been contentious for a number of years. The main reason is the use of the Material Product approach "inherited" from the Soviet-type accounting. This approach, by focusing on the production of tangible goods and disregarding production of "unproductive" services, gives a lower overall level of income, but generally exaggerates growth rates because productivity improvements in services are slower than in the production of goods. Another reason is the Chinese National Statistical Bureau's use of "comparable" prices, which are not well defined and are again thought to exaggerate growth through underreporting of inflation. The third problem, alluded to in the text, is that the nation-wide and the sum of the provincial GDPs that should, of course, be the same, tend to diverge in the recent period (with the sum of provincial GDPs yielding higher overall level of income). All of these problems render the Chinese official data unreliable despite the fact that the Chinese official statisticians adopted the SNA system several years ago, and that there are some recent improvements and recalculations of the official aggregates. As Maddison (2003, p. 151) writes, "Misstatement [of Chinese GDP] is not deliberate, but is a transitional problem in moving from a detailed reporting practice inherited from the long period in which the norms of the Soviet material product system (MPS) prevailed."[141]

These problems have led to alternative estimates of Chinese historical growth rates and GDP levels. Maddison (2001), basing himself on a very detailed study in Maddison (1998), rejected official rates and produced alternative calculations that have been maintained in the most recent compendium (Maddison 2003). Heston (2001) in his explanations of the calculations underlying the Penn World Tables 6.1 explicitly rejects the official Chinese growth rates and calculates, following to a large extent Maddison's lead, a significantly lower growth. Thus the two sources (Penn World Tables 6.1 and Maddison) give approximately the same evolution of the Chinese GDP since 1952. If the 1952 level is taken as 100, the 1978 level is 276 in PWT6.1, and 306 in Maddison; in 1998, the levels are respectively 1239 and 1258 (see Heston 2001, pp. 8–9). This is vastly different from the official Chinese sources (reported in two different versions in table A7.1), which—taking again 1952 as

**TABLE A7.1.**
Implied Growth Rates of China's Real GDP according to Different Sources

| | *Official1* | *Official2* | *PWT 6.1* | *Maddison* | *World Bank* |
|---|---|---|---|---|---|
| 1952–78 | 6.2 | 6.0 | 4.0 | 4.4 | 6.2 |
| 1978–98 | 9.7 | 9.6 | 7.8 | 7.3 | 9.5 |
| 1952–98 | 7.7 | 7.6 | 5.6 | 5.7 | 7.7 |

*Note:* Rates calculated as simple geometric average. *Sources:* The Official1 data from Hu and Khan (1996). The Official2 data, 1952–78, real national income from Chinese Statistical Yearbook 1985, p. 34; and 1978–1998, real GDP from Chinese Statistical Yearbook 2002, p. 58. Penn World Tables 6. 1 downloaded from http://pwt.econ.upenn.edu/. (the variable RGDPCH). Maddison (2001, p. 304). World Bank from SIMA (Statistical Information Management and analysis) database (World Development Indicators).

100—give 472 or 453 for the year 1978; and 3,010 or 2,900 for the year 1998. The World Bank (World Development Indicators as reported in SIMA data are largely the same as the official Chinese data. Accordingly, the official and World Bank growth rates are always higher than the Penn World Tables and Maddison's growth rates (see Table A7.1).

That different sources do not always agree is not uncommon, as illustrated in tables A7.2 to A7.4. However, the discrepancies for China are of an entirely different order of magnitude than for India or the United States.[142] Thus for 1952, for example, all the sources are within 13 percentage points for the United States and 18 percentage points for India; the ratio for China is 3.35 to 1 however. As mentioned before, Maddison, who calculates relatively low growth for the post-1952 period, gives a fairly high GDP per capita level for 1952, and probably relatively high income levels for the earlier period as well. For example, Maddison's (2003) 1900 GDP per capita is 2.43 times higher than the World Bank's 1952 level (table A7.4). These disagreements are caused by the different views of Chinese post-1952 growth. But while the Penn World Tables and Maddison almost wholly agree on the Chinese growth path, they seem to disagree on the initial *level* of income. In 1952, Penn World Tables give Chinese GDP per capita as $PPP 522 (in 1995 prices), and Maddison as $PPP 877 (at same prices). The discrepancy in levels, although not as great as between these sources and the World Bank, persists for other years.

Next, the differences in the estimation of China's growth rates have obvious implications for our assessment of economic performance during various subperiods, e.g., if we wish to place the recent, post-1978 Chinese growth record in a context by comparing it to the pre-1978 period. As figure A7.1 shows, while the past twenty years of Chinese growth have been impressive, they have not been very different, if we

**TABLE A7.2.**
GDPs Per Capita of China, India and the United States in Different Sources (as shown in the original sources)

| | *China* | | | | | *India* | | | | *United States* | | | |
|---|---|---|---|---|---|---|---|---|---|---|---|---|---|
| | *Maddison (1995)* | *Maddison (2001)* | *Maddison (2003)* | *Penn 6.1* | *World Bank SIMA* | *Maddison (1995)* | *Maddison (2001)* | *Penn 6.1* | *World Bank SIMA* | *Maddison (1995)* | *Maddison (2001)* | *Penn 6.1* | *World Bank SIMA* |
| 1820 | 523 | | 600 | | | 531 | 533 | | | 1237 | 1257 | | |
| 1900 | 652 | | 545 | | | 625 | 599 | | | 4096 | | | |
| 1913 | 688 | | 552 | | | 663 | 673 | | | 5307 | 5301 | | |
| 1929 | 779 | | 562 | | | 665 | 728 | | | 6907 | | | |
| 1938 | 778 | | 562 | | | 619 | 678 | | | 6134 | | | |
| 1950 | 614 | | 439 | | | 597 | 619 | 705 | 604 | 9573 | 9561 | 10702 | 12549 |
| 1952 | 752 | 537 | 537 | 584 | 262 | 609 | 629 | 740 | 621 | 10596 | 10316 | 11279 | 12594 |
| 1960 | 878 | 673 | 673 | 681 | 497 | 735 | 753 | 847 | 655 | 11193 | 11328 | 12272 | 14227 |
| 1978 | 1352 | 979 | 979 | 925 | 754 | 972 | 966 | 1177 | 857 | 18168 | 18373 | 21004 | 21790 |
| 1998 | | 3117 | 3117 | 3275 | 3646 | | 1746 | 2284 | 1586 | | 27331 | 31090 | 30160 |
| 2000 | | | 3425 | 3747 | 4144 | | | 2478 | 1693 | | | 33292 | 31519 |

*Sources:* Maddison (1995): for China and India, pp. 204–5; for the United States, pp.196–97. Maddison (2001); for India, p. 203, for China, p. 304, for the United States, pp. 185 and 279. Maddison (2003) for China, pp. 180–84. Penn World Tables: version 6.1 from http://pwt.econ.upenn.edu/, (real GDP per capita chain index method). SIMA, as explained in the text. Maddison (2003) data for India and the United States are the same as in Maddison (2001). All of Maddison's data in 1990 Geary-Khamis are in international dollars; Penn World Tables are in Geary-Khamis 1996 international dollars; SIMA in EKS 1995 international dollars.

**TABLE A7.3.**
GDPs Per Capita of China, India and the United States in Different Sources, Converted in 1995 International Dollars

| | *China* | | | | | *India* | | | | *United States* | | | |
|---|---|---|---|---|---|---|---|---|---|---|---|---|---|
| | *Maddison (1995)* | *Maddison (2001)* | *Maddison (2003)* | *Penn 6.1* | *World Bank SIMA* | *Maddison (1995)* | *Maddison (2001)* | *Penn 6.1* | *World Bank SIMA* | *Maddison (1995)* | *Maddison (2001)* | *Penn 6.1* | *World Bank SIMA* |
| 1820 | 610 | | 700 | | | 619 | 621 | | | 1442 | 1467 | | |
| 1900 | 760 | | 636 | | | 729 | 698 | | | 4776 | | | |
| 1913 | 802 | | 644 | | | 773 | 785 | | | 6188 | 6186 | | |
| 1929 | 908 | | 656 | | | 775 | 849 | | | 8054 | | | |
| 1938 | 907 | | 656 | | | 722 | 791 | | | 7152 | | | |
| 1950 | 716 | | 512 | | | 696 | 722 | 684 | 604 | 11162 | 11158 | | 12549 |
| 1952 | 877 | 627 | 627 | 566 | 262 | 710 | 733 | 718 | 621 | 12355 | 12039 | 10941 | 12594 |
| 1960 | 1024 | 785 | 785 | 661 | 497 | 857 | 878 | 822 | 655 | 13051 | 13220 | 11904 | 14227 |
| 1978 | 1576 | 1142 | 1142 | 897 | 754 | 1133 | 1126 | 1142 | 857 | 21184 | 21441 | 20374 | 21790 |
| 1998 | | 3637 | 3638 | 3177 | 3646 | | 2036 | 2215 | 1586 | | 31895 | 30157 | 30160 |
| 2000 | | | 3997 | 3635 | 4144 | | | 2404 | 1693 | | | 32293 | 31519 |

*Note:* All of Maddison's data expressed in 1990 Geary-Khamis international dollars; Penn World Tables in Geary-Khamis 1996 international dollars; SIMA in EKS 1995 international dollars (see table A7.2). In order to convert to 1995 international dollars, PWT data are multiplied by 0.97, and Maddison's data by 1.167.

**TABLE A7.4.**
Confrontation of the Four Sources (World Bank SIMA 1952 = 1)

| | *China* | | | | | *India* | | | | *United States* | | |
|---|---|---|---|---|---|---|---|---|---|---|---|---|
| | *Maddison (2001)* | *Maddison (2001)* | *Maddison (2003)* | *Penn* | *World Bank SIMA* | *Maddison (1995)* | *Maddison (2001)* | *Penn* | *World Bank SIMA* | *Maddison (1995)* | *Penn* | *World Bank SIMA* |
| 1820 | 2.33 | | 2.67 | | | 1.00 | 1.00 | | | 0.11 | | |
| 1900 | 2.90 | | 2.43 | | | 1.17 | 1.12 | | | 0.38 | | |
| 1913 | 3.06 | | 2.46 | | | 1.24 | 1.26 | | | 0.49 | | |
| 1929 | 3.47 | | 2.50 | | | 1.25 | 1.37 | | | 0.64 | | |
| 1938 | 3.46 | | 2.50 | | | 1.16 | 1.27 | | | 0.57 | | |
| 1950 | 2.73 | | 1.95 | | | 1.12 | 1.16 | 1.10 | 0.97 | 0.89 | | 1.00 |
| 1952 | 3.35 | 2.39 | 2.39 | 2.16 | 1.00 | 1.14 | 1.18 | 1.16 | 1.00 | 0.98 | 0.87 | 1.00 |
| 1960 | 3.91 | 3.00 | 3.00 | 2.52 | 1.90 | 1.38 | 1.41 | 1.32 | 1.05 | 1.04 | 0.95 | 1.13 |
| 1978 | 6.02 | 4.36 | 4.36 | 3.42 | 2.88 | 1.82 | 1.81 | 1.84 | 1.38 | 1.68 | 1.62 | 1.73 |
| 1998 | | 13.88 | 13.89 | 12.13 | 13.92 | | 3.28 | 3.57 | 2.55 | | 2.39 | 2.39 |
| 2000 | | | 15.26 | 13.87 | 15.82 | | | 3.87 | 2.73 | | 2.56 | 2.50 |

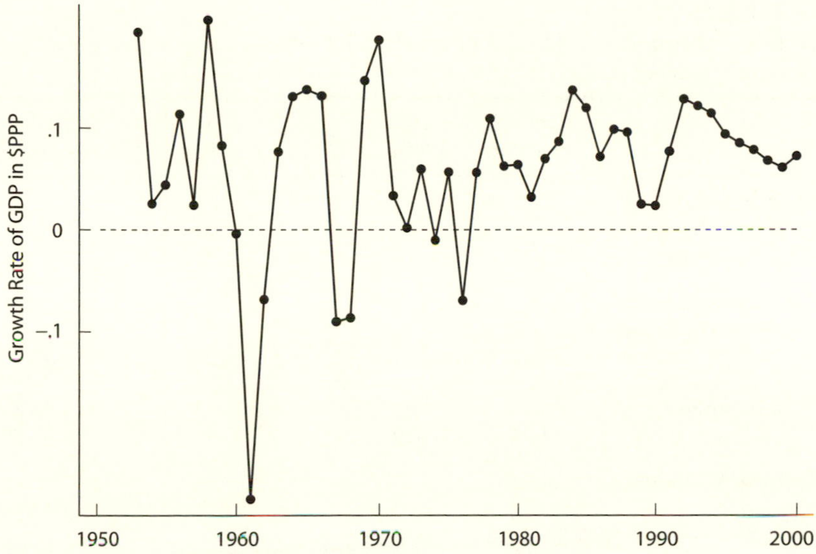


**Figure A7.1.** Chinese GDP per capita growth rate, 1953–2000.

believe the World Bank data, from the 1952–78 period except that there were no politically motivated GDP declines as in 1961 (the aftermath of the Great Leap Forward and the Sino-Soviet split), 1967–68 (the Cultural Revolution) and 1976 (the power struggle against the "Gang of Four"). The trend in growth rate did not change much. If we consider our three periods (1950–60, 1961–78, 1979–2000) which luckily also correspond to a meaningful periodization from the Chinese perspective, the World Bank calculated average growth rates were respectively 8.6, 3.0, and 8.2 percent (with standard deviations of 8, 11.3, and 3.2 percent). So, the past twenty years have been much more stable than the earlier periods, but their record was not out of character for China. Once we account (the best we can) for political disruptions, it turns out that the difference in the growth performance of the pre- and post-reform China is much less dramatic (this is the point argued by Borensztein and Ostry 1996).

Table A7.5 shows growth rates for different political and economic periods. The maximum overstatement, and probably the source of major discrepancies, are the data for the early stage of socialism between 1952 and 1958, and for the "readjustment" after the disaster of the Great Leap Forward. It is interesting, though, that the decline in income caused by the Great Leap Forward appears more severe if we use the official or World Bank sources than if we use the more cautious PWT or Maddison.

**TABLE A7.5.**
Chinese Performance in Different Periods (GDP or real national income growth in percent per annum)

| *Period* | *Official Statistics* | *Maddison (2001)* | *PWT6.1* | *World Bank* | *Official "Overestimate"* |
|---|---|---|---|---|---|
| Socialist beginnings to Great Leap Forward (1952–58) | 10.9 | 4.3 | 3.4 | 11.6 | 4.5 |
| Great Leap forward and its aftermath (1958–63) | –5.0 | –3.1 | –1.7 | –3.1 | –2.4 |
| "Readjustment" (1963–66) | 16.8 | 8.3 | 6.5 | 16.2 | 6.5 |
| Cultural Revolution (1966–78) | 5.8 | 2.2 | 1.3 | 5.2 | 2.9 |
| Reform (1978–94) | 9.8 | 6.0 | 6.8 | 9.7 | 2.3 |
| Advanced reform period (1994–2000) | 7.8 | 5.7 | 6.0 | 8.8 | 1.0 |

*Note:* Results based on official statistics calculated from Hu and Khan (1996, appendix), and SIMA (World Bank) database; Maddison (2001, p. 304), Penn World Tables: version 6.1 from http://pwt.econ.upenn.edu/, and World Bank (SIMA), as explained in the text. The official "overestimate" is calculated as the difference between the official growth rate and the average of the other three estimates.

# *Notes*

1. The Gini coefficient (named after Corrado Gini, an Italian economist of the early twentieth century) is a measure of *in*equality. Consequently, when its value increases, inequality goes up. The coefficient ranges between the two theoretical values of 0 and 100. If zero, all individuals have the same incomes; if 100, the entire income of a community is appropriated by one person only. Both values are, of course, impossible. The usual range of Gini values for country-wide distributions is between 25 and 60. The most egalitarian are Nordic European countries with Gini values in the mid-twenties. Western and Central Europe, Canada, Australia, New Zealand, as well as a number of Asian countries (Japan, Taiwan, India), have values around 30 to 35. The United States is an outlier among the rich countries, with the Gini in the lower 40s, about the same as that for Russia. Countries in Latin America and Africa are generally the most unequal, with Ginis in the 50s; and in some countries like Brazil, South Africa, or Botswana, inequality reaches a Gini of almost 60. Inequality among individuals in the world is in the mid-60s. We shall discuss later the exact definition and other characteristics of the Gini coefficient.

2. The first, to my knowledge, international Concept 2 calculation was done by Kuznets (1954).

3. Also, the fact that the United States is a highly unified country with easy mobility of labor between the states means that the importance of Concept 1 inequality is limited (because there are strong "self-equilibrating" mechanisms in the event that some states were to become much richer than others).

4. If (poor) countries A and B are compared using the price reference of a (richer) country C, then the more distant the reference vector C from the price structures in A and B, the smaller the income differences between A and B will appear. In other words, the Geary-Kramis method also leads to a bias when the incomes of two countries are valued at prices of a third country (see Dowrick and Akmal 2001, Proposition 3, p. 11).

5. Point made in a personal communication.

6. For example, Concialdi (1997, 261) writes that the best available French household surveys conducted by the *Institut National de Statistique et Etudes Economiques* underestimate capital incomes by about 40 percent. Wagner and Grabka (1999) write that German property income in surveys is underestimated by almost one-half compared to National Accounts data.

7. In calculating concepts 1 and 2, we could compare either GDPs per capita or personal consumption per capita.

8. A particular problem is location. Location is, as we all know, probably the most important element in housing or rental prices. Yet surveys cannot capture it better than by giving information on whether the house is located in rural or urban areas.

9. This is, of course, because average household size tends to be smaller in rich countries.

10. The Gini coefficient seems a fairly complicated measure when written out, but what it does can be explained relatively simply. First, it sums absolute income differences across all *N* individuals. Thus, if one person's income is 10 and another's 6, there would be two interpersonal comparisons, and the results will be (10 – 6) = 4 and |6 – 10| = 4. All of these distances are then added up, and to find the average distance their total sum is divided by the total number of such comparisons ($N^2$). The result is in turn "mean-normalized," that is, divided by the mean income of the group, and is further divided by 2 to make the value of the coefficient lie between 0 and 1 (or 0 and 100 if expressed in percents as is done here). This is why the Gini can be written as

$$\frac{1}{\mu}\frac{1}{N^2}\frac{1}{2}\sum_{i=1}^{N}\sum_{j=1}^{N}|y_j - y_i|,$$

where $\mu$ = mean income, and $y_i$ = income of *i*-th individual.

11. In some cases, the maximum inequality can be written as 1. We prefer to write it as percentage: thus, inequality of say 40.3 rather than 0.403.

12. Germany, with the largest population, will have a population weight of 0.22 and income weight of 0.23. Hence even for Germany the total weight would be only 0.05.

13. Notice that if instead of using *i* to represent countries, we use it to represent individuals and take $\mu$ to be country-wide mean income rather than world-wide mean income, the expression (6) is the formula for a country-wide Theil coefficient.

14. Obviously, this is true for all values greater than *e*. Note also that strictly speaking, the measure is not bounded from above because it would approach infinity as N approaches infinity. Also, the assumption is that the lowest $y_i$'s are infinitesimally small and not equal to 0 for otherwise the Theil would approach minus infinity.

15. We have a total of 6149 GDP per capita observations: 4836 (78.6 percent) are taken from the World Bank database, 1055 (17.2 percent) from various countries' statistical yearbooks, and 258 (4.2 percent) from other sources (Penn World Tables, Maddison [1995, 2001], and the IMF). In the latter two cases, the data are real growth rates (in domestic prices) that, together with population numbers, are used to compute GDP per capita levels. All data are available from the author on request.

16. Summers and Heston's Penn World Tables version 6 can be downloaded from http://pwt.econ.upenn.edu/. For some countries (Iraq, Cuba) Maddison (2001) gives the 1950–98 estimates, but since I lacked the benchmark 1995 GDP PPP values for these countries, I could not use Maddison's real growth rates.

17. In the text that follows, GDP will, unless explicitly stated otherwise, always refer to GDP at 1995 international prices ($PPP).

18. Several problems with the formerly Communist countries need to be noted. Romania and Bulgaria show very high growth rates respectively for the period 1950–75 and 1950–80 (after these dates, the data are available in World Bank SIMA). For Romania, we have used official statistics between 1950 and 1960 (the only GDP data available), and for the period 1960–75, Penn World Ta-

bles. For Bulgaria, we have used Maddison's (1995) data for the entire 1950–80 period. A combination of (unrealistically) high growth rates during most of the communist period, and presumably accurate GDP per capita later, yields very low initial (1950) GDPs per capita: $605 for Romania and $1045 for Bulgaria (all in 1995 $PPP). This fact needs to be flagged although little can be done about it. In the case of the former Soviet republics, we also rely on the (most likely) exaggerated official statistics because these are the only available historical data for the constituent republics of the USSR. For other communist countries the official statistics are more reliable. We have used the official growth rates (when no SIMA data were available) for Czechoslovakia and the former Yugoslavia since again this was the only way to obtain consistent data for the constituent republics. Data for USSR, Yugoslavia and Czechoslovakia are available (see appendix 1), but they are not used in the calculations (since individual republics are included). This explains the discrepancy between 141 countries listed in the appendix and 138 countries used in our calculations.

19. In the context of the discussion of the convergence literature, we shall argue that a much more direct test on (inequality) of distribution of countries' GDPs per capita via the Gini coefficient is preferable to a regression-based estimate of the so-called convergence parameters. This point was made early on in the discussion by Quah (1993b, 1996) and was reiterated recently by Wodon and Yitzhaki (2002). Note also that the Gini coefficient was used in the first paper published on the topic of convergence (Summers, Kravis, and Heston 1984).

20. Moreover, one could easily argue that the cost borne by the citizens of the poorer country, Indonesia, is greater because their starting point is lower, and hence the loss of marginal utility is greater.

21. The correlation between world and U.S. growth rate is 0.76.

22. Between 1978 and October 1981, oil prices increased from about $12 to $34 per barrel (Bairoch 1997, vol. 2: 702), and their all-time high (at constant prices) was reached in mid-1979.

23. Between 1970 and 1980, U.S. real interest rate on deposits never exceeded 2 percent per annum. In 1981, real interest rate increased to 8 percent and with the exception of the period 1992–94, the rate never dropped below 2 percent again (source: IMF *International Financial Statistics*, various volumes).

24. For a recent discussion of the Chinese 1959–61 famine, see Lin and Yang (2000). Lin and Yang quote Ashton et al (1984) calculations which, based on demographic data, estimate the total death toll to be about 30 million people. Yet they note that the disaster of such proportions went almost unnoticed by the outside world since the famine was limited to rural areas (whose food was requisitioned to feed the cities). Lin and Yang (p. 145) describe how at a recent conference where their research was presented, a senior official from FAO, who was in China during 1959–61, still could not believe that the famine took place. His travels in China, though, were limited to cities only. On a personal note, a friend of my parents was a Yugoslav diplomat stationed in Beijing over the same period. He never noticed a hint of famine.

25. If $\frac{dU}{dy} = \frac{1}{y}$, then $U = \ln y$, where $U$ = utility and $y$ = GDP per capita.

26. Notice that this rate of growth will tend by definition to be higher in the earlier periods when the overall levels of income were lower and thus utility from a given growth rate was greater.

27. This concept is very similar to the σ convergence used in the growth literature. The difference consists in the inequality statistic used: σ convergence uses standard deviation (or variance); here we use the Gini and Theil coefficients. The latter two are the standard measures of inequality. This allows us to move seamlessly between the different inequality concepts: from inequality within a nation, to inequality among the nations, to inequality among world individuals.

28. Unweighted cross-country inequality is calculated without Kuwait. Its extremely high GDP in the 1960s and 1970s is due, on the one hand, to huge oil revenues (many of which were repatriated outside of Kuwait) and, on the other, to the use of only citizen (not resident) population in the denominator. One such observation—Kuwait's GDP per capita in 1962 was $PPP 67,000!—would both bias the calculations and mislead us as to the direction of overall change in cross-country inequality. Kuwait is included in the population-weighted calculations since its effect on these, on account of its tiny population, is minimal.

29. In 2000, only four transition economies (Poland, Hungary, Slovak Republic, and Slovenia) were at their historical income peak (see appendix 3).

30. The average lost time (defined as the number of years elapsed between the year when the 2000 level of GDP per capita was first achieved by a country and the year 2000) for Latin America and the Caribbean is almost twelve years; for Africa, almost seventeen years (see appendix 4).

31. The effect on the Gini of "stacking up" these regions is discussed in appendix 2.

32. Calculated as I have done here—because this calculation of contributions depends on the order in which the regions are stacked.

33. The story is taken from Abba Lerner's *Flation: Not Inflation of Prices, not Deflation of Jobs* (Hammondsworth, England: Pinguin's), 1972.

34. See the excellent review of the convergence literature by Islam (2003).

35. Note that the use of the variance of logs to assess whether the distribution is shrinking or widening is a singularly bad choice. The variance of logs does not even satisfy the Dalton criterion, namely that the measure of inequality should always go down if there is a transfer of income from a rich to a poor country such that their rankings are not reversed). Since σ convergence is about the dispersion of a distribution, the use of the standard measures of distribution inequality like the Gini or Theil coefficients would have made much more sense.

36. The terminological confusion (which we addressed in chapter 1) is illustrated by Jones's (1997) article, which deals entirely with inequality among countries' mean incomes and is entitled "On the Evolution of World Income Distribution."

37. Examples include Barro (1991), Mankiw, Romer, and Weil (1992), and Barro and Sala-i-Martin (1995)

38. However, to conclude that $\beta < 0$ must imply a shrinking of *distribution* is wrong. As shown by Quah (1993b), this interpretation amounts to Galton's fallacy, where a regression toward the mean appears regardless of the fact that the distribution of countries' incomes may be constant or diverging. Quah nicely il-

lustrates it by pointing out that this was indeed a problem that puzzled Galton when he noticed that the sons of tall fathers tended to regress toward the mean, and yet the distribution by height did not show any obvious shrinking. Friedman's (1992) proposed solution is to do a regression on the final, and not on the initial, value ($\ln y_t - \ln y_{t-1} = \alpha + \beta \ln y_t$) and to accept the convergence hypothesis if $\beta < 0$ (for a critique of this approach see Bliss [1999] and the further discussion by Cannon and Duck [2000] as well as Bliss's [2000] rejoinder). Or very simply suppose that there is such a change that makes the rich and the poor trade their places, with the new poor becoming poorer than the old, and the new rich richer than the old. Then there would be a negative relationship between growth in income and initial income level, and yet the overall distribution would widen. Wodon and Yitzhaki (2002) argue that β convergence is uninformative because it can exist when the distribution converges, diverges, or stays the same (in other words, it is compatible with the presence or absence of σ convergence). Sala-i-Martin (1996) argues that there is a case for β convergence. According to Islam (2003, p. 314), β convergence is a necessary but not a sufficient condition for σ convergence.

39. See Quah (1996b) and Dowrick and de Long (2001).

40. See also the review of findings in Barro and Sala-i-Martin (1995).

41. Bairoch's (1981, 1993, pp. 102–6) estimate of income differences prior to the industrial revolution is smaller (2 to 1). It was questioned by Maddison (1995, p. 31), but whether the ratio is 2 to 1 or 3 to 1, the gap was several orders of magnitude less than at the end of the twentieth century.

42. Maddison (1995) divides the world in seven regions: Western Europe, Western offshoots, Southern Europe (basically poorer OECD countries), Eastern Europe, Latin America, Asia, and Africa.

43. According to Islam (2003, p. 328), the problem with this "extended specification" is that the variables that are included are often purely conjectural and have no guidance from the theory of growth. Some researchers argue that these additional variables stand for the technological shift parameter in the growth regressions, which was found by Islam (1995) to vary by the ratio of 40 to 1 among the countries. Thus, for example, one can argue that better legal protection explains why the level of technology in one country is higher than in another, which in turn justifies the use of legal protection on the right-hand side of the growth regressions.

44. This point is not universally acknowledged. Some authors, and in particular those who have worked on the issue of convergence, hold that the statement "everything else being the same, a poor country will grow faster than a rich country" is meaningful and important. But while I can see that it may be meaningful if "everything else being the same" includes say, fiscal balance—for one can sensibly entertain the view that there is nothing that would predispose poor countries to have larger or smaller budget deficits—it is difficult to see how meaningful it is when other things include such clear correlates of income level as average level of education, stability of political institutions, or even government expenditures as a share of GDP. All these factors are not randomly distributed, with some poor countries being highly educated, others badly educated, and likewise for the rich world. On the contrary, they do come as a package: high level of education, strong institutions, high income, etc. Thus the

phrase "everything else being the same" is not meaningful in any other than an econometric sense.

45. The sample size cannot be the cause of these changes because it is fairly stable for all the regions. The number of countries in 1960, 1978, and 2000 varies between 40 and 42 for Africa, 20 and 25 for Asia, 23 and 24 for Latin America and the Caribbean, 19 and 22 for transition countries, and is constant for WENAO (23 countries).

46. According to Dowrick and de Long (2001, pp. 43–46), the first period was also characterized by a positive growth premium to openness (2 percent per annum) with poor countries benefiting more from openness than the rich (as argued also by Sachs and Warner 1995). The more recent period, however, saw both the decline of the openness premium (to 1.3 percent per annum) and the premium becoming larger for the rich than poor countries.

47. We would expect to see this positive relationship because more successful countries will move upward in the income distribution (and the less successful countries will tend to move down).

48. The same fact of low growth for developing economies over the past twenty-year period provides the background for the analysis of different rentier experiences in Isham et al. (2002, pp. 3–4). It also motivates Easterly (2001).

49. In an intriguing note, the *Moscow Times* (September 30, 2002) describes how President Putin announced in 2001 that Russia's medium-term economic goal should be to catch up with Portugal (somewhat of a comedown from Khrushchev's "catching up and overtaking the United States"). The newspaper dryly commented, "At its current pace, he [Putin]—and his daughters—will be long dead before the country achieves parity with the European Union's poorest nation." Portugal is often used by Russian commentators as a yardstick. In a *Nezavisimaya Gazeta* article, Andrei Savitsky (2003), after discussing the fact that there are nine Russian tycoons on the list of Europe's 200 richest people in 2002, ironically concludes, "The Portuguese economy is often used as a criterion for measuring the growth of the Russian economy. So we have outpaced Portugal according to the number of billionaires—nine-fold."

50. Czechoslovakia as well belonged to the rich club, but for the year 1960 it is not included in our data because we do not have separate GDPs per capita for the Czech republic and Slovakia. The separate information for the two republics is available only from 1984.

51. African countries' incomes in the early 1960s and before must be taken with a strong dose of caution. The reason is not only the usual problem of national accounting in the not-fully monetized economies, but also the large difference between domestic and national income. A large chunk of profits made by foreign-owned companies were repatriated: this income adds to the domestic product but not to national income and standard of living of the local population. Barber ([1961] 1984) documents this very persuasively using the example of Southern and Northern Rhodesia (Zimbabwe and Zambia) and Nyasaland (Malawi). Thus, in 1959 in Northern Rhodesia, net domestic money income (then called "geographical income") exceeded net national money income by 29 percent (and on the eve of the Second World War, by more than 100 percent!); in Nyasaland, in the mid-1950s, the difference was more than 50 percent. Very high profits realized by colonially owned, mostly extractive, compa-

nies are also reflected in a heavily unbalanced factoral distribution of income. Barber (p. 159) reports, for example, that net profits of corporations in the three countries combined amounted to almost one-third of net domestic income. This share is three times as high as that in the United States. Huge differences in the standard of living between European and African populations (amounting to a ratio in excess of 30 to 1, according to Kuznets [(1954) 1965, p. 155] who quotes a UN report) were further evidence not only of an extremely skewed distribution of income, but also of accounting problems—namely, a relatively high domestic product, yet an abysmal standard of living for the indigenous population. Furthermore, under colonial conditions, it is unclear who is the citizen, that is, how to treat colonists who are residing there temporarily. Thus both the denominator (population) and the numerator (GDP) are dubious.

52. In 1870, when Argentina is for the first time included in Maddison (2001, p. 195) estimate of its GDP per capita ($PPP 1,311, at 1990 prices) was higher than that of Portugal, Finland, and Norway. For earlier years, Maddison presents the data for Mexico and Brazil alone (from among the Latin American countries), both of which were poorer than the poorest WENAO country. Yet, Argentina and Uruguay were already then significantly richer than Mexico or Brazil and probably richer than several West European countries.

53. The only "overlap" is provided by Turkey, which is classified as a WENAO country and yet belongs to the Third World.

54. In addition to Tunisia, whose position was stable throughout the whole period.

55. For Nicaragua the decline continued even further, until 1994.

56. But in 1960, both were within the striking distance of Portugal: Nicaragua's GDP per capita was $PPP 3,023; Iran's, $PPP 2,787; and Portugal's, $PPP 3,205.

57. The list of the ten most and least successful countries over the period 1960–2000 is as follows (note that 8 out of the 10 most successful countries are Asian, and 7 out of the 10 worst performers are African):

| *Top Ten Performers* | *GDP Per Capita in 2000 (compared to its 1960 level = 1)* | *Average Per Capita Growth Rate, 1960–2000* | *Ten Worst Performers* | *GDP Per Capita in 2000 (compared to its 1960 level = 1)* | *Average Per Capita Growth Rate, 1960–2000* |
|---|---|---|---|---|---|
| Taiwan | 11.53 | 6.3 | Niger | 0.49 | −1.7 |
| Botswana | 11.08 | 6.2 | Angola | 0.54 | −1.5 |
| Singapore | 10.97 | 6.2 | Sierra Leone | 0.58 | −1.3 |
| South Korea | 10.50 | 6.1 | Zambia | 0.64 | −1.1 |
| China | 8.34 | 5.4 | Madagascar | 0.64 | −1.1 |
| Hong Kong | 8.04 | 5.3 | Haiti | 0.67 | −1.0 |
| Thailand | 5.95 | 4.6 | Nicaragua | 0.75 | −0.7 |
| Ireland | 5.60 | 4.4 | Chad | 0.75 | −0.7 |
| Japan | 5.24 | 4.2 | Turkmenistan | 0.77 | −0.7 |
| Malaysia | 4.66 | 3.9 | Central Africa | 0.77 | −0.7 |

*Note:* For some countries like the Congo, I did not have 2000 data; the Congo would certainly qualify as one of the greatest failures.

58. The table refers to the period prior to 1980. Unfortunately, the political system variable from the *Database of Political Institutions* (see note to table 7.5) begins its coding from 1975 only.

59. I did not have the average tariff data for the period before 1980.

60. See Bairoch (1997, vol. 2, chapt. 21) for a discussion of African incomes at the time of the industrial revolution in the West.

61. The same point regarding the importance of the Pacific trade with the United States for Korea's and Taiwan's export-driven success is made by Hsiao and Hsiao (2003, p. 237).

62. While all but one WENAO country are at their historic income peak in 2000, and Asia is only 3.5 percent below the peak, Latin America and the Caribbean are 10 percent below the peak, Africa 17 percent, and Eastern Europe and FSU a whopping 30 percent (all of these are unweighted figures; see appendix 3).

63. Net Official Development Assistance (ODA) to sub-Saharan Africa, which in the 1980s averaged $33 per person annually, was about $20 in the second half of the 1990s (all figures in 2001 constant U.S. dollars; data kindly provided by Xiao Ye from the World Bank).

64. No less of a mainstream authority than Stanley Fischer, the former de facto supremo of the IMF, writes, "The international trading system *is* biased against developing countries" (2003, p. 24; emphasis in the text). On asymmetric rules of the games, particularly with the advent of WTO, see Nayyar (1997), Third World Network (2001), Jomo (2002), and Birdsall (2002).

65. Another source of complaint often voiced by the Third World countries is the imposition of very high standards concerning, for example, child labor, union rights, and environment. Here, however, their case is much weaker since the standards represent (what may be called) the *acquis humanitaire* and as such are desirable even in poor countries.

66. It is not irrelevant that a recent negative utopia *Jennifer Government* by Max Berry has the world divided into three blocs: the first world composed of the United States, Russia, Latin America, and Asia (without China), which is a technologically sophisticated area with no taxation and no government, ruled by a score of large corporations; the second world: Europe and China, countries with strong governments and welfare states; and the third world: Africa and the Middle East, where anomie reigns supreme. It is notable that no migration nor travel is allowed from Africa into the United States (and the rest of the First World).

67. The same conclusion holds if instead of Gini, we use Theil index.

68. It may not be quite clear why adding China to the sample of countries reduces (in the 1990s) Concept 2 inequality while (as we shall see later) China's contribution to overall Concept 2 inequality is pretty substantial. To explain this, consider the definition of Concept 2 inequality

$$G = \frac{1}{\mu} \sum_{i}^{n} \sum_{j>i}^{n} (y_j - y_i) p_i p_j.$$

This can be rewritten as

$$G = \frac{1}{2\mu}\sum_{i\neq k}^{n}\sum_{j\neq k}^{n} | y_j - y_i | p_j p_i + \frac{1}{2\mu}\sum_{i=1}^{n} | y_k - y_i | p_k p_i = A + \frac{1}{2\mu}\sum_{i=1}^{n} | y_k - y_i | p_k p_i, \quad (8)$$

where the entire first right-hand side term is written as $A$, and $k$ is the relevant country (China) . All other terms are defined as before. Now, once China is dropped from the sample, all population shares ($p_i$'s) will increase by a factor of ß (about 1.29 for the year 2000), and the world mean income will change, too, by a factor α (in the year 2000 if China is dropped, μ will go up by 11 percent). The new Gini will be

$$G_1 = \frac{1}{2\alpha\mu}(\beta)^2 \sum_{i\neq k}^{n}\sum_{j\neq k}^{n} | y_j - y_i | p_i p_j = \frac{1}{\alpha}(\beta)^2 A. \quad (9)$$

The issue then becomes under what conditions equation (9) can be greater than (8). We know that in 2000, the second term in equation (8), summing all absolute income differences between China and all other countries and then normalizing them by mean world income, amounts to 14.6 Gini points. The overall 2000 Gini was 50.2. Thus $A = 50.2 - 14.5 = 35.7$, which, multiplied by $(\beta)^2/\alpha$ [1.48 * $(1.29)^2/1.1$] as per equation (9), gives $G_1 = 52.8$, and $G_1 > G$. The Gini without China is thus indeed shown to be greater than the Gini that includes China (even if China's contribution to inequality is very large).

69. I am using 1965 as the start-up year because it is the year when the steady decline in Concept 2 inequality begins. If one were to use 1960, there would have been practically no difference in Concept 2 inequality between 1960 and 1978.

70. Note as a curiosity that this is the same relative level as that attained by Japan around 1950.

71. Notice that throughout, the interaction within the "triangle" alone explains about a fifth of Concept 2 international inequality. To get to the overall contribution of China, India, and the United States, we need to include the "interactions" (the ICT terms) between each member of the triangle and all other (100+) countries. Then, the contribution is about one-half of total inequality.

72. More exactly, the distance between the United States and Germany increased by about as much as the distance between the United States and Japan went down, and Japan and Germany switched places. German decline was due to the unification with a poorer country (the former German Democratic Republic).

73. All in 1995 international dollars.

74. 1952 is the first year for which the World Bank and the official Chinese data are available.

75. This is, however, less radical than the 1995 Maddison data which give an even higher 1952 GDP per capita (see appendix 7). As the appendix makes clear, the discrepancies between the sources are far greater in the case of China than other countries (and Maddison's revisions between 1995 and 2001 versions are also much greater than for other countries).

76. The data were kindly supplied by Tamar Manuelyan Atinc, Roberto Zagha, and Bala Bhaskar Naidu, all from the World Bank.

77. Interestingly, the all-India and all-China price levels in 1995 are almost identical: 21 percent of international (U.S.) level in India and 22 percent in China. Thus nominal dollar incomes in both countries (and all their regional units) are boosted by a factor of almost five.

78. Using provincial CPIs to convert 1978 into 1995 values is in principle possible. However, that would make sense only if we had data on different PPP exchange rates by province. Short of that, using a provincial CPI will simply give a boost to incomes of high-inflation provinces: their incomes would be shown higher in real terms than warranted. This would be akin to using the same PPP exchange rate for two countries that, starting with the same price level, have experienced different inflation rates.

79. After 1993, the sum of provincial GDPs exceeds the all-China values by an ever-increasing percentage. Growth rates of all-China GDP are therefore also higher when obtained by the summation of provincial GDPs than when given for the country as a whole. The difference amounts to about two percentage points per annum. This is yet another point that sheds doubt on the accuracy of Chinese GDP numbers (see the estimates in Maddison [1998, 2001] and the comment by Xu [1999]). Broadly speaking. Maddison's adjustment shaves some two to three percentage points off the official all-China growth rate after the 1978 reforms. The rising discrepancy between provincial and all-national statistics confirms what Heston (2001, p. 3) calls "winds of falsification," which became more common after 1995. Heston, in the new version 6.1 of Penn World Tables, explicitly rejects Chinese official growth rates (see appendix 7).

80. Indian states throughout were below world mean income. They too were becoming relatively richer, however. While in 1980 the range was from 10 percent of world mean income (Bihar) to 29 percent (Punjab), in 2000 the range was from 10 (Bihar) to 43 (Punjab). The average population-weighted ratio, reflecting India's rise, went up too.

81. If we use the same provincial- and state-level data to calculate Concept 2 inequality for China and India, we find that between 1980 and 2000 India's population-weighted inter-state inequality has grown by a half, and China's by a quarter.

82. See Bourguignon and Morrisson (1999) for a pioneering attempt that calculates world inequality from 1815 until practically today and that, of course, relies on many approximations and strong assumptions.

Since the same source of data (household surveys) is used to calculate world poverty, the same problem, namely, the lack of reliable data on world poverty prior to the late 1980s, is true as well. This is why the first, and by now famous, World Bank calculations of the number of people with income less than $PPP1 per capita per day were done only in the 1990 *World Development Report* (World Bank 1990, chapt. 2). As we lack a single world survey from which we could directly calculate both poverty and inequality statistics, we need to approximate a world survey by "piecing" together as it were individual country surveys. The relationship between world poverty and world inequality is then, in principle, the same as between poverty and inequality within a country. An increase in inequality need not indicate an increase in poverty for at least two reasons: (1) mean income might increase, so even the income of the poor might go up and some of them might cease to be poor, and (2) what happens to poverty critically depends on where we draw the poverty line and thus what happens to the incomes of the people that are close to the poverty line. It is in theory possible, although not very likely, that poverty declines even if average income is unchanged and inequality measured by the Gini coefficient goes up. We do not deal with poverty here except very briefly, and mostly for illustrative purposes, in chapter 10.

83. After noticing that a lognormal approximation does a rather poor job in predicting the poverty gap Bourguignon (2002, p. 14) concludes, "if one wants to go beyond the poverty headcount in poverty measurement, then functional [lognormal] approximations to growth and distribution elasticity of poverty reduction may simply be unsatisfactory. Dealing with the issue of the determinants of poverty reductions will then require working with the full distribution of income or living standards rather than a few summary measures. This will probably prove to be the only satisfactory solution in the long run and the sooner poverty specialists will get used to dealing systematically with distribution data . . . the better it will be."

84. In the United States, the maximum capital gain that can be recorded in the survey is $99,999 per household annually. Similar top-coding exists in surveys of many rich countries.

85. On the additional problems with the use of averages from national accounts data and distributions from household surveys, see Ravallion (2000) and Deaton and Drèze (2002).

86. The number of "cross-overs," i.e., countries that are in one year represented with an expenditure- (or income-) based survey and in another year with a different type survey is rather small. There are nine such cases accounting for 2.8 percent of total population and 1.4 percent of world $PPP income in 1993, and thirteen cases in 1998 accounting for 1.7 percent of total population and the same percentage of world $PPP income. Thus the bias imparted by the "cross-over" countries must be minimal.

87. It may be worth noting that most of the PPPs are extrapolations since the only true global International Comparison Project (ICP) exercises were held just twice: in 1985 and then in 1993/96 (the second round was not simultaneously conducted in all countries). In addition, one should note that China has never officially participated in ICP and that estimates of China's PPP are based on surveys conducted in several cities only (see Dikhanov 2003). The 1993 PPP data used here are the same as those used in the most recent revision of World Bank $PPP 1 and $PPP 2 poverty estimates (see World Bank 2001).

88. The PPP data were obtained from the World Bank. In view of the debate regarding the bias imparted by various PPP formulas (see chapter 2 above and Dowrick and Akmal 2001; Pogge and Reddy 2002), it is important to mention that the PPP rates were calculated by the EKS formula. Dowrick and Akmal (2001) argue that the Geary-Khamis approach used in the Penn World Tables calculations overestimates incomes of poor countries. They suggest instead the use of the Afriat index. According to a personal communication by Yuri

Dikhanov from the World Bank, the EKS formula gives results that are quite similar to the Afriat index.

89. About 70 percent of surveys were conducted within a year of the benchmark. That percentage is quite stable in each benchmark year.

90. The mean incomes of the groups just below and above this one are respectively Yuan 550 and 892, so we can reasonably assume that the 180 million people have incomes that probably range between, say Yuan 600 and 750. Still, this is only an educated guess, nothing more. We have to stick with the single estimate of Yuan 695 for all.

91. Even if we know that such an error can be relatively limited (see Davies and Shorrocks 1989, pp. 100–3, who show that with ten to twelve optimally distributed data points one approximates the "true" Gini within 2–3 percent), there is almost certainly a greater underestimation of inequality in our case because the data points are not necessarily optimally distributed.

92. Obviously, this issue is of much less importance when we deal with smaller countries. The reason why we "divided" up China, India, Indonesia, and Bangladesh is that their data points are particularly large and the downward bias to the world Gini would therefore be larger too.

93. Rural and urban China (or rural and urban India, for example) are each treated as separate "countries." Similarly, in keeping with the approach adopted in the earlier calculations of concept 1 and 2 inequality, the currently existing countries are projected backward: e.g., all the republics of the former Soviet Union, Yugoslavia, and Czechoslovakia for which the data are available are treated as independent countries in 1988.

94. The common-sample coverage cannot increase because it is limited by the number of countries included in 1988.

95. The estimate of how much world $PPP GDP they account for is impossible to make due to the lack of PPP data for the countries that are not included in our calculations. However, since these are mostly poor countries, their GDPs expressed in $PPP are greater than their GDPs expressed in current dollars. Hence, the true coverage is less than 94 percent.

96. The term "income" is used for simplicity even if the welfare aggregate is either income or expenditures.

97. This is the growth rate of world per capita income as calculated from household surveys. To obtain real dollar amounts, the $PPP values for each year are deflated by U.S. Consumer Price Index.

98. It is important to note that the composition of each ventile changes between the years. Thus, the growth incidence curve simply shows whether people who belonged to a given ventile in one year had a higher or lower income than the people who belonged to the same ventile five years before, not whether the people who belonged to one ventile in, say, 1988 had a positive income growth rate or not. In effect, people who belong to any given ventile in a year would typically experience very different growth rates: some might go up, others down, in the overall distribution.

99. The implication of these results is that there is no first-order dominance of any distribution.

100. Recall that these calculations treat as "countries" rural and urban parts of four large Asian countries (China, India, Bangladesh, and Indonesia). The between-country component is thus made significantly larger than it would have been if we had used actual countries only.

101. If we had kept income levels and inequality in Eastern Europe/FSU at their 1988 levels, world Gini (full sample) would have been 64.6 instead of 65.2.

102. Note that strictly speaking rural incomes in China grew slightly faster than urban incomes. But even when this is the case, the individual Gini term (the inter-country term) can go up if the absolute distance between the two countries (in this case, urban and rural China) increases by more than mean world income (see Milanovic 2002, p.85 ).

103. Had they remained at their 1993 level, inequality would have been 0.3 Gini points higher. The Asian crisis too had some, albeit rather small, impact on overall inequality: for example, the intercountry term between urban Indonesia and the United States increased by 0.08 Gini points.

104. Datt and Ravallion (2002, p. 4) calculate that over the 1972–97 period, consumption from national accounts rose 0.74 percent per annum faster than consumption calculated from household surveys. To complicate the matter further, the methodology used to collect household survey data (the recall period in particular) had changed and made comparisons even more difficult.

105. Interestingly, the two most populous countries, China and India, exhibit the same declining household surveys/national accounts ratio but for opposite reasons. For India, the coverage of expenditures by household surveys might have gradually declined; for China, statistical upward bias of national accounts has gone up.

106. Note that when we do so, we need to recombine, into a single unit, the countries that are "broken" into rural and urban areas, and then to scale up the "whole country" mean household incomes to the level of GDP per capita.

107. They are available respectively at http://www.worldbank.org/research/growth/dddeisqu.htm. and http://www.wider.unu.edu/wiid/wiid.htm.

108. This was an anonymous paper I reviewed for a journal.

109. The lognormal distribution is defined by two parameters: the mean $\mu$, and the standard deviation $\sigma$, or $\Lambda(\mu,\sigma)$. The relationship between the Gini coefficient and the standard deviation is given by

$$Gini = 2\Phi\left(\frac{\sigma}{\sqrt{2}}\right) - 1,$$

where $\Phi$ is the distribution function of a normally distributed variable with the mean = 0 and the standard deviation = 1. Once we know the Gini coefficient, we can easily calculate the standard deviation and thus know both parameters of $\Lambda$. For example, if Gini = 0.5, then $\Phi\left(\frac{\sigma}{\sqrt{2}}\right) = 0.75$, which is the case if $\sigma = 0.96$. For the global Gini of 0.65 and lognormal distribution, the standard deviation would be 1.33. It can be easily verified that with Gini = 0, $\Phi(.) = 0.5$ and thus $\sigma = 0$.

110. And, in some cases, even distributions of households ranked by their per capita income/expenditures.

111. The same point is made by Atkinson and Brandolini (2003, p. 18). For countries where Sala-i-Martin has quintiles from one year only, the quintile shares are supposed to remain the same for the entire twenty-seven year period; if a country has no income distribution data at all, its inequality is assumed to be zero (all individuals receive GDP per capita).

112. Annual values of Concept 3 Gini for the period 1950–2000 are shown in figure 11.1 (Bhalla, 2002, p. 174). The benchmark year distributions and Ginis are given in Appendix C, Table C1.

113. The following table (calculated from Bhalla's [2002] appendix C) shows that for twenty-eight countries Bhalla had only one income distribution that he first "assigned" to each benchmark year, and then assumed to hold constant, for that country, during fifty years. Of course, the lack of income distribution data is most common in sub-Saharan Africa; least common for the industrialized countries. There are in total only 286 independent distributions that are used to approximate 6,800 distributions (136 countries times 50 years). Thus, on average, each distribution is "stretched" to stand for no fewer than twenty-four

| | *Number of Independent Income Distributions per Country* | | |
|---|---|---|---|
| | *Three* | *Two* | *One* |
| Asia | 11 | 7 | 2 |
| Sub-Saharan Africa | 0 | 19 | 16 |
| Middle East and North Africa | 0 | 6 | 5 |
| Latin America and Caribbean | 10 | 15 | 2 |
| Eastern Europe | 4 | 14 | 3 |
| Industrialized world | 17 | 5 | 0 |
| *Total countries* | *42* | *66* | *28* |

*Note:* The value in each cell gives the number of countries in that region with three, two, or one independent income distributions.

distributions! As argued in Milanovic (2003) regarding Sala-i-Martin's calculations, the art of approximation is thus indeed taken to new heights.

114. Firebaugh (2003, p. 215) also estimates global inequality. Most of his important book is concerned with Concept 2 and Concept 1 inequality as well as with within-nation inequality. In the last chapter, however, he rather cursorily puts these estimates together and concludes that global inequality must have decreased because the decline in Concept 2 inequality was greater than the av-

| | *(1) 1980* | *(2) 1995* | *(3) Change (Theil points)* | *(4) Change (in %)* |
|---|---|---|---|---|
| Between-nation (Concept 2) | 65 | 52 | −13 | −20 |
| Within-nation | 19 | 22 | +3 | |
| Global | 84 | 74 | −10 | |

erage increase in within-national inequalities. He uses the Theil index, which is fully decomposable. His results are reproduced in the table above. Columns (1) and (3) are taken directly from the book (p. 215, table 11.1); columns (2) and (4) are calculated.

The odd thing, in view of the rest of the book, where the calculations are quite clear, is that the 1995 inequality level must be inferred from the change given in the table. Moreover, when we begin to look for the source of these values, the plot thickens. The between-nation component of 65 is not given in table 6.1 (p. 102), which presents Firebaugh's Concept 2 calculations. This is because of the break in the series. For the period 1960–89, Firebaugh uses the Penn World Tables (PWT) data; for the period after 1990, the World Bank data. However, what we know from his own calculations (table 6.1) is that between 1980 and 1989, Concept 2 Theil (based on PWT) was stable and that between 1990 and 1998 it decreased by 11.4 percent (see table 6.3, p. 107). If we apply this decline to the Theil value *shown* for 1980 by Firebaugh, we get the new values for the between-component (see the table below). The decline in Concept 2 is now 5.8 Theil points, not 13 as claimed.

Moreover, when we go to the source of Firebaugh's numbers for the within-nation component (table 9.3, p. 164), we find that he uses a panel of fifty-seven countries. If he were to select the data coming from the repeated cross-sections whose country-coverage is much greater, the second line changes substantially too. The outcome is now an *increase* in global inequality, rather than a decline. This illustrates how fragile these results are, and how, within the data provided by the same author, an equally plausible choice of methods easily reverses the conclusions.

| | *(1)*<br>*1980* | *(2)*<br>*1995* | *(3)*<br>*Change* | *(4)*<br>*Change (in %)* |
|---|---|---|---|---|
| Between-nation (Concept 2) | 53.1 | 47.3 | –5.8 | –11.4 |
| Within-nation | 18.0 | 25.0 | +7.0 | |
| Global | 71.1 | 72.3 | +1.2 | |

115. As well as their use of the Penn World Tables rather than Maddison's data. The use of the latter reverses the conclusion of declining Concept 2 and Concept 3 inequality as shown both by Bourguignon and Morrison (2002) and by Sutcliffe (2003).

116. Reproduced from figure 8.5 in this book.

117. Note that these are 1998 international dollars, while the GDP per capita statistics discussed earlier are expressed in 1995 international dollars. The conversion between the two is about 1.07 to 1.

118. Which in the case of the world (whose median income in 1998 was $PPP 1328) turns out to be between $PPP 1000 and $PPP 1660.

119. The lowest country value obtains for Brazil: the average income of the middle class is 46 percent of the country average.

120. The rich are those with per capita income higher than the mean per capita income of Portugal.

121. The former is obtained as the ratio of 10 to 15.9 percent, the latter as the ratio of 13 to 16 percent (see table 10.1).

122. While the poorest ventile in South Africa is near the world's bottom: it has an income higher than only 7.4 percent of world population.

123. All standard contingency statistics, however, are significant at a 1 percent level.

124. The same argument was recently made by Peter Singer (2002, pp. 174–75): "We can increase taxes on rich . . . [individuals] who have higher incomes or leave large sums to their heirs, and use the revenue to increase aid to those people in the world's poorest nations who have incomes well below average even for the nation in which they are living. That would reduce inequality both in poor nations [and rich too; my addition] and between nations."

125. These countries are Australia, Austria, Bangladesh, Belgium, Brazil, Canada, China, Denmark. Finland, France, Germany, India, Indonesia, Ireland, Italy, Japan, Mexico, the Netherlands, Norway, Pakistan, Spain, Sweden, United Kingdom, United States, the former Czechoslovakia, and the former USSR.

126. These are the same twenty-six countries as in the previous note plus Argentina, Bulgaria, Chile, Colombia, Greece, Hungary, South Korea, Burma, New Zealand, Peru, Philippines, Poland, Portugal, Romania, Switzerland, Taiwan, Thailand, Turkey, Venezuela, and former Yugoslavia.

127. Kuznets (1954) was the first to have explicitly calculated Concept 2 inequality. If we use his figures provided in table 7 of the quoted article and compute the Concept 2 Ginis, we obtain 28.3 for the year 1894–95, 37.2 for the year 1938, and 35.7 for the year 1949. The results refer to the developed world only, since these are the only countries included by Kuznets (world population coverage is around 30 percent).

128. According to Maddison's (2003) data, China's per capita income in 1950 was 20 percent less than in 1913. On the other hand, U.S. income—which by 1913 was already the second highest in the world after Australia's—increased by 80 percent.

129. The 1952–78 values are obtained from the thirty-three "countries" as defined by Bourguignon and Morrisson (2003). These values seem to underestimate world inequality, particularly so in 1952 when the within-county component (difference between concepts 3 and 2) amounts to an implausible 7 Gini points only.

130. Actually, the 1988 value may not be a dip, but rather the minimum reached following ten years of fast Chinese growth and before the collapse of Eastern Europe contributed to global inequality.

131. As Sen (2002) writes, "[T]he concept of private property on ideas and the corresponding entitlement to incomes generated therefrom is full of delicious vulgarities," not the least being that it "goes right against the spirit of scientific enterprise, and against the idea that knowledge is for all, rather than for the profit of some 'owner.'" The incentive argument in favor of intellectual property rights—namely that the production of inventions will suffer if the inventors are not sufficiently remunerated—must be, Sen writes, taken seriously. Yet an almost negligible amount of money is generated for the large pharmaceutical companies from their sales in poor countries; hence insistence on high prices

there to the detriment of the health of the people has scant commercial justification. Its main rationale is avoidance of a precedent-setting.

132. Notice that the income Lorenz curve and Gini calculated here are equivalent to Concept 2 inequality.

133. The U.S. population share is 4.8 percent, and the U.S. share in the IMF voting rights is 17.7 percent.

134. Karl Deutsch's (1955) work on how denser networks of communication helped create national consciousness is a classic in this line of thought.

135. To see that, write the Gini as

$$G = \frac{1}{2\mu n^2} \sum_{i=1}^{n} \sum_{j=1}^{n} | y_i - y_j |.$$

136. "In a free society in which the position of the different individuals and groups is not the result of anybody's design—or could, within such a society, be altered in accordance with a generally applicable principle—the differences in rewards simply cannot meaningfully be described as just or unjust" (Hayek 1976, 2: 70).

137. See his interview in the French newspaper paper *La Tribune*, November 13, 2003.

138. Of course, if we believed in an entirely anonymous global world, the responsibility of the rich from poor countries is no greater than that of the rich from rich countries. Yet it is not unreasonable to assume that a poor country's "own" rich might have a bit more to do with its poverty than other countries' rich.

139. So to a researcher, a few decades hence, who would have access to a world household survey, issues with which we had to grapple here would seem quaint and, obviously, unnecessary.

140. Suppose that in the extreme case, the new country's income is 0. Then the first term in equation (A3) becomes

$$\frac{1}{n^2\mu_1 + n\mu_1} \sum_{i}^{n} \sum_{j>i}^{n} (y_j - y_i),$$

which is obviously less than G from equation (A1).

141. However, as mentioned before, Heston (2001, p. 3) writes of the "winds of falsification," particularly after 1985.

142. Note, however, that the Penn World Tables imply a significantly higher real growth for India than do the World Bank data. According to the former, in 2000 India's GDP per capita was 3.3 times greater than in 1952, as opposed to 2.7 times using the World Bank data.

# *References*


Abramovitz, Moses. 1989. *Thinking about Growth*. Cambridge: Cambridge University Press.

Alesina, Alberto, and Perotti, Roberto. 1994. "The Political Economy of Growth: A Critical Survey of the Recent Literature." *The World Bank Economic Review* 8 (3): 350–71.

Ali, A.A.G., C. Malvanda, and Y. Suliman. 1999. "Official Development Assistance to Africa: An Overview." *Journal of African Economies* 8, no. 4 (December): 504–27.

Anderson, Edward. 2001. "Globalisation and Wage Inequalities, 1870–1970." *European Review of Economic History* 5: 91–118.

Arrighi, Giovanni. 2002. "The African Crisis: World Systemic and Regional Aspects." *New Left Review* (May–June 2002).

Ashton, Basil, Kenneth Hill, Alan Piazza and Robin Zeitz. 1984. "Famine in China 1958–61." *Population and Development Review* 10 (December 11): 613–45.

Atkinson, Anthony T., and Andrea Brandolini. 1999. "Promise and Pitfalls in the Use of 'Secondary' Data-Sets: Income Inequality in OECD Countries." Typescript, July.

Atkinson, Anthony T., and Andrea Brandolini. 2003. "The Panel-of-Countries Approach to Explaining Income Inequality: An Interdisciplinary Research Agenda." Paper presented at 2003 Siena Summer School on Global Inequality, July.

Bairoch, Paul. 1981. "The Main Trends in National Economic Disparities since the Industrial Revolution." In *Disparities since the Industrial Revolution*, edited by Paul Bairoch and M. Levy-Leboyer. London: Macmillan.

———. 1993. *Economics and World History: Myths and Paradoxes*. Chicago: University of Chicago Press.

———. 1997. *Victoires et déboires. Histoire économique et sociale du monde du XVIe siècle à nos jours*. 3 volumes. Paris: Folio Histoire Gallimard.

Banerjee, Abhijit, and Thomas Piketty. 2003. "Top Indian Incomes, 1956–2000." Mimeo, version June 2003.

Barber, William J. [1961] 1984. *The Economy of British Central Africa*, Westport, Conn.: Greenwood; originally published by Stanford University Press.

Bardhan, Pranab. 2000. *Social Justice in the Global Economy*. ILO Social Policy Lecture. Geneva: ILO, International Institute for Labor Studies. Available at www.ilo.org/public/english/inst/papers/socpolecs/bardhan/index.htm.

Barrett, David B. 1982. *World Christian Encyclopedia*. New York: Oxford University Press.

Barro, Robert. 1991. "Economic Growth in a Cross Section of Countries." *Quarterly Journal of Economics* 106 (2): 407–43.

Barro, Robert, and Xavier Sala-i-Martin. 1992. "Convergence." *Journal of Political Economy* 100 (2): 223–51.

Barro, Robert, and Xavier Sala-i-Martin. 1995. *Economic Growth*. New York: McGraw Hill.

Baumol, William. 1986. "Productivity Growth, Convergence, and Welfare: What the Long-run Data Show." *American Economic Review* 76 (December): 1072–116.

Baumol, William, and Edward Wolff. 1998. "Productivity Growth, Convergence, and Welfare: Reply." *American Economic Review* 78 (December): 1155–59.

Beck, T., G. Clarke, A. Groff, P. Keefer, and P. Walsh. 2000. "New Tools and New Tests in Comparative Political Economy: The Database of Political Institutions." World Bank Policy Research Working Paper No. 2283.

Berry, Albert, and John Serieux. 2003. "Riding the Elephants: The Evolution of World Economic Growth and Income Distribution at the End of the 20th Century (1980–2000)." Available at http://www.gsb.columbia.edu/ipd/povertywk.html.

Bhalla, Surjit. 2000. "Growth and Poverty in India—Myth and Reality." Available at http://www.oxusresearch.com/economic.asp.

———. 2002. *Imagine There Is No Country*. Washington, D.C.: Institute for International Economics.

Birdsall, Nancy. 2002. "A Stormy Day on an Open Field: Asymmetry and Convergence in Global Economy." Paper presented at G-20 Workshop: Globalization, Living Standards, and Inequality: Recent Progress and Continuing Challenges, Sydney, Australia May 26–28.

Birdsall, Nancy, Carol Graham, and Stefano Pettinato. 2000. "Stuck in the Tunnel? Have New Markets Muddled the Middle Class?" Typescript, June 6, 2000 version. Available at http://www.ceip.org/programs/polecon/recentpapers.htm.

Birdsall, Nancy, and John Williamson. 2002. *Delivering on Debt Relief: From IMF Gold to New Aid Architecture*. Washington, D.C.: Center for Global Development and Institute for International Economics.

Bliss, Christopher. 1999. "Galton's Fallacy and Economic Convergence." *Oxford Economic Papers* 51: 4–14.

———. 2000. "Galton's Fallacy and Economic Convergence: A Reply to Cannon and Duck." *Oxford Economic Papers* 52: 420–22.

Boltho, Andrea, and Gianni Toniolo. 1999. "The Assessment: The Twentieth-Century Achievements, Failures, Lessons." *Oxford Review of Economic Policy* 15, no. 4. (Winter): 1–17.

Borensztein, Eduardo, and Jonathan D. Ostry. 1996. "Accounting for China's Growth Performance." *The American Economic Review* 86, no. 2 (May): 224–28. From the Papers and Proceedings of the Hundredth and Eighth Annual Meeting of the American Economic Association, San Francisco, Calif., January 5–7, 1996.

Bourguignon, François. 2002. "The Growth Elasticity of Poverty Reduction: Explaining Heterogeneity across Countries and Time Periods." February 2002 version; forthcoming in *Growth and Inequality*, edited by T. Eichler and S. Turnovsky. Cambridge, Mass.: MIT Press.

Bourguignon, François, and Christian Morrisson. 1999. "The Size Distribution of Income among World Citizens, 1820–1990." Mimeo, June; published in *American Economic Review* (September 2002): 727–44.

Braudel, Fernand. [1979] 1984. *The Perspective of the World: Civilization and Capitalism, 15th–18th Centuries.* New York: Harper and Row.

Cannon, Edmund S., and Nigel W. Duck. 2000. "Galton's Fallacy and Economic Convergence." *Oxford Economic Papers* 52: 415–19.

Castles, Ian. 2001. Email sent on March 15, 2001, regarding B. Milanovic's calculations of world inequality.

Chotikapanich, D., R. Valenzuela, and D.S.P. Rao. 1997. "Global and Regional Inequality in the Distribution of Income: Estimation with Limited and Incomplete Data." *Empirical Economics* 22: 533–46.

Cline, William R. 2004. *Trade Policy and Global Poverty.* Washington, D.C.: Center for Global Development and Institute for International Economics.

Concialdi, Pierre. 1997. "Income Distribution in France: The Mid-1980s Turning Point." In *Changing Patterns in the Distribution of Economic Welfare. An International Perspective,* edited by Peter Gottschalk, Bjorn Gustafson, and Edward Palmer. Cambridge: Cambridge University Press.

Datt, Gaurav, and Martin Ravallion. 2002. "Is India's Growth Leaving the Poor Behind?" World Bank Policy Research Paper No. 2846, May.

Davies, J. B., and A. F. Shorrocks. 1989. "Optimal Grouping of Income and Wealth Data." *Journal of Econometrics* 42: 97–108.

Deaton, Angus. 2000. "Preliminary Notes on Reporting Periods in the Indian NSS 52nd through 54th Rounds." Mimeo, Research Program in Development Studies, Princeton University.

———. 2003. "Measuring Poverty in a Growing World (or Measuring Growth in a Poor World)." NBER Working Paper 9822, June. Available at http://www.wws.princeton.edu/~deaton/working.htm.

Deaton, Angus, and Jean Drèze. 2002. "Poverty and Inequality in India: A Reexamination." *Economic and Political Weekly* (September 7): 3729–48.

Deininger, Klaus, and Lyn Squire. 1996. "A New Data Set Measuring Inequality." *World Bank Economic Review* 10: 565–91.

Deininger, Klaus, Lyn Squire, and Tao Zhang. 1995. "Measuring Income Inequality: A New Data Base." Mimeo, August.

Deutsch, Karl. 1955. *Nationalism and Social Communication.* Cambridge: Harvard University Press.

Dikhanov, Yuri. 2003. "PPP in Global Inequality Measurement." PowerPoint presentation at the Conference on Global Poverty, Columbia University, New York, March 31–April 1, 2003. Available at http://www.gsb.columbia.edu/ipd/povertywk.html.

Dikhanov, Yuri, and Michael Ward. 2001. "Evolution of the Global Distribution of Income, 1970–99." August 2001 draft.

Diven, Polly J. 2001. "The Domestic Determinants of U.S. Food Aid Policy." *Food Policy* 26, no. 5 (October): 455–74.

Dowrick, Steve, and Muhammed Akmal. 2001. "Contradictory Trends in Global Income Inequality: A Tale of Two Biases." Draft March 29, 2001. Available at http://ecocomm.anu.edu.au/economics/staff/dowrick/dowrick.html.

Dowrick, Steve, and J. Bradford de Long. 2001. "Globalization and Convergence." Paper prepared for NBER conference on Globalization in Historical Perspective, Santa Barbara, Calif., May 4–5.

Dowrick, Steve, and Duc-Tho Nguyen. 1989. "OECD Comparative Economic Growth 1950–85: Catch-up and Convergence." *American Economic Review* 79 (December): 1010–30.

Easterly, William. 2001. "The Lost Decades. Developing Countries' Stagnation in spite of Policy Reform, 1980–98." *Journal of Economic Growth* 6 (2): 135–57.

Easterly, William, and Ross Levine. 2001. "It's Not Factor Accumulation: Stylized Facts and Growth Models." *World Bank Economic Review* 15 (2): 177–220.

Estrin, Saul, and Giovanni Urga. 1997. "Testing for Ongoing Convergence in Central and Eastern Europe, 1970–95." CEPR Discussion Paper No. 1616.

Feldstein, Martin. 1998. "Overview." Introduction to the Federal Reserve Conference on Income Inequality: Issues and Policy Options, Symposium Proceedings.

Firebaugh, Glenn. 1999. "Empirics of World Income Inequality." *American Journal of Sociology* 104: 1597–630.

———. 2003. *The New Geography of Global Income Inequality*. Cambridge: Harvard University Press.

Fischer, Stanley. 2003. "Globalization and its Challenges." Ely Lecture delivered at the American Economic Association meeting in Washington, D.C., January 3, 2003. Forthcoming in *American Economic Review Papers and Proceedings*. Available at http://www.iie.com/fischer/pdf/fischer011903.pdf.

Fong, Christina, Samuel Bowles, and Herbert Gintis. 2003. "Reciprocity, Self-interest and the Welfare State." Forthcoming in *Handbook on Economics of Giving, Reciprocity and Altruism*, edited by C. A. Gerard-Varrett. Dordrecht: Elsevier, 2004.

Fourastié, Jean. 1963. *Le grand espoir du XXième siècle.* Paris: Gallimard, édition definitive.

Friedman, Milton. 1992. "Do Old Fallacies Ever Die?" *Journal of Economic Literature* 30: 2129–32.

Fuente, Angel da la. 1998. "Convergence Equation and Income Dynamics: The Sources of OECD Convergence, 1970–95." Centre for Economic Policy Research. Discussion Paper Series, no. 1794, January.

Galbraith, James K. 2002. "A Perfect Crime: Inequality in the Age of Globalization." *Deadalus* (Winter): 11–25.

Galbraith, James K., and Hyunsub Kum. 2002. "Inequality and Economic Growth: Data Comparisons and Econometric Tests." Mimeo, version April 5.

Goerlich, Francisco J., and Matilde Mas. 2001. "Inequality in Spain, 1973–91: Contribution to a Regional Database." *Review of Income and Wealth*, series 47, no. 3 (September).

Gottschalk, Peter, Bjorn Gustafsson, and Edward Palmer, eds. 1997. *Changing Patterns in the Distribution of Economic Welfare. An International Perspective.* Cambridge and New York: Cambridge University Press.

Hayek, Augustus. 1976. *Law, Legislation and Liberty: Volume 2. The Mirage of Social Justice.* Chicago: Chicago University Press.

Heston, Alan. 2001. "Treatment of China in PWT 6.1." December. Available at http://pwt.econ.upenn.edu/.

Hobsbawm, Eric. 1990. *Nations and Nationalism since 1780: Programme, Myth, Reality*. Cambridge: Cambridge University Press/Canto.

Hoff, Karla. 1996. "Market Failures and the Distribution of Wealth." *Politics and Society* (December): 411–32.

Hroch, Miroslav. 1993. "From National Movement to Fully-fledged Nation." *New Left Review*, no. 198 (March–April).

Hsiao, Frank S. T., and Mei-Chu W. Hsiao. 2003. " 'Miracle Growth' in the Twentieth-Century International Comparison of East Asian Development." *World Development* 31 (2): 227–57.

Hu, Zuliu F., and Mohsin Khan. 1996. "Why Is China Growing So Fast?" IMF Working Paper No. 96/75, Washington, D.C.: IMF. Also published in *IMF Staff Papers* 44, no. 1 (March 1997).

Isham, Jonathan, Michael Woolcock, Lant Pritchett, and Gwen Busby. 2002. "The Varieties of Rentier Experience: How Natural Resource Endowments Affect the Political Economy of Economic Growth." Mimeo, January 8.

Islam, Nazrul. 1995. "Growth Empirics: A Panel Data Approach." *Quarterly Journal of Economics* 110: 1127–70.

———. 2003. "What Have We Learnt from the Convergence Debate?" *Journal of Economic Surveys* 17 (3): 309–62.

IWM (Institut fur die Wiessenschaften von Menschen) Newsletter. 2003. "Morality and Politics." Review of Conference on Morality and Politics. No. 79, p. 2. Vienna, December 6–8, 2002.

Jomo, K. S. 2002. "Globalisation for Whom? A World for All." Ishac Shari Memorial Lecture at the Institut Kajian Malaysia dan Antarabangsa. IKMAS. Bangi, Selangor, Malaysia, June 11, 2002. Available at www.networkideas.org.

Jones, Basil. 2002. "Economic Integration and Convergence of Per Capita Income in West Africa." *African Development Review* 14, no. 1 (June 2002): 18–47.

Jones, Charles. 1997. "On the Evolution of World Income Distribution." *Journal of Economic Perspectives* 11, no. 3 (Summer): 19–36.

Kapstein, Ethan. 2002. "Models of International Economic Justice." Forthcoming in *Perspectives on Politics*.

Keefer, Phil, and Stephen Knack. 2002. "Polarization, Politics, and Property Rights: Links between Inequality and Growth." *Public Choice* 111, nos. 1–2 (March): 127–54.

Khor, Martin. 2001. "The Multilateral Trading System: A Development Perspective." Mimeo, World Network, December.

Krueger, Anne O. 2002. "Supporting Globalization." Remarks at the 2002 Eisenhower National Security Conference on "National Security for the 21st Century: Anticipating Challenges, Seizing Opportunities, Building Capabilities," September 26. Available at http://www.imf.org/external/np/speeches/2002/092602a.htm.

Krugman, Paul. 1991. *Geography and Trade*. Cambridge: MIT Press.

Kuznets, Simon. 1954. "Regional Economic Trends and Levels of Living." In *Economic Growth and Structure: Selected Essays*, edited by Simon Kuznets. New Delhi: Oxford and IBH, 1965.

Kuznets, Simon. 1965. *Economic Growth and Structure: Selected Essays.* New Delhi: Oxford and IBH.

Lambert, Peter, and J. Richard Aronson. 1993. "Inequality Decomposition Analysis and the Gini Coefficient Revisited." *Economic Journal* (September): 1221–27.

Leech, Dennis. 2002. "Voting Power in the Governance of International Monetary Fund." *Annals of Operations Research* 109, pp. 375–97.

Li, Qing, and David Papell. 1999. "Convergence of International Output: Time Series Evidence for 16 OECD Countries." *International Review of Economics and Finance* 8 (3): 267–80.

Lin, Justin Yifu, and Dennis Tao Yang. 2000. "Food Availability, Entitlements and the Great Chinese Famine of 1959–61." *Economic Journal* 110, no. 1 (January): 136–58.

Lindert, Peter H., and Jeffrey G. Williamson. 2001. "Does Globalization Make World More Unequal?" National Bureau of Economic Research. Working paper no. 8228, April.

Lucas, Robert. 1990. "Why Doesn't Capital Flow from Rich to Poor Countries?" *American Economic Review Papers and Proceedings* 80 (2): 92–96.

———. 1998. "The Industrial Revolution: Past and Future." Mimeo, University of Chicago.

———. 2002. *Lectures on Economic Growth.* Cambridge: Harvard University Press.

Maudos, Joaquin, José Manuel Pastor, and Lorenzo Serrano. 2000. "Convergence in OECD Countries: Technical Change, Efficiency and Productivity." *Applied Econometrics* 32, no. 6 (May).

Maddison, Angus. 1991. *Dynamic Forces in Capitalist Development.* Oxford: Oxford University Press.

———. 1995. *Monitoring the World Economy, 1820–92.* Paris: OECD Development Centre Studies.

———. 1998. *Chinese Economic Performance in the Long Run.* Paris: OECD Development Centre Studies.

———. 2001. *The World Economy: A Millenial Perspective.* Paris: OECD Development Centre Studies.

———. 2003. *The World Economy: Historical Statistics.* Paris: OECD Development Centre Studies.

Mankiw, G., David Romer, and D. Weil. 1992. "A Contribution to the Empirics of Economic Growth." *Quarterly Journal of Economics* 107 (2): 407–37.

Melchior, Arne, Kjetil Telle, and Henrik Wiig. 2000. "Globalisation and Inequality: World Income Distribution and Living Standards, 1960–1998." Royal Norwegian Ministry of Foreign Affairs, Studies on Foreign Policy Issues, Report 6B:2000, October.

Milanovic, Branko. 1999. "True World Income Distribution, 1988 and 1993: First Calculation Based on Household Surveys Alone." World Bank Policy Research Working Paper No. 2244, November.

———. 2002. "True World Income Distribution, 1988 and 1993: First Calculation Based on Household Surveys Alone." *Economic Journal* 112, no. 476 (January): 51–92.

———. 2003. "The Ricardian Vice: Why Sala-i-Martin's Calculations of World Income Inequality Are Wrong." Mimeo. Available at http://econpapers.hhs.ee/RAS/primi44.htm

Milanovic, Branko, and Shlomo Yitzhaki. 2001. "Decomposing World Income Distribution: Does the World Have a Middle Class?" World Bank Policy Research Working Paper No. 2561, February.

Mistiaen, Johan, and Martin Ravallion. 2003. "Survey Compliance and the Distribution of Income." World Bank Working Paper No. 2956, January.

Morrisson, Christian. 2000. "Historical Perspectives on Income Distribution: The Case of Europe." In *Handbook of Income Distribution*, edited by Anthony Atkinson and François Bourguignon. Dordrecht: Elsevier.

Myrdal, Gunnar. 1970. *The Challenge of World Poverty: A World Anti-Poverty Program in Outline*. New York: Pantheon Books, Random House.

Nayyar, Deepak. 1997. "Globalization: The Game, the Players and the Rules." In *The Political Economy of Globalization*, edited by Satya Dev Gupta. Boston, Dordrecht, and London: Kluwer.

———. 2003. "The Existing System and the Missing Institutions." In *Governing Globalization: Issues and Institutions*, edited by D. Nayyar. Oxford: Oxford University Press.

Omoruyi, Leslie O. 2001. *Contending Theories on Development Aid: Post–Cold War Evidence from Africa*. Aldershot, U.K.; Burlington, Vt.; and Sydney: Ashgate.

Pen, Jan. 1971. *Income Distribution: Facts, Theories, Policies.* New York, Washington, D.C.: Praeger.

Perotti, Roberto. 1993. "Political Equilibrium, Income Distribution, and Growth." *Review of Economic Studies* 60 (October): 755–76.

———. 1996. "Growth, Income Distribution, and Democracy: What the Data Say." *Journal of Economic Growth* 1 (June): 149–87.

Pogge, Thomas W. 2002. " 'Assisting' the Global Poor." Mimeo.

Pogge, Thomas W., and Sanjay Reddy. 2003. "Unknown: The Extent, Distribution, and Trend of Global Income Poverty." Version July 26. Available at http://www.columbia.edu/~sr793/povpop.pdf.

Pomeranz, Kenneth. 2000. *The Great Divergence: China, Europe, and the Making of the Modern World Economy.* Princeton Economic History of the Western World series. Princeton and Oxford: Princeton University Press.

Prados de la Escosura, Leandro. 2000. "International Comparison of Real Product, 1820–1990: An Alternative Data Set." *Explorations in Economic History* 37: 1–41.

Pritchett, Lant. 1997. "Divergence, Big Time." *Journal of Economic Perspectives* 11 (3): 3–17.

Quah, Danny. 1993a. "Empirical Cross-Section Dynamics in Economic Growth." *European Economic Review* (April): 426–34.

———. 1993b. "Galton's Fallacy and Tests of the Convergence Hypothesis." *Scandinavian Journal of Economics* 94, no. 4 (December): 427–43.

———. 1996a. "Convergence Empirics Across Countries with (Some) Capital Mobility." *Journal of Economic Growth* 1: 95–124.

———. 1996b. "Empirics for Economic Growth and Convergence: Stratification and Convergence Clubs." *European Economic Review* 40: 427–43.

Quah, Danny. 1999. "$6 \times 10^9$: Some Dynamics of Global Inequality and Growth." Typescript, December. Available at http://econ.lse.ac.uk/staff/dquah/p/9912sbn.pdf.

———. 2002. "One-third of the World's Growth and Inequality." Mimeo, London School of Economics, Economics Department, March.

Ravallion, Martin. 2000. "Should Poverty Measures Be Anchored to the National Accounts?" *Economic and Political Weekly* 34 (August 26): 3245–52.

———. 2001. "Growth, Inequality and Poverty: Looking Beyond Averages." *World Development* 29 (11): 1803–15.

Rawls, John. 1999. *The Law of Peoples*. Cambridge: Harvard University Press.

Rawski, Thomas G. 2001. "What's Happening to China's GDP Statistics?" *China Economic Review* 12: 347–54.

Reddy, Sanjay G., and Thomas W. Pogge. 2002. "How Not to Count the Poor." Manuscript, version May 1, 2002. Available at www.socialanalysis.org.

Rodrik, Dani. 1999. "Where Did All the Growth Go? External Shocks, Social Conflicts, and Growth Collapses." *Journal of Economic Growth* 4: 385–412.

Romer, Paul M. 1990. "Are Nonconvexities Important for Understanding Growth?" *American Economic Review Papers and Proceedings* 80, no. 2.

Sachs, Jeffrey, and Andrew Warner. 1995. "Economic Reform and the Process of Global Integration." Brookings Papers on Economic Activity, pp. 1–95.

Sala-i-Martin, Xavier. 1996. "Regional Cohesion: Evidence and Theories of Regional Growth and Convergence." *European Economic Review* 40: 1325–52.

———. 2002. "The Disturbing 'Rise' of World Income Inequality." NBER Working paper No. 8904, April. Available at www.nber.org.

———. 2002a. "The World Distribution of Income." NBER Working Paper No. 8905, May. Available at www.nber.org.

Savitsky, Andrei. 2003. "A Billionaire in Russia Is More than an Oligarch." *Nezavisimaya Gazeta*, January 20, 2003; translated in *Johnson Russia List* (electronic publication) No. 7025, January 20, 2003.

Schultz, T. P. 1998. "Inequality in the Distribution of Personal Income in the World: How It Is Changing and Why." *Journal of Population Economics* 11 (3): 307–44.

Sen, Amartya. 2002. "Globalization and Poverty." Transcript of a lecture given at Santa Clara University, October 29, 2002. Available at www.scu.edu/gloabalization/speakers/senlecture.cfm.

Sid-Ahmed, Mohamed. 2002. "Has World War III Begun?" *Al Ahram*, November 7–13, 2002. Available at http://www.ahram.org.eg/weekly/2002/611/op3.htm.

Singer, Peter. 2002. *One World: The Ethics of Globalization*. New Haven: Yale University Press.

Solimano, Andres. 2001. "The Evolution of World Income Inequality: Assessing the Impact of Globalization." Mimeo, draft: October 18, 2001.

Solow, Robert. 1956. "A Contribution to the Theory of Economic Growth." *Quarterly Journal of Economics* 70: 65–94.

Stiglitz, Joseph. 2002. *Globalization and Its Discontent.* New York: Norton.

Summers, Robert, Irving Kravis, and Alan Heston. 1984. "Changes in World Income Distribution." *Journal of Policy Modeling* (May 1986): 237–69.

Sutcliffe, Bob. 2003. "A More or Less Unequal World? World Income Distribution in the 20th century." University of Massachusetts Amherst, Political Economy Research Institute, Working Paper Series, no. 54.

Szekely, Miguel, and Marianne Hilgert. 1999. "What's behind the Inequality We Measure: An Investigation Using Latin American Data for the 1990s." Mimeo, version: December 3. Washington, D.C.: Inter-American Development Bank.

Third World Network. 2001. "The Multilateral Trading System: A Development Perspective," edited by Martin Khor. United Nations Development Program, background paper for the UNDP project on Trade and Sustainable Human Development, December.

Thomas, Vinod, Xibo Fan, and Yan Wang. 2001. "Measuring Education Inequality: Gini Coefficients of Education." World Bank Working Paper No. 2525, January. Available at http://econ.worldbank.org.

Tocqueville, Alexis de. 1978. *Souvenirs*. Paris: Gallimard; First published in 1893, written in 1850.

Tsangarides, Charalambos. 2001. "On Cross-country Growth and Convergence: Evidence from African and OECD Countries." *Journal of African Economies* 10, no. 4 (December): 355–89.

Wagner, Gert, and Markus Grabka. 1999. "Robustness Assessment Report. (RAR) Socio-Economic Panel 1984–1998." Available at http://www.lisproject.org/techdoc/ge/ge94survey.doc.

Walsh, Carl E. 1993. "What Caused the 1990–1991 Recession?" *Economic Review*, Federal Reserve Bank of San Francisco, No. 2, pp. 33–48.

Wesseling, H. L. 1996. *Divide and Rule: The Partition of Africa, 1880–1914*. Westport, Conn.: Praeger.

Wodon, Quentin, and Shlomo Yitzhaki. 2002. "Growth and Convergence: An Alternative Empirical Framework." Mimeo, March.

World Bank. 1990. *World Development Report 1990: Poverty.* New York and Washington, D.C.: Oxford University Press and World Bank.

———. 2001. *World Development Report 2000/2001: Attacking Poverty*. New York and Washington: Oxford University Press and World Bank.

Xu, Xianchun. 1999. "Evaluation and Adjustments of China's Official GDP by the World Bank and Prof, Maddison." *Journal of Econometric Study of Northeast Asia* 1 (2).

Yemtsov, Ruslan. 2002. "Quo Vadis: Inequality and Poverty Dynamics across Russian Regions." Mimeo, World Bank.

Yitzhaki, Shlomo. 1994. "Economic Distance and Overlapping of Distributions." *Journal of Econometrics* 61: 147–59.

Yitzhaki, Shlomo, and Robert I. Lerman. 1991. "Income Stratification and Income Inequality." *Review of Income and Wealth* 37 (3): 313–29.

# *Index of Authors*

# *Index of Subjects*